# On Spirituality

**Essays from the third Shi'i Muslim Mennonite Christian Dialogue**

## ANABAPTIST AND MENNONITE STUDIES

Anabaptist and Mennonite Studies is a publication series sponsored by the Institute of Anabaptist Mennonite Studies, Conrad Grebel University College, University of Waterloo, published in cooperation with Pandora Press. The aim of the series is to make available significant academic works relating to Anabaptist and Mennonite history and theology.

1. A. James Reimer, *Mennonites and Classical Theology: Dogmatic Foundations for Christian Ethics* (Kitchener, ON: Pandora Press, 2001) ISBN 0-9685543-7-7

2. Helen Martens, *Hutterite Songs* (Kitchener, ON: Pandora Press, 2002) ISBN 1-894710-24-X

3. Karl Koop, *Anabaptist-Mennonite Confessions of Faith: The Development of a Tradition* (Kitchener, ON: Pandora Press, 2004) ISBN 1-894710-32-0

4. John Howard Yoder, *Anabaptism and Reformation in Switzerland* (Kitchener, ON: Pandora Press, 2004) ISBN 1-894710-44-4

5. Rodney James Sawatsky, *History and Ideology: American Mennonite Identity Definition through History* (Kitchener, ON: Pandora Press, 2004) ISBN 1-894710-53-3

6. Harry Huebner, *Echoes of the Word* (Kitchener, ON: Pandora Press, 2005) ISBN 1-894710-56-8

7. Werner O. Packull, *Peter Riedemann: Shaper of the Hutterite Tradition* (Kitchener, ON: Pandora Press, 2007) ISBN 978-1-894710-76-3

8. Neal Blough, *Christ In Our Midst: Incarnation, Church and Discipleship in the Theology of Pilgram Marpeck* (Kitchener, ON: Pandora Press, 2007) ISBN 978-1-894710-77-0

9. Astrid von Schlachta translated by Werner and Karin Packull, *From the Tyrol to North America* (Kitchener, ON: Pandora Press, 2008) ISBN 978-1-926599-01-4

10. Willem de Bakker, Michael Driedger, and James Stayer, *Bernhard Rothmann and the Reformation in Münster* (Kitchener, ON: Pandora Press, 2009) ISBN 978-1-926599-06-9

11. M. Darrol Bryant, Susan Kennel Harrison, A. James Reimer, eds., *On Spirituality* (Kitchener, ON: Pandora Press, 2010) ISBN 978-1-926599-13-7

# On Spirituality

**Essays from the third Shi'i Muslim
Mennonite Christian Dialogue**

Edited by
M. Darrol Bryant
Susan Kennel Harrison
A. James Reimer

On spirituality : essays from the third Shi'i Muslim Mennonite Christian Dialogue / edited by M. Darrol Bryant, Susan Kennel Harrison, A. James Reimer.

Based on papers presented at the Shi'a Muslim/Mennonite Christian Dialogue III, held at Conrad Grebel University College, Waterloo, Ont. on May 27-30, 2007.
Includes bibliographical references.
ISBN 978-1-926599-13-7

1. Islam--Relations--Christianity.  2. Christianity and other religions-- Islam.  I. Bryant, M. Darrol  II. Harrison, Susan Kennel, 1965-  III. Reimer, A. James (Allen James), 1942-

BP172.O7 2010                   297.2'83                   C2010-902669-1

Article: "Building an understanding; Once the protesters departed, Muslim and Mennonite scholars meeting in Waterloo exchanged kind words," © 2007 *Waterloo Region Record, Ontario Canada*

Book design by Christian Snyder
Cover photo © Karl Griffiths-Fulton, 2010
ISBN 978-1-926599-13-7
ON SPIRITUALITY.

PANDORA
PRESS

Published by Pandora Press
33 Kent Avenue
Kitchener, Ontario N2G 3R2
All rights reserved.
www.pandorapress.com
All Pandora Press publications are printed on FSC certified paper.

19 18 17 16 15 14 13 12 11 10                        3 4 5 6 7 8 9 10

# Table of Contents

Readers will detect some differences in the orthography of Arabic terms transliterated in the various articles gathered in this volume. To avoid the possibility of introducing errors, the editors have generally chosen to retain the particular styles used by the authors themselves and not to impose unnecessary uniformity. Experts agree that there is no one "correct" style. However, terms that are common to many of the pieces, such as Shi'a and Shi'ite, are rendered in that now widely-accepted English form, with a few exceptions. Other terms appear as the authors presented them in their texts.

# Preface

## A. James Reimer

The third dialogue between Shi'a Muslims from Qom, Iran, and Mennonite Christians from Canada and United States took place at Conrad Grebel University College (CGUC) in Waterloo, Ontario, from May 27 to 31, 2007. The theme of this dialogue was "Spirituality," and fourteen scholarly papers were presented, seven from each of the two traditions and all of which are published in this volume. The conference was sponsored on the Iranian side by the Imam Khomeini Education and Research Institute (IKERI) of Qom, a most important Shi'a seminary for training Muslim clerics in the Islamic world, located in Iran's most holy city. On the Christian side, the dialogue was co-sponsored by the Mennonite Central Committee (MCC).

The first such dialogue had taken place in Toronto in October 2002, on "The Challenge of Modernity." Background to the exchange, the content of the conversations, and a number of the essays appeared in *The Conrad Grebel Review* 21.3 (Fall 2003). The dialogue was co-sponsored by MCC, the Toronto Mennonite Theological Centre, and IKERI. A good part of that first encounter was spent by participants from two very different traditions beginning to get to know one another, and this process included not only academic discussions but visits to a worship service in a Toronto mosque, a worship service in a Mennonite church, a modest Old Order Mennonite farm, an upscale Niagara Mennonite farm, and Niagara Falls.

What we discovered to our surprise were the number of commonalities we had with each other, especially in our respective ambivalence toward modernity. The 1979 revolution that established the Islamic Republic of Iran was particularly critical of the western, liberal assumptions of individual freedom derived from the Enlightenment. What the Muslims found so interesting was that Mennonites too have a critical relation to modernity, especially evident among the Old Orders, whom they visited with great delight. However, as I have tried to show in my work, the Anabaptist-Mennonite tradition also has a side that is quite open to valuable, emancipatory insights from the Enlightenment – the emphasis on religious freedom and pluralism, for instance.

The friendship and trust between the two sides was cemented further in the second dialogue, which occurred in Qom on the theme "Revelation and Authority" and was held February 15-16, 2004, as part of a two-week visit. Eight North American Mennonites joined a similar number of Muslim scholars for an intensive but cordial two-day discussion at the IKERI, with accompanying visits to a prisoner-of-war camp from the time of the Iran-Iraq war (now a museum), the former American Embassy grounds in Tehran, palaces of the former Shahs, and the simple dwelling of the late revolutionary leader Ayatollah Khomeini. We also visited the beautiful cities of Kashan with its lavish pre-revolutionary homes, and Esfahan with its 17th-century square and market, exquisite ancient mosques, the old Armenian Christian Church, and the Zoroastrian "Temple of Fire."

A full report of this encounter, with a number of essays, can be found in *The Conrad Grebel Review* 24.1 (Winter 2006). In my Introduction to this second dialogue in that issue, I expand on similarities and differences between the two traditions, and reasons that dialogue is so important. There is a common search for truth; we as Christians can learn from Muslims' strong emphasis on the absolute transcendence of God, without giving up on our notion of the Trinity; both have a strong moral-ethical consciousness; each values the importance of reason and understanding for the life of faith; for both the sacred text as revelation is important; we share a common hope in the coming of the Kingdom of God on earth; both have a positive anthropology (Muslims have no concept of original sin comparable to the Christian one, and the Anabaptist-Mennonites too rejected the harsh view of original sin and the accompanying doctrine of predestination so dominant in early Protestantism, and have emphasized human free will, more like Roman Catholicism and Islam); and, finally, Muslims and Mennonites share a common emphasis on the importance of community (the corporate nature of the believing community).

There are, however, also important differences, such as the Christian doctrine of the Trinity, the deity of Christ, and Christ's sacrificial atonement, which Muslims reject. These ought not to be avoided for the sake of dialogue, but when faced openly can enhance the discourse, respect, and trust, and can open opportunities to learn from each other even about our own traditions.

The 2007 dialogue, on "Spirituality," began under a storm of protest by about fifty members of the expatriate Iranian community from the Toronto and Kitchener-Waterloo areas. The protesters objected to Mennonites having friendly conversations with what they considered to be conservative scholars from Iran who are friendly to the present regime. Some of the protesters and their acquaintances had experienced persecution during the 1979 revolution. They in effect shut down the first event – a panel discussion between Mennonite and Muslim scholars. This unsuccessful event, which was open to the public, was followed by two days of highly productive closed sessions. There was considerable coverage in local and national news media, the most supportive being the *Waterloo Region Record*, which in an editorial promoted the dialogue. Its religion editor covered the conference, and devoted a full page (June 2, 2007) to summarizing each of the papers presented.

What we discovered in the third dialogue was that for both communities spirituality is important but each has a somewhat different understanding of the nature of spirituality. For Anabaptist-Mennonites, spirituality is closely linked to the doctrine of the Holy Spirit, the source of a regenerated life of Christian discipleship, including nonviolent love in human relations. Spirituality is largely experiential. Shi'ah Muslims, while not rejecting the experiential nature of spirituality altogether, tend towards a more philosophical, mystical, and ritual form of spirituality. Spirituality, rationality, and the political life of the community are not as strictly separated as in they are in many forms of Christianity. Here too we can learn from each other. I, for one, have been deeply moved by the piety and spiritual faithfulness of my Iranian Muslim friends who pray five times a day, come what may.

The editors of this volume want to thank both the Institute of Anabaptist Mennonite Studies at Conrad Grebel University College and

*On Spirituality*

the Mennonite Central Committee for providing substantial grants in support of this publication. I also want to add a special word of thanks to my co-editors, Susan Kennel Harrison and M. Darrol Bryant. When illness prevented me from completing my editorial tasks, they took over and readied the manuscript for publication.


                                              *A. James Reimer*
                                              January 15, 2010

# Introduction

## M. Darrol Bryant and Susan Kennel Harrison

On May 27-30, 2007, Shi'a Muslim/Mennonite Christian Dialogue III was held at Conrad Grebel University College in Waterloo, Ontario. It was the third meeting of Mennonites and Shi'a Muslim scholars, the first since a 2004 meeting in Iran. These meetings had grown out of Mennonite relief efforts in northwest Iran after an earthquake that had shaken the region in the early 1990s. The collegial relations established between Mennonites and Muslims in Iran led eventually to a student exchange with students from the Imam Khomeini Education and Research Institute coming to study in Canada at the Toronto School of Theology, and Mennonites from Canada (and the United States) going to study in Qom. In this volume, the preface by A. James Reimer gives a fuller account of the background to this third meeting, as does the contribution by Susan Kennel Harrison. The 2007 Dialogue built on the earlier meetings and a shared history over the preceding fifteen years.

The overall theme for the 2007 meeting was "spirituality," a theme that has become popular in the West in recent decades. The conference convener, Lydia Harder, had circulated to representatives of both communities a proposal suggesting this focus for the third meeting. The Shi'a scholars noted it was not a theme that was well known with the Muslim world, but they were willing to accept it, understanding that the desire was to avoid an overly philosophical and abstract focus for the gathering.

The thematic focus on spirituality had initially been generated during a meeting with Mohammad Ali Shomali when he visited Canada for other purposes. He met with a group at the Toronto Mennonite Theological Centre, including Reimer and Harrison, and they felt that this would be a good theme to address. Shomali then reported back to Qom, and Aboulhassan Haghani Khaveh and the Qom scholars gave their approval. The Qom scholars were invited to pose questions they would like to see addressed by the Mennonite scholars, since they had now known many of them for several years. The Mennonites were also invited to submit to the planning committee the questions they had about spirituality in Shi'ite Islam. From a list of questions generated by conversations in both communities the committee came up with specific topics for the papers. Then the committee requested specific Mennonite scholars to write papers on the assigned topics or questions arising from the Muslims. And in Qom they likewise assigned specific scholars to address questions that the Mennonites had posed. It was a dialogical process throughout, one made possible by relationships that had developed over a long period.

The essays in this volume were first presented at the May 2007 meeting; they have since been revised for publication here. They represent a range of perspectives on the theme of spirituality in relation to the religious traditions, ritual practices, mystical dimensions, ethical practices, prayer, and politics.

The opening essays by Hajj Muhammad Legenhausen on spirituality in Shi'a Islam and by C. Arnold Snyder on spirituality in the Mennonite faith community provide masterful introductions to the overall conference theme. Legenhausen rightly points out that the theme of spirituality (as something separate from religious practice) is new to Islam and is not a topic regularly addressed in Islamic philosophy and theology. He understands spirituality in Shi'a Islam as "direction to ever deeper levels of meaning," a "spiritual journey from the outward to the inward." Snyder sees Christian spirituality as it "enfolds and includes the inner and outer lives of Christians," noting that Mennonite spirituality involves both the "inner work of the living spirit of God and the outer work of obedience and discipleship." While Muslim teaching concerning spirituality goes back to the beginnings of Islam in relation to the prophet Muhammad (c. 570-630), Mennonite spirituality is rooted in the Anabaptist movement during the Reformation and the efforts of figures like Menno Simons (1496-1561) to recover the spirituality of early Christianity. Both papers then unfold the manifold dimensions of spirituality within their respective traditions.

It is worth observing that both of these essays emphasize the collective or communal nature of spirituality. Legenhausen points to the importance of the guidance of the Imams for the spiritual journey in his tradition of Shi'a, while Snyder points to the community of believers as the context for Mennonite spirituality. This is significant. In many discussions of contemporary forms of spirituality there is an emphasis on its radical subjectivity and individuality, but here it is spirituality-in-community that is central.

The third essay in this opening trilogy is by A. James Reimer, who insists that Mennonite spirituality is rooted in the Trinity; just as Legenhausen emphasized that the relation to Allah is fundamental to spirituality within Shi'a Islam. Reimer acknowledges the rejection of Trinitarian understandings of God among Muslims – Shi'a and Sunni – but wonders if we might not find some unexpected common ground. As he notes, Trinitarian thought for Mennonites is not important for its own sake but because it is the "necessary framework for and ground of regenerated life," the regenerated life known within the community of believers. Other essays in the volume make clear that building bridges of understanding between Christian Trinitarian thought and the Muslim teaching concerning *tawhid* [the unity of God] remains a distant hope. What is valuable here are the sustained conversations towards this end.

The next three articles form another trilogy. Ali Mesbah explores the conjunction between knowing and loving God, a conjunction that on the human level discloses the connection between submission and a growth, a deepening, of the inner meaning of the spiritual journey. While much of his essay engages Western thinkers, it is to Muslim figures like Ayatollah Murtaza Mutahhari (d. May 1, 1979) whom he turns in order to ground his conclusions. This is followed by an essay by David Shenk, who explores what he calls "biblical spirituality" – a right, joyous, loving, repentant, and obedient relationship with God the Creator – by recounting his own spiritual formation. Drawing upon his Mennonite tradition and the East African Revival Fellowship, he presents a multi-faceted understanding of spirituality. The third essay, by Mohammad Fanaei Eshkevari, explores the relationship of mysticism and religion. He looks at various theories, especially among Western scholars, and then argues that both religion and mysticism seek a "nearness to God" but that it is essential in the Shi'a tradition that it not fail to observe the *shari'a* [the code of law based on the Qur'an]. Where it does, it loses its authenticity.

The next two essays explore prayer. The focus of Jon Hoover's contribution is the Lord's Prayer. Hoover offers a detailed commentary that draws upon the writings of Mennonites on the Lord's Prayer and notes that, though it is employed differently in different communities, it is the most widely used prayer among Mennonites. Aboulhassan Haghani Khaveh draws attention to prayers of supplication in the "Words of the Infallibles." In his tradition, the "Infallibles" are the twelve Imams following Ali who were the authentic successors of the Prophet Muhammad. And since they were "without sin," it is to these figures that Shi'a Muslims turn for guidance.

The essays by Mahmoud Namazi Esfahani and Harry Huebner turn our attention from prayer to politics in a unique way as they relate to the interface of spirituality and politics. Namazi seeks to outline the dimensions of spirituality found in Imam Khomeini and the Islamic Revolution of 1979, while Huebner offers a Mennonite perspective on Christian politics. For Huebner, the Anabaptist-Mennonites' view of politics was grounded in their view of Jesus, who was the model for the Christian's relationship to the political order. Known for their commitment to nonviolence, Huebner shows that the relationship of Mennonites to governance is nuanced, ad hoc, and varied. Namazi struggles to clarify his use of the term "spirituality," but stresses the deep personal spirituality of Iman Khomeini and sees spirituality as an important dimension of the Iranian Revolution. He emphasizes the Shi'a view that all life is in God's hands.

Then we have two papers on spiritual poverty. The first, by Mohammad Ali Shomali, offers a Shi'a perspective while the second, by Thomas Finger, delves into the background of spiritual poverty in the Mennonite tradition. Shomali takes us into the Qur'an and the Hadith to unpack this important Muslim teaching, while Finger looks at the biblical teachings on the subject. Finger also identifies Rhineland mysticism as an important but neglected source for the "unarticulated spirituality of many Mennonites." Here again, as in other essays in this volume, the communal nature of spirituality in both traditions is emphasized.

The last pair of essays are by Aboulfazl Sajedi on "The Roles of Islamic Rituals in Cultivating Morality and Spirituality" and Irma Fast-Dueck on "Spirituality, Ritual, and Ethics in the Anabaptist-Mennonite tradition." There is an interesting convergence here in the way each tradition sees ritual activity as intimately related to ethical formation; there is no sense of ritual for its own sake.

These essays, then, provide a glimpse into the substance of the exchange that occurred during the conference. But that is all they can do, since they can only suggest something of the rich conversation that these essays generated – a conversation that at times skirted becoming a ruckus yet always returned to a place where respect prevailed, even around issues of significant difference. While the exchange and conversation that is the living heart of events like this remain hidden to the reader, the essay by Susan Kennel Harrison, who has been integral to the long journey of these Shi'a Muslims and Mennonite Christians, provides some hints of what occurred. She also takes us behind the scenes to elements of the pre-conference and post-conference dimensions of the event. The reader will find her "Dialogue of Life: Recalling the Living Exchange in 2007," immensely useful, though teasing, because it can only highlight a few moments from the rich, at times conflictual conversation that developed around the event.

The final essay, by M. Darrol Bryant, offers an outsider's perspective on the conference. A long-time colleague and friend of James Reimer, he had pleaded to be part of the event. He was graciously invited by the organizers to serve on the Listening Committee. His reflections bring the volume to a close, offering some observations – but no conclusions. All the participants would have their own perspectives on the event, and its real conclusion will be reached only as the conference finds its ways into the ongoing life and thought of those who were its participants.

The Appendix contains a number of documents that provide further information on the process leading up to Dialogue III, the participants, a reprint of an article that appeared in the *Waterloo Region Record*, and several photographs.

# Spirituality in Shi'a Islam: An Overview

## Hajj Muhammad Legenhausen

*By grace of the Holy Spirit, if aided,*
*Others too, would do what the Messiah did.*
– Hafez

## Spirit and Meaning

None of the major important ideas of Christianity and modern Western culture map very neatly onto those of Islam, and the notion of *spirituality* is no exception. This makes an introduction to Islamic spirituality a bit misleading if not prefaced by a discussion of what the term could mean, given that the concept has its home in a cultural milieu alien to the Muslim world.

Even among Christians, the concept of spirituality is difficult to pin down, for it has evolved rather rapidly from the second half of the twentieth century until the present. From its earliest usages, however, we find that the "spiritual" was contrasted with the "worldly." In the Middle Ages, the term "spirituality" was sometimes used for the Church hierarchy, in contrast to secular authorities. By the twelfth century, things of this world were considered to be corporeal, and a contrasting attention to religious values would make one *spiritual*. So, in Aquinas we find that "spirituality" (Latin, *spiritualitas*) has both a metaphysical and a moral sense that are never clearly distinguished.

In the metaphysical sense, the spiritual is what is incorporeal, spiritual as opposed to material. In the moral sense, one may adopt worldly or spiritual values. Furthermore, there is a theological sense of being spiritual that derives from the Pauline Epistles, e.g., Rom 8:9: "But ye are not in the flesh, but in the Spirit, if so be that the Spirit of God dwell in you." (Also see 1 Cor. 2:10f. and 12:13.)

In the later Middle Ages the use of the term "spirituality" declined, but it was revived in 17th-century France, where it was sometimes used pejoratively for those considered to have fanatically heretical beliefs. Voltaire is reported to have used the term mockingly, and it continued to be associated with Quietism in Spain, France, and Italy, and Enthusiasm in England. However, in the nineteenth century the term "spiritual theology" became established as the study of Christian life and prayer.

Over the past fifty years or so, discussions of "spiritual theology" have given way to more inclusive discussions of "spirituality," which is understood in a more *ecumenical* manner than "spiritual theology" and has even come to be used in interfaith discussions (such as ours). It is associated with religious experience (but in a much broader sense than that of "mysticism"), with depth of character, personal piety, and morality. A recent tendency among Christian theologians concerned with spirituality is to expand the notion to include all areas of human experience to the extent that they are connected with religious values, rather than focusing on prayer and the inner life. Nevertheless, there is a tendency to view spirituality as contrasting with the institutional and doctrinal aspects of religion, and to give prominence to personal religious feelings and experiences. Philip Sheldrake sums up his own review of Christian spirituality and its history with this comment:

> Christian spirituality derives its specific characteristics from a fundamental belief that human beings are capable of entering into relationship with a God who is transcendent yet dwelling in all created reality. Further, this relationship is lived out within a community of believers that is brought into being by commitment to Christ and is sustained by the active presence

of the Spirit of God. Put in specific terms, Christian spirituality exists in a framework that is Trinitarian, pneumatological, and ecclesial.[1]

Needless to say, if we can identify anything as Islamic spirituality, it will be neither Trinitarian, pneumatological, nor ecclesial. Nevertheless, these features of Christian spirituality may assist us in our efforts to recognize Islamic spirituality.

The term in Arabic and Persian that is best translated into English as "spiritual" is *ma'navi*, and "spirituality" is best translated into Persian as *ma'naviyyat*. These are derived from the word for *meaning, ma'na,* which in turn is derived from the root *'ana*, which means a concern. So, a meaning (*ma'na*) is literally a locus of concern, that to which concern is directed, a purport; the spiritual (*ma'navi*) is that which pertains to inner meaning, as opposed to the outward literal form; and spirituality (*ma'naviyyat*) is the quality of being inwardly meaningful or of possessing a purport to which concern is directed.

The spiritual (*ma'navi*) is opposed to the literal (*lafzi*), and like "spiritual" in English, it can be used to mean that something is immaterial or incorporeal. (Also, the term *ma'nawiyyat* is used in Arabic in one sense for immaterial entities and in another sense to indicate what in English would be called "team spirit.") The most well-known use of ma'navi in the sense of indicating spirituality is in the title that has come to be given to the great compendium of poetry by Mawlavi Jalal al-Din Rumi (d. 1273), the *Mathnavi Ma'navi*, or *Spiritual Couplets*.[2]

> If you are thirsting for the spiritual (*ma'navi*) ocean (or ocean
>    of meaning)
> Make a breach in the island of the *Mathnavi*.
> Make such a breach that with every breath
> You will see the *Mathnavi* as spiritual (*ma'navi*) only.

The etymological differences between the English "spirituality" and the Persian *ma'naviyyat* may be understood as symbolic of a fundamental difference between Christian and Islamic spirituality. Christians understand spirituality as the work of the Holy Spirit, while

Muslims understand spirituality as direction to ever deeper layers of meaning. For Christians, spirituality is to be found through the inward life because of the indwelling of the Holy Spirit; for Muslims, spirituality will be found within, because the soul is a sign that indicates God. Christian spirituality is the result of inspiration – the spirit comes into one; Muslim spirituality is the result of another kind of movement, not an external spirit coming in but the self's delving within as it is guided to meaning. To change the direction of the metaphor, we could say that Islamic spirituality is a kind of explication or *exegesis* – the bringing out of inner or hidden meaning, not exclusively in the sense of interpretation of scripture but in the broader, more literal sense of being guided to a meaning. However, it is not so much that a meaning is brought out as that one becomes conversant with a more interior world of meaning.

Christian spirituality is the characteristic of a life that expresses the work of the spirit within, so that it is not the believer's own will but God's that is done. Muslim spirituality is the characteristic of the spiritual journey of Islam from the outward to the inward – a hermeneutic trail of openings to insights and unveilings. In both cases a divine guide is required, but the nature of this divine guidance is understood somewhat differently. Christian spirituality is found in the manifestation of signs and in the affective indications of right guidance due to the effects of the spirit within; Muslim spirituality is found in the understanding of signs, which is cognitive although having both conceptual and presentational or experiential aspects. Right guidance for the Muslim is evidenced in certainty and understanding, and by adherence to the path indicated by the guide. The Christian becomes spiritual as the soul is sanctified through the gifts of grace brought by the Holy Spirit. The Muslim becomes spiritual as the mirror of the soul is polished to reflect the image of God hidden beneath the dust that covered it. In Christianity the soul becomes sanctified as the Spirit enters into it, while in Islam it becomes sanctified as it is led to enter the spiritual realm.

I have exaggerated these differences between Christian and Islamic spirituality in order to make their distinctive characters clearer. In doing so, one may get the false impression that Christian and Islamic spiritualities are mutually exclusive. However, it is not too difficult to find images typical of Islamic spirituality expressed by Christian writers or expressions of spiritual life by Muslims that seem typically Christian, or mixtures of both. In fact, the differences are more a matter of emphasis than distinction. There are cognitive and affective aspects to both Christian and Islamic spirituality, and interpretation as well as inspiration have a place in the spiritualities of both religious traditions, yet the differences in accentuation are significant.

Let's return to Sheldrake's characterization of Christian spirituality in order to find Islamic counterparts to it. Muslims also have a fundamental belief that human beings are capable of entering into a relationship with a God who is transcendent and yet immanent. For Sheldrake, the immanence of God is found in the doctrine of the Trinity: God approaches man by becoming incarnate in Christ. For Muslims, however, the doctrine of the strict unity of God, *tawhid*, is no obstacle to an appreciation of the immanence of God expressed in such verses of the Qur'an as "Wherever you turn, there is the face of Allah" (2:115) and "We are closer to them than their jugular vein" (50:16). However, to find God in all things requires guidance, and so Muslims live out their relation to God in a community of seekers under the guidance of those sent by God for this purpose, pre-eminently the Prophet Muhammad. For the Shi'a, the community is sustained in its relation to God through the continuing guidance of the divinely appointed Imams.

## Spirit and Guide

Both Christianity and Islam are covenantal religions. In all three Abrahamic religions, human beings set out on the spiritual journey by entering into a covenant with God and at the invitation of God. Entering into the covenant is a kind of initiation by which God brings the person or people initiated onto the path toward him. It is a path of return to the origin. Although the covenant takes different forms during the ages of the different prophets, acceptance of the covenant by man was prior to the earthly sojourn of humanity: "When your Lord took from the Children of Adam from their loins, their descendents and made them bear witness over themselves, [He asked them,] 'Am I not your Lord?'

They said, 'Yes indeed! We bear witness!'" (7:172). The divine guide is one who can lead us back to the unseen realm from which we came, on a path whose goal is the divine encounter (*liqa Allah*).

The "initiatic" aspect of the religious life becomes especially prominent in Shi'a Islam. Initiation takes place on various levels, and may be considered as a kind of vocation or divine appointment. Initiation normally marks the beginning of a spiritual training or wayfaring, but in the case of the prophets and Imams the training takes place prior to the formal beginning of their mission.

At the highest level, there is the calling and appointment of the Prophet Muhammad. Even the Prophet is guided by God along a spiritual path. In the collections of sermons, letters, and sayings attributed to Imam 'Ali, *Nahj al-Balagha*, it is reported that in one of his sermons 'Ali said:

> From the time of his weaning, Allah had appointed a greater angel from His angels to guide him (*yasluku*) along the path (*tariq*) of nobility (*al-makarim*) and excellence of moral character (*akhlaq*), throughout his nights and days. And I would follow him like a young camel following in the footprints of its mother.[3]

In this report the training of the Prophet Muhammad is linked with that of Imam 'Ali. Following this passage is reference to knowledge of hidden significance:

> And I heard the moan of Satan when the revelation came down upon him (s), and I said, "O Apostle of Allah! What is this moan?" Then he answered, "That is Satan who despairs of being worshipped. Verily, you hear what I hear and you see what I see, except that you are not a prophet but you are a deputy and you are on [the path of] goodness.[4]

Here we find that the Prophet is privileged in having concourse with what is not perceived by ordinary people. He is guided by an angel and he hears the moan of Satan. Imam 'Ali shares the privilege with the Prophet, but as one who *follows* the Prophet. He hears the moan of Satan, but the Prophet tells him its inner meaning.

Sometimes the guiding angel is identified with the Holy Spirit (*ruh al-qudus*). In his *Shi'ite Creed*, Shaykh Saduq (d. 991) writes:

> And our belief concerning the prophets (*anbiya*), the messengers (*rusul*) and the Imams is that there were five spirits within them: the Holy Spirit, the spirit of faith, the spirit of strength, the spirit of appetite, and of motion.[5]

Shaykh Saduq continues that the true believers have the latter four, but the Holy Spirit is found only in the prophets and Imams. He continues:

> For verily it is a creation greater than Gabriel and Michael. It always accompanies the Messenger of Allah and the angels and the Imams, and it belongs to the angelic domain (*malakut*).[6]

The Shi'ite Imams are each appointed by God, and this appointment is announced by the Prophet and then by each Imam in succession. The prophets and Imams are all able to guide others because of the guidance they have been given through which they acquire moral excellence and knowledge of the unseen (*ghayb*). Ordinary people see only the exterior of things or their surfaces (*zahir*), while the divine guides lead people to knowledge of the interior or inward aspects of things (*batin*). The spiritual path is one that takes the adept from the world of exterior things to an interior world, a world of hidden meanings, and traveling this path builds character.

The term *Shi'i* literally means *partisan* or *adherent*, and is understood as indicating the adherents of Imam 'Ali, the Commander of the Faithful; and by implication the Shi'a are followers of the Imams, each of whom is designated by his predecessor according to divine direction. Sectarian differences among the Shi'a occur over disputes about the identities of those appointed. The vast majority of Shi'a are known as Twelvers (*ithna'ashari*). There are also two main branches of Isma'ili Shi'ism, found mostly in India and Pakistan, and there is the Zaydi Shi'ism of Yemen. Our discussion of expressions of Shi'ite spirituality will be confined to that of Twelver Shi'ism.

To describe the Shi'a in this way, however, is only to give a verbal account based on outward allegiances. There are many narrations about what it means to be a true Shi'ite. Imam Baqir is reported to have said:

> The Shi'a of 'Ali are those who are giving because of their friendship for us, who are loving because of their affection for us, those who, when angry, do not oppress, and who, when satisfied, do not waste. They are a blessing to their neighbors, and peace (or safety) to those with whom they associate.[7]

In another narration, the Imam reportedly said:

> Would it suffice for someone to be a Shi'a that he loves us, the Household of the Prophet? By Allah! No one is of our Shi'a unless he fears God and obeys Him, and they will not be known (as Shi'a) except by their modesty and humility, keeping their trusts, profuse remembrance of God, fasting and prayer, kindness to parents, helping their neighbors, especially the poor, destitute, the indebted, and orphans, by the truth of their reports, recitation of the Qur'an, holding their tongues about people except for what is good, and they are the most trusted tribesmen of their tribes.[8]

It is also narrated that the Prophet Muhammad said:

> Whoever loves 'Ali, God will fix wisdom in his heart, He will make what is right flow from his tongue, and He will open for him the gates of mercy. And whoever loves 'Ali, in heaven and on earth will be called the captive of God.[9]

The difference between Sunni and Shi'i Islam is often portrayed as a disagreement over the political leadership of the Muslim community after the Prophet, and it is alleged that the Shi'a believe in something like royal succession through an inherited right to rulership. However, the issue of communal leadership is only the manner in which a more fundamental difference came to the surface. This difference is the religious authority the Shi'a attribute to the Imams on the basis of their selection, esoteric knowledge, and precedence in virtue. So, we could say that the most fundamental characteristic of Shi'ite spirituality is the particular way in which the Shi'a view what in contemporary English is called *spirituality*, for what distinguishes the Shi'a is precisely the belief that the spiritual life of Islam – individually and collectively – can be sustained only through the guidance of the Imams. S.H.M. Jafri concludes his study of *The Origins and Development of Shi'a Islam* with this comment:

> The actual disagreements between the Shi'is and the Sunnis in certain details of theology and legal practices were not as important as the "Spirit" working behind these rather minor divergences. This "Spirit", arising from the differences in the fundamental approach and interpretation of Islam ... issued forth in the Shi'i concept of leadership of the community after the Prophet. It is this concept of divinely-ordained leadership which distinguishes Shi'i from Sunni within Islam....[10]

The fundamental difference of which Jafri speaks, and which is the basis for the Shi'i ideas about religious leadership (*Imamat*), is the belief that divine guidance is given to the community through the person of the Prophet as well as the revelation of the Qur'an, and continues after the Prophet by virtue of the divine selection and esoteric knowledge transmitted to the Imams. In a famous *hadith* it is reported that the Prophet said: "I am leaving you with two weighty things (*thaqalayn*). If you take hold of them, you will not stray after me: the Book of Allah and my kindred, my household (*ahl al-bayt*)."[11] This is sometimes explained, in part, in terms of the esoteric knowledge of the proper interpretation of the Qur'an transmitted through the Imams. In the Qur'an it is written:

> It is He who has sent down to you the Book. Parts of it are definitive verses [literally signs (*ayat*)], which are the mother

of the Book, while others are metaphorical. As for those in whose hearts is deviance, they pursue what is metaphorical in it, courting temptation and courting its interpretation (*ta'wil*). But no one knows its interpretation except Allah and those firmly grounded in knowledge (*al-rasikhuna fi al-'ilm*); they say, "We believe in it; all of it is from our Lord."(3:7)

The Shi'a interpret "those firmly grounded in knowledge" as referring to the prophets and Imams.[12] After naming the twelve Imams, Shaykh Saduq writes:

Our belief regarding them is that they are in authority (*ulu al-amr*). It is to them that Allah has ordained obedience, they are the witnesses for the people and they are the gates of Allah and the road to Him and the guides thereto, and the repositories of His knowledge and the *interpreters of His revelations* and the pillars of His unity.[13]

The idea of the Imam as one who can lead others to a correct understanding of the Qur'an is only one instance of the general function of the Imam as divine guide, but it is a pivotal one.[14] The knowledge possessed by the Imams and by which they guide is an esoteric knowledge, not only in the sense that it involves going beyond the surface literal meaning to a deeper meaning, but in the sense that it cannot be completely communicated to anyone but the next Imam, and the guidance of the Imams must be calibrated so as to impart only as much knowledge as the follower has the capacity to receive.

In many ways the spirituality of Shi'i Islam is like the spirituality of Sufi Islam among Sunni Muslims, and for good reason. All of the Sufi Orders trace their initiatic chains to Imam 'Ali. The Sufis accept the most fundamental claim of the Shi'a, namely that divine guidance continued after the revelation of the Qur'an through the work of specially appointed divine guides. Furthermore, in Iranian culture, the influence of Sufi ideas has been pervasive for centuries, and there is a great complex history of the interactions between Sufis and Shi'ites, to such an extent that on many issues it is impossible to sort out the lines along which ideas have been passed.[15]

The problem of sorting is made more difficult because many prominent Shi'i ulama – from Khwaja Nasir al-Din Tusi (d. 1273), through Mulla Sadra (d. 1640), to Imam Khomeini (d. 1989) – have drawn heavily on Sufi teachings about the understanding and practice of Islam. The difference between Shi'i and Sufi spiritualities is largely confined to questions about the identities of these guides after Imam 'Ali, and the function of the guide. For the Shi'a, although the Imams do not bring any new book or religious law, their authority extends to all the areas of religion: interpretation of the Qur'an, interpretation of the law, theology, politics, and morals. Their authority is exegetical, doctrinal, legal, moral, and social, and all of these aspects are based on divine appointment. God chooses those who will become guides, and sees to it that they receive training in which they acquire wisdom and perfect their morals.

For the Sufis in the Sunni world, the guidance of the divine guides after the Prophet is limited: the four Sunni schools of jurisprudence are followed on issues of Islamic law rather than the Ja'fari legal code (named after the sixth Imam), and usually no claims are made to political authority (although there have been important exceptions of politically active Sufi Orders among both Sunnis and Shi'ites, such as that of the Safavid dynasty; and generally appeal is often made to the Sufi shaykhs to arbitrate disputes among their followers).

The Sufi and Shi'ite Sayyid Haydar Amuli (d. ca. 786/1384) describes the spiritual path of Islam as consisting of three levels: *shari'at, tariqat,* and *haqiqat* in his *Inner Secrets of the Path,*[16] where he reports a narration attributed to the Prophet: "The *shari'ah* is my words, *tariqah* my actions, *haqiqah* my states."[17] *Shari'at* is literally "the way," but it is used to refer to the exterior or legal dimension of Islam. *Tariqat* also means *way,* but is used to indicate a spiritual discipline, the interior way, and is commonly used for the Sufi orders. *Haqiqat* is truth or reality, and Sayyid Haydar uses this term to indicate the goal of the exterior and interior ways. His book applies this threefold distinction to both doctrine and practice. Among the religious practices, for example, he first considers the *hajj* from the point of view of its outward rules as discussed by the jurists (*fuqaha*). Next he considers the *hajj* for the people of *tariqat* as an inner journey toward the purified heart of the wayfarer. Finally, he turns to the *hajj* at a cosmic level, in which one seeks to attain access to the heart of the "Great Man," also known as the "Universal Soul" and the *Bayt al-Ma'mur* (the House in heaven above the Ka'bah) or the "Guarded Tablet." In each of these three discussions the course of the performance of the rituals is reviewed but each time at a more profound level.

About a century before Haydar Amuli, Mawlavi referred to the same tripartite division in the preface to the fifth book of the *Mathnavi*;

> This volume is the fifth of the books of the *Mathnavi* and the spiritual (*ma'navi*) exposition which declares that the *shari'at* is like a candle that shows the way. Without taking the candle in your hand, you cannot travel the way. When you come to the way, your traveling on it is the *tariqat*. When you reach the goal, that is the *haqiqat*.[18]

More recent Shi'ite writers have also made use of this tripartite division in order to elaborate views about Islamic spirituality, particularly to assert the harmony between Islamic spirituality and Islamic law.[19] Seyyed Hossein Nasr[20] compares this division to that of islam (submission, or as our Mennonite friends say, *Gelassenheit*), *iman* (faith), and *ihsan* (William Chittick translates this as *doing the beautiful*, and it could also be understood as beneficence or active kindness), and the comparison can also be found in the works of Haydar Amuli.[21] Sachiko Murata and Chittick use the themes of *islam, iman,* and *ihsan* to organize an introduction to Islam that is at once profound, elementary, concise, and wide-ranging.[22]

It also seems that Shi'i views are the source for much that later found its way into Sufism, although there is scholarly debate about how this has taken place and the mechanisms of mutual influence as the traditions developed. As just one example, we might consider early Sufi exegesis of the Qur'an, since we have already seen that the Shi'a view the Imams as interpreters of divine revelation. The sixth Shi'i Imam, Ja'far al-Sadiq (d. 148/765), is reported to have referred to four levels of exegesis:

an apparent level (*zahir*) for the common people, and three esoteric levels (*batin*) corresponding to the levels of the mystic, the imam, and the prophet. In practice, what is usually reported, however, are only references to the apparent and esoteric meanings generally. One of the early Sufi interpreters of the Qur'an, Sahl al-Tustari (d. 283/896) makes essentially the same distinctions both in theory and in practice. In his study of Tustari's exegesis, Gerhard Böwering concludes:

> Although Tustari does not cite Ja'far al-Sadiq in his *Tafsir*, neither by name nor anonymously, he seems to follow the principles of Qur'anic interpretation employed by Ja'far al-Sadiq…. the Qur'anic commentaries of both Ja'far and Tustari are characterized as mystical, Sufi interpretation of the Qur'an, independent of each other in their content, but related in their method.[23]

The ability to understand hidden meanings is not merely an aptitude for textual hermeneutics, for the Qur'an itself repeatedly enjoins its readers to think, to reason, and in other ways to ponder on the signs of God as they appear in nature, history, and all creation. Reason (*'aql*) is seen as a gift of God. One can acquire knowledge, but not reason. In an important narration, Imam Musa Kazim presents reason as a faculty for perception of divinity, insight, and a light in the heart that enables one to recognize and understand the signs of Allah.[24] The degree of reason possessed by the believer is sufficient for him to recognize that the prophets and Imams are in possession of knowledge (*'ilm*), and hence to seek guidance from them.[25]

## Spirit Overflowing

Spirituality displays itself in numerous ways in Islamic cultures. Here, we might take a glance at how a more specifically Shi'ite spirituality is manifest in contemporary Iranian culture. What we are looking for is not just any expression of religious feeling, but how the major Shi'ite themes of the spiritual journey and the guide through levels of meaning are expressed. Before doing so, however, another characteristic element of Shi'i spirituality needs to be discussed: martyrdom and oppression.

All of the Shi'ite Imams (except the last, who is in occultation [a state of hiddenness from humanity]) were martyred, and subject to unjust treatment by those who abused religion. They are described as *shahid* (martyr) and *mazlum* (oppressed). Two of them, Imam 'Ali and Imam Husayn, were killed by swords, and the rest were poisoned. The sword that struck Imam 'Ali while he prayed was also poisoned. All of them were killed by those who outwardly professed Islam.

So, the spiritual path of the Shi'a is a dangerous one, and the danger comes from those who outwardly profess Islam while inwardly are oriented toward worldly instead of divine aims. As a result, the Imams cautioned their followers to be secretive about their true beliefs when threatened (*taqiyyah*). They also encouraged their followers to weep for those who had been martyred, especially Imam Husayn. As a result, Shi'ite spirituality is characterized by esotericism, secretiveness, and mourning.

What may be called the Shi'ite liturgical year is organized around the major Islamic holidays at the end of Ramadan and at the culmination of the *hajj*, the celebrations of the birthdays of the fourteen *Ma'sumin* (literally, those protected from sin, the Prophet, his daughter Fatima, and the twelve Imams), and mourning ceremonies to commemorate their martyrdoms, especially that of Husayn during the first ten days of the lunar month of Muharram, and that of 'Ali on the 19th and 21st of Ramadan (when he was struck and died, respectively). Mourning is expressed by the wearing of black, by breast-beating (and self-flagellation during Muharram), and by the recitation of poetry and stories about the sufferings of the martyrs and their families. At some point in such gatherings the lights are turned down and people weep.

The spiritual journey is symbolized through pilgrimages (*ziyarat*, literally "visitations") to the shrines of the Ma'sumin and members of their families or other notable descendents.[26] There people seek the intercession of the divine guides, read devotions, and picnic and watch children run around. The shrines also serve as places where mourning ceremonies are held and holidays are publicly celebrated. The shrines are sacred spaces, but the spirit one finds at them is less one of solemnity and more one of an unburdening of need expressed through formal and informal supplications.

Supplications play an important role in public and personal devotions, and may be purely inward or expressed verbally. True supplication requires attention of the heart, whether or not accompanied by spoken words. When supplication takes place with the attention of the heart, its effect on the heart is to produce a spiritual state (*hal*). The recitation of special supplications attributed to the Ma'sumin is especially valued,[27] and such supplications serve as models by which to learn the proper etiquette of prayer and intimate conversation with God. Supplication encourages the supplicant to turn his attention inward, to recognize his own sinfulness, to seek refuge in God, and to ask for his own forgiveness and for the forgiveness of others. One also prays that the prayers of others will be answered.

In the visual arts, geometrical figures indicate intellectual abstraction, and the mirroring of patterns in carpets, architecture, and calligraphy reflects the soul's mirroring of divinity. Floral themes with birds symbolize the flight of the mystic toward divine beauty. A central underlying theme expressed in many variations can symbolize divine unity and its manifestations. Often a phrase of the Qur'an, a Name of God, or an appellation of one of the *Ma'sumin* is hidden in brickwork or calligraphy in such a way that it can be deciphered only after some study; and this, too, reflects the spiritual quest and the esoteric truth.

Allusions to the spiritual journey are also very common in Iranian film, poetry, and stories. On television one often sees a movie or serial in which something is lost or misplaced. Help is needed to find it. A guide is sought, and what is found is surprisingly much more than was imagined to have been lost. A story is told in which someone tells another story, and sometimes this goes on for several levels to give an indication of the levels of meaning that are traversed on the spiritual path. These are just a couple of examples of the many ways in which spiritual themes appear in Iranian media, literature, and art.

In this regard, the long and rich tradition of Sufi poetry in Farsi provides an invaluable treasury of imagery, motifs, and ideas that are elaborated in constantly changing variations. Classical Persian poetry is often set to music and becomes popular entertainment. Many Iranians also memorize impressive quantities of poetry, and are easily prompted to recite at social gatherings. Although there are important

Sufi poets who wrote in Arabic, the bulk of the corpus of Sufi poetry is in Persian. While many of these poets followed a Sunni school of jurisprudence, due to the concordance of Sufi and Shi'i spirituality, they are understood as giving voice to central spiritual themes and values for the Shi'a, too.

The spirituality of Shi'ite society is so pervasive that one even finds it in sports. In a traditional Iranian sports center, called a *zur khaneh* (literally, "house of strength"), exercises are performed to the recitation of poetry, and the coach also plays the role of spiritual guide. The entrance to the *zur khaneh* is intentionally made low so that those entering must humble themselves. Virtue is encouraged as much as strength, and the model of the champions is Imam 'Ali, whose spiritual chivalry (*futuwwat*) is taken as an ideal. Even in sports that are not traditional in Iran, such as karate, one often finds that the trainer acts as a guide to moral character as well as technique, and sessions are begun or ended with salutations of the Prophet and his family: O Allah, peace be with Muhammad and with the folk of Muhammad.

Spiritual virtues are especially prized among Iranian Muslims. Humility and asceticism are especially praiseworthy, as are generosity, clemency, and prayerfulness. Conversely, arrogance, conceitedness, wastefulness, extravagance, hard heartedness, and vengefulness are particularly loathed vices. One of the works dubiously attributed to Imam Ja'far al-Sadiq that interweaves spirituality and ethics and continues to be popular is *Misbah al-Shari'ah (The Lantern of the Path)*.[28] It features discussions of the spiritual merits of some of the Islamic rules of behaviour interwoven with brief articles on such virtues and vices as truthfulness, humility, generosity, repentance, greed, hypocrisy, avarice, patience, and wisdom.

On the relation between the spiritual path and ethics, Shahid Mutahhari wrote a very important concise introduction to '*irfan* in which he compares Sufism and ethics.[29] Before we review his comparison, however, a terminological point is in order. The term "Sufism" (*tasawwuf*) is often associated with the institutionalized spirituality of the various Sufi Orders, and thus many Shi'ite authors prefer the use of the term '*irfan* (*gnosis*). Sometimes *Sufism* is used for the practical instructions for spiritual wayfaring, while '*irfan* is used for the theory; other authors use the terms interchangeably. I will use "Sufism" in the broadest way as synonymous for *'irfan* and having both practical and theoretical branches. Using "Sufism" in a similar way, Seyyed Hossein Nasr points out that "Islamic spirituality ... has revealed itself in Islamic history most of all in Sufism";[30] nevertheless, it is important to recognize that spirituality pervades Islamic society and is by no means confined to those who self-consciously concern themselves with what is generally understood as *'irfan* or *tasawwuf*.

Sufism, even in its most general sense, is a particular way in which spirituality was refined in Shi'i society. As Shahid Mutahhari points out, there have always been Sufis among the Shi'a, many of whom do not designate themselves as such or distinguish themselves in any outwardly recognizable way, e.g., by association with a particular Sufi hospice or *khanaqah*, or by some particular manner of dress, and yet they are deeply involved in spiritual wayfaring (*sayr o suluk*) and the study of Sufi texts.[31]

Practical Sufism is similar to a system of religious ethics, in that both are oriented toward the agent's relationship with God and the obligations and virtues ensuing from this relationship. However, as Mutahhari points out, Sufism is dynamic while ethics is static. Sufism considers the origin and destination of man, and the numerous stages along the way that must be traversed in succession. The Sufi sees the human spirit as a living organism to be nurtured in accordance with a particular order of development. In ethics, on the other hand, we find descriptions of the virtues and obligations, their interrelations and consideration of how they are to be applied, but scant detailed discussion of what practical steps can be taken to acquire them. According to Mutahhari, while Sufism sees the soul as an organism to be cultivated, ethics sees it as a house to be furnished. Another difference mentioned by Mutahhari is that Sufism pays particular attention to the heart, what is understood by the heart, and the heart's states. A full understanding of this requires experience on the path, while the discussions of moral psychology found in ethics tend to focus on questions of conscience and moral conflict that are comparatively commonplace. Consequently, recognition of the need for a guide is much more pronounced in Sufism than in ethics. Both ethics and practical Sufism, however, are concerned with human excellence.

The methods of practical Sufism are not only employed by members of Sufi orders; there are also teachers of practical Sufism both among Shi'ite clergy and laity, and their students are drawn from various segments of society. Most are fairly orthodox, as far as the doctrines and practices of Shi'ite Islam are concerned, although it is not difficult to find individuals and groups who hold beliefs or condone practices falling outside of what most Shi'a would consider acceptable, such as the *ghullat* (extremists), who claim that Imam 'Ali was divine, or those who claim that when one reaches a certain stage on the path, obligatory prayer and fasting may be abandoned. Here we confine our discussion to what is common among the forms of practical Sufism that do not conflict in theory or practice with Shi'ism as taught in the seminaries.

Practical Sufism requires one to pay attention to the heart. The heart is understood as the locus of spiritual understanding, in accord with the verse of the Qur'an: "Know that Allah intervenes between a man and his heart" (8:24). There is also a narration, according to which Imam Sajjad said: "There are four eyes for a servant: two eyes with which to see his other worldly affairs, and two eyes with which to see his worldly affairs. So, when Allah, the Mighty and Magnificent, wills good for a servant, He opens the two eyes in his heart, and then he sees faults by them."[32] According to this and many other verses and narrations, the heart is the receptacle for divine grace. God grants his grace to the human heart through guidance by which the heart finds its way, understands its wrong turns, and "sees" the right direction. In order for the heart to function properly, however, one must cleanse it, or polish it, or chop away the debris that covers it, and this is accomplished by wielding the double-edged sword of *dhikr* (remembrance) and *fikr* (contemplation). In Shi'i spirituality, it is not uncommon for military imagery to be taken to symbolize various facets of the inner journey: so, the sword of Imam 'Ali, *Dhu al-Faqar*, is taken to indicate remembrance of God and contemplation of him in the heart, and the struggle against the base elements of the soul is called "the greatest jihad."[33]

Another feature of practical Shi'ite spirituality is *intizar*, which means "waiting" or "expectation" and is associated with the belief that the Mahdi, the twelfth Shi'ite Imam, is alive but in *occultation*. The Shi'a are encouraged to await the appearance of the hidden Imam, and in their practical Sufism, this means not only to expect the outward appearance of the hidden Imam but to prepare oneself by seeking the grace to be the Imam's worthy companion, with the consciousness that he may be hidden in the appearance of the least among us.

As the seeker awaits the companionship of the Imam, he should also develop companionship with others involved in the spiritual journey, and should attune his interests to the personalities of those more advanced on the path, especially the Prophet and his folk, known as the fourteen impeccable ones, the Ma'sumin.

Observing the customs of one's society, proper etiquette, and morals is seen at one level as a prerequisite for following the spiritual path under the guidance of the divinely appointed guide. One conforms one's behaviour to the principles of morality and Islamic law because without doing so, there can be no progress on the spiritual path. However, as one travels the path, further motivation is found for worship and love of God and respect and kindness to his creatures. As the heart becomes illuminated through the guidance of those appointed by God for this purpose, virtues appear as outward signs of steady travel on the path. In order for this to happen, the wayfarer (*salik*) must be continually engaged in the examination of conscience and in taking care that base motives do not get the upper hand.

As an aid in wayfaring, it is highly recommended to visit cemeteries and to ponder death. The intended effect of this is to instill the idea of the transience of worldly goods and strengthen the wayfarer's remembrance of God.

There are many other sorts of instructions for spiritual wayfaring, for example, regarding humility and a disdain for ostentation, repentance, how to keep proper attention during worship, recitation of the Qur'an, maintaining ritual purity, and other acts going beyond the requirements of religious law. Many of these instructions are contained in manuals such as the frequently reprinted *Zad al-Salik* (Provisions of the Wayfarer) by Muhsin Fayd Kashani (d. 1680).[34] A more recent example is that of Ayatullah Ibrahim Amini's *Self-Building: An Islamic Guide for Spiritual Migration towards God*.[35]

There is some disagreement about instructions for spiritual wayfaring, with regard to *who* gives the instructions and *what* instructions are to be given. Some believe that the instructions can only be taken directly from the Prophet or an Imam, and that when none is available for consultation (as in the current age of *ghaybat al-kubra* [major occultation]), we must confine ourselves to what can be found in the books of narrations attributed to them. Traveling on the spiritual path requires the performance of works recommended but not religiously obligatory, such as reading supplications and fasting on particular days. These sorts of instructions are most popularly found in the book *Mafatih al-Jinan.* However, instructions found in other manuals (such as those of Kashani and Amini, mentioned above) combine instructions for supererogatory works with attention to moral considerations and the spiritual states appropriate to these works at a particular stage of the spiritual path, somewhat along the lines of the division of *shari'at, tariqat,* and *haqiqat* (though not necessarily making this threefold distinction explicit).

Others hold that particular instructions personally suited for the individual should be given by an *ustad* (teacher). There is also some difference of opinion about the sorts of instructions that would be suitable for an *ustad* to give. For example, some hold that the *ustad* should restrict instructions to those that can be found in narrations, while others hold that he could issue other instructions, e.g., to abstain from meat for some period or to remain in a certain city for some time. According to Sayyid Husayni Tehrani, the *salik* should have two *ustads,* a general one who is not specially appointed but has more experience and can help the *salik* through the first stages of spiritual wayfaring, and a special *ustad,* who is the Twelfth Imam, with whom the *salik* is to develop a lifelong relation by traveling "within the planes of the Imam's luminosity."[36]

Although there are differences of opinion about the identities of those from whom it is appropriate to seek instructions for wayfaring, and about the extent of the instructions it is appropriate for a spiritual advisor to give, agreement about the general contours of the spiritual path is much more extensive than the area of disagreement. Instructions can be found in manuals of the sort mentioned, but also in more specific works about particular types of worship, such as fasting[37] and prayer,[38] and in commentaries on parts of the Qur'an[39] or on narrations attributed to or describing the lives of the Ma'sumin.[40]

If practical Sufism is comparable to ethics, theoretical Sufism is comparable to metaphysics, for the subject of both is existence. Theoretical Sufism today as studied in Iran is dominated by the school of the Shaykh al-Akbar (the greatest master) Ibn 'Arabi (d. 1240). Theoretical Sufism (*'irfan nazari*) is also like metaphysics in that it is an academic field of study in which degrees are granted at universities and research is conducted at the many research centers in Iran. Texts in this field are also studied in the Islamic seminaries, from Ibn 'Arabi's *Bezels of Wisdom*[41] to Ayatullah Javadi Amuli's commentary on a treatise by Ibn Turkah (d. 1432).[42]

Sufi theory is complex, and a common error is to label it as pantheism.[43] Suffice it to say that according to Sufi theory, God is existence, but existence is to be understood neither as the collection of all existing things nor as a universal whose instances are individual existents. Instead, the relation between individual things and God is understood as a relationship between sign and signified. All creatures signify God and have no existence of their own.

Sufi theory is criticized by Muslim philosophers and theologians, but this is not the place to go into the charges and replies. However, Shi'ite spirituality, in the broad sense elaborated here, is pursued on various sides of the debates about theory. There are Shi'a philosophers, jurists, and theologians with a very intense spiritual life who find Sufi theory implausible, based on their own studies.[44] No matter how much they may disagree with the proponents of Sufi theory, they all have in common the spirituality of religious study. The study of religious texts – pre-eminently the Qur'an, then hadiths, but also texts in jurisprudence, its principles, philosophy and theology, and the great commentary literature – is itself an enterprise taken up with devotion. The study of the "Islamic sciences," especially as traditionally undertaken, is also a facet of Islamic spirituality. To dedicate oneself to the study of the Islamic sciences is not only to strive to attain mastery of a scholarly discipline but to live a kind of life informed and transformed by one's studies. Study is carried out as a form of complying with the divine imperatives found in the Qur'an and the narrations of the Ma'sumin. To teach the Islamic sciences is not just a form of employment; rather, ideally, it is a way of living in which one has daily proceedings with the sacred.

The fruits of the spiritual life of Shi'ite Islam should be evident in all the pursuits of the believer. We fall far short, but pray that God may grant us his spiritual gifts to share with our Mennonite friends.

## Endnotes

1   Philip Sheldrake, "Spirituality and Theology," in *Companion Encyclopedia of Theology*, ed. Peter Byrne and Leslie Houlden (London: Routledge, 1995), 514-35, 521. Much of the historical information given above about the term "spirituality" is drawn from this article.

2   In the text of Rumi's *Mathnavi*, the term *ma'navi* occurs twenty-five times, in several of which he refers to his couplets (*mathnavi*) as being *ma'navi*, e.g., in the prefaces to the fifth and sixth books, and in the following two couplets, VI:67-68.

3   *Nahj al-Balagha*, ed. Subhi al-Salih (Qom: Dar al-Hijrah, 1412/1991), 300.

4   Ibid., 301.

5   Asaf A. A. Fyzee, *A Shi'ite Creed* (Tehran: WOFIS, 1982), 48. A similar narration is reported in *Al-Kafi*, to which reference is made in Fayd Kashani's *Kalimat Maknuneh* (Ch. 30): "Among the references to this is that which has been narrated in al-Kafi from the Commander of the Faithful (*'a*): 'The prophets and the foremost [*al-sabiqin*, i.e., the Imams, in accordance with the Shi'i interpretation of (56:10)] have five spirits: the Holy Spirit, the spirit of faith, the spirit of strength, the spirit of desire and the spirit of motion.' He said that it is by the Holy Spirit that the prophets are commissioned and by it that they know the things, and by the spirit of faith they worship Allah and do not associate anything as a partner to Him; and by the spirit of strength they struggled against their enemies and they earned their livings; and by the spirit of desire they are inclined toward delicious food and they marry those who are permitted (*halal*) of the young women; and by the spirit of motion they creep and walk." Then he said, 'The believers who are the companion of the right hand possess the first four, and the infidels and companions of the left hand have the last three of them, such as the animals,' or words to this effect." Muhsin Fayd Kashani, *Kalimat Maknuneh* (Tehran: 1981).

6   Asaf A. A. Fyzee, *A Shi'ite Creed*, 48.

7   Hassan ibn Fazl ibn Hassan Tabarsi, *Mishkat al-Anwar* (Qom: Ansariyan, 2002), narration 296. My translation.

8   Shaykh Saduq, *Sifat al-Shi'ah*, in *Al-Mawaaizh, Sifat al-Shi'ah and Fadhaail*

*al-Shi'ah* (Qom: Ansariyan, 2001), narration 22. My translation.

9   Shaykh Saduq, *Fadhaail al-Shi'ah* in above source, narration 1. My translation.

10  S.H.M. Jafri, *The Origins and Development of Shi'a Islam* (Qom: Ansariyan, 1409/1989), 312.

11  *Tafsir al-Ǽàfí*, Vol. 1, 473, after the verse (5:67).

12  For the dispute about interpretation of this verse, see Mahmoud M. Ayoub, *The Qur'an and Its Interpreters, Vol. II, The House of Imran* (Albany: SUNY, 1992), 39-46.

13  *A Shi'ite Creed*, 85.

14  According to Martin McDermott, the difference between the Shi'ite view of *imamate* (as detailed in the works of Shaykh Mufid (d. 1022) and the Mu'tazilite view is that the Shi'a view the *Imam* as educator and guide for mankind. For the Mu'tazilie 'Abd al-Jabbar, the Imam is merely one who holds authority in administrative, military, and judicial affairs. The authority to guide and teach is the key to understanding the rest of Shi'ite theological claims about the Imamate, such as the doctrine that Imams are protected from sin and error, and that all people need to have a living Imam. See Martin J. McDermott, *The Theology of Al-Shaikh al-Mufid* (Beirut: Dar el-Machreq, 1986), 105.

15  See Carl W. Ernst, *The Shambhala Guide to Sufism* (Boston and London: Shambhala, 1997), 138.

16  Sayyid Haydar Amuli, *Inner Secrets of the Path*, Asadullah ad-Dhaakir Yate, trans. (Dorset, UK: Element Books, 1989).

17  Scholars of hadiths generally consider this one to be apocryphal.

18  *Mathnavi*, Bk. V, preface, my translation.

19  See Martyr Murtada Mutahhari, *An Introduction to 'Irfan*, tr. 'Ali Quli Qara'i, *Al-Tawhid*, 4:1 (1407/198?): http://al-islam.org/al-tawhid/default.asp?url=irfan.htm.

20  Seyyed Hossein Nasr, "The Interior Life in Islam," *Al-Serat*, Vol. III, Nos. 2 and 3, URL= http://www.al-islam.org/al-serat/interior-nasr.htm.

21  Sayyid Haydar Amuli, *Jami' al-Asrar wa Manbi' al-Anwar* (Tehran: Intisharat 'Ilmi wa Farhangi, 1989), 343ff., 586ff. In this work, Haydar Amuli makes the distinction between *islam, iman,* and *iqan* (certainty); but he identifies *ihsan* with the highest stage of *iman* (faith), in accordance with the famous narration: "*Ihsan* is to worship Allah as if you see Him; and if you do not see Him, then verily, He sees you" (597).

22  Sachiko Murata and William C. Chittick, *The Vision of Islam* (New York: Paragon House, 1994).

23  Gerhard Böwering, *The Mystical Vision of Existence in Classical Islam: The Qur'anic Hermeneutics of Sahl At-Tustari (d. 283/896)* (Berlin: Walter de Gruyter, 1980), 141-42.

24  See Mohammad Ali Amir-Moezzi, *The Divine Guide in Early Shi'ism* (Albany:

SUNY Press, 1994), 9. The narration is reported as the twelfth narration of the first part of Kulayni's *Usul al-Kafi*.

25　See Andrew J. Newman, *The Formative Period of Twelver Shi'ism* (Richmond, UK: Curzon, 2000), 94-112. Newman argues that Kulayni's position was actually taken in opposition to the rationalism of the Baghdadi Shi'i scholars.

26　There are also books of religious instruction on how to make a visit to a shrine that discuss this activity with regard to what is and is not proper to do according to *shari'at*, discuss the virtues associated with such visits, and give a few hints of the deeper significance of visiting the shrines in the lives of believers today. See, for example, *Decorum for Visiting the Shrine of Imam Rida ('a)*, prepared by the Islamic Research Foundation of Astan Quds Radavi (Mashhad, Iran: Astan Quds, 2002).

27　Such as those in the collection attributed to the fourth Imam, *Al-Sahifah al-Sajjadiyyah*, translated by William C. Chittick as *The Psalms of Islam* (London: Muhammadi Trust, 1987).

28　The work is in Arabic, and has been published with a Persian commentary and translation by Hasan Mustafavi as *Misbah ash-Shari'ah wa Miftah al-Haqiqah* (Tehran: Iranian Academy of Philosophy, 1981). Another Persian translation is by Zayn al-'Abedin Kazemi Khalkhali, *Misbah al-Shari'ah* (Tehran: Hijr, 1982). There is also an English translation: *The Lantern of the Path*, Muna Bilgrami, trans. (Dorset, UK: Element, 1989), available at http://al-islam.org/lantern-of-the-path/.

29　Martyr Murtada Mutahhari, *An Introduction to 'Irfan*, trans. 'Ali Quli Qara'i, *Al-Tawhid*, 4:1 (1407/198?). See: http://al-islam.org/al-tawhid/default.asp?url=irfan.htm.

30　See the introduction by Seyyed Hossein Nasr to *Islamic Spirituality: Manifestations* (New York: Crossroad, 1997), xv.

31　For more on the mutual influences of Shi'ism and Sufism, see Seyyed Hossein Nasr, "Shi'ism and Sufism: their Relationship in Essence and in History," in his *Sufi Essays* (Albany: SUNY, 1991), 104-20. For a Sufi pronouncement on the inner identity of Islam with Shi'ism and of Shi'ism with Sufism, see Majdhub 'Alishah, "Shi'ism, Sufism and Gnosticism," in *The Sufi Path*, ed. Shahram Pazouki (Tehran: Haqiqat, 2002), 23-45.

32　Shaykh Saduq, *Al-Tawhid*, Bab 60, narration 4.

33　See Imam Ruhollah Khomeini, *The Greatest Jihad: Combat with the Self*, URL = http://www.al-islam.org/al-tawhid/jihadeakbar/.

34　A translation of this work is found in the *Journal of Shi'ite Islamic Studies* 1.1 (2006): 68-80.

35　Available on line at: http://najaf.org/english/book/16/

36　Sayyid Muhammad Husayn Husayni Tihrani, *Kernel of the Kernel* (Albany: SUNY, 2003), 109.

37　See, for example, Mirza Javad Agha Maliki Tabrizi, *Spiritual Journey of the*

*Mystics (Suluk-i Arifan): Etiquette of the Holy Month of Ramadhan* at http://al-islam.org/suluk/

38  For example, Imam Ruhollah Khomeini, *Adab al-Salat: The Disciplines of the Prayer* (Tehran: The Institute for the Compilation and Publication of Imam Khomeini's Works, 2002).

39  For an example of a modern Shi'ite Sufi work of this genre, see Fadhlalla Haeri, *Beams of Illumination from the Divine Revelation* (Blanco, TX: Zahra, 1985).

40  See Muhammad Legenhausen, "A Mystic's Insights on the Words of the Shi'i Imams: A Selection of Narrations from the First Chapter of Al-Tawhid of Shaykh Saduq and Commentary by Qadi Sa'id Qummi (d. 1696)."

41  Ibn al-'Arabi, *The Bezels of Wisdom,* trans. R.W.J. Austin (Lahore: Suhail, 1988).

42  Javadi Amuli, *Tahrir Tamhid al-Qawa'id* (Qom: Zahra, 1993).

43  The best introduction in English is the pair of volumes by William Chittick, *The Sufi Path of Knowledge* (Albany: SUNY, 1989) and *The Self-Disclosure of God* (Albany: SUNY, 1998).

44  As an example of the sort of criticism of Sufi theory raised from the perspective of Islamic philosophy, see Ayatullah Misbah Yazdi, *Philosophical Instructions* (Binghamton, NY: Global Publications, 1999), 247f.

# Spirituality in the Mennonite Faith Community

## C. Arnold Snyder

I would like to speak about the historical foundations of Mennonite spirituality, focusing my comments on a description of the spiritual vision of our Mennonite faith parents. Other participants in this conference will be looking more closely at present Mennonite spirituality and practice.

Our Mennonite Christian tradition has its origins in the sixteenth century, now almost 500 years ago, at the time of the so-called Protestant Reformation. In many ways, our faith tradition was part of the Protestant reform; like Protestant Christians, our faith parents also left the Roman Catholic Church. But in its spirituality, our tradition continues many emphases seen in the Catholic orders and monastic communities – especially the emphasis on a visible community life that tries to live faithfully in accordance with the teachings of Jesus and the practice of the Apostles. Our tradition has sometimes been described as "neither Catholic nor Protestant," or as "both Catholic and Protestant." I will try to describe the spiritual foundations of this tradition for you, as briefly as I can.

## Spirituality

One of the subjects that we will no doubt be discussing throughout this conference is what we mean, individually and collectively, by the term "spirituality." One description that I find helpful is adapted from Philip Sheldrake, and applies to Christian spirituality generally: The Christian spiritual life is lived in relationship with God, in Jesus Christ, through the indwelling of the Holy Spirit, within a community of believers, embracing the entire world. Christian spirituality encompasses all of life and relates all of life to the creator.

Christian spirituality enfolds and includes the inner and the outer lives of Christians – that is, both their contemplative and their active lives. This dual emphasis on the inner work of the living Spirit of God and the outer work of obedience and discipleship comes to expression and is put into practice in different ways among Christian churches, but the dual emphasis is especially important to Mennonite spirituality. It is true that with the passing of some centuries, our tradition did begin to emphasize obedience and discipleship more strongly than the cultivation of the inner, contemplative side of the spiritual life. The visible features of the Mennonite understanding of the faithful Christian life – the baptism of committed adults and following after Jesus' teachings of love and nonviolence, in a communal commitment – are certainly the best-known and most easily recognized marks of Mennonite spirituality. However, they are only a part of the story. Our spiritual tradition also has an interior dimension and foundation that is less well known. I will try to describe some of its features here.

## Framework

The Christian story of creation, fall, and redemption provided the framework for the spiritual life of our faith tradition. Our earliest writings repeat a story familiar to all Christians. God, the creator and sustainer of all that is, originally created humanity in his image, and created human beings good. This original harmony was destroyed by the disobedience and rebellion of our human parents, and resulted in alienation from God, the only source of life. This rebellion persisted, in spite of the law, the covenant, and the sending of the prophets. With the life and death of Jesus Christ, however, the alienation of human beings from God was overcome for all time. The sacrifice of Jesus on the cross corrected the cosmic wrong, and opened the way back to God for those who believe in Christ and are prepared to follow him.

Our faith tradition implicitly accepted this biblical account of creation, fall, and redemption and placed the spiritual life within that framework. The spiritual life was often described as a journey back to God; it was a journey that progressed by a series of steps or stages. It was described as a journey from disobedience to obedience, from natural human rebellion to a supernatural yielding to God's will by God's grace and power.

## Inward Journey

The spiritual journey in our tradition begins with an inward journey, which itself begins with the negative condition in which all human beings find themselves: there is a time for all human beings when the spiritual life has not yet been consciously accepted. This is the original state of alienation, rebellion, or sin in which all of us come to live, following our inherited human inclinations. Our tradition maintained that in order for the spiritual life to begin, human beings must come to an awareness of the situation of disobedience that exists between them and their creator. The awakening of this awareness was often described as coming to a "fear of God." That is, when human beings realize the greatness of God and their own smallness and state of disobedience, it is clear that eternal death is the only possible reward. "Fear of God" is a phrase that encompassed these many meanings: the awesomeness and greatness of God, the admission of human failure, and the recognition of human dependence on God. Our faith parents often quoted the book of Proverbs: Fear of the Lord is the beginning of wisdom (Prov.1:7).

Following from the fear of God comes heartfelt repentance and sorrow for disobedience. We could call this the second stage in the inward spiritual journey: Those who have truly come to an understanding of the greatness of God and their own smallness and disobedience respond first with sorrow and penitence. Our Mennonite spirituality was, at its origins, a penitential spirituality, based on the sincere and heartfelt repentance of individuals who had come face to face with the overwhelming greatness of God the creator. These people often were called "the God-fearing" in the writings of our tradition. In a letter written from prison, Soetgen van den Houte, a mother who knew she was going to be put to death for her faith, wrote to her children in 1560 that God would not leave them without parents. They were to "seek out the God-fearing" and all would be well.

> My most beloved, always ... be instructed by those who fear the Lord; then you will please God, and as long as you obey

good admonition and instruction, and fear the Lord, He will be your Father and not leave you orphans.[1]

The fear of God and coming to repentance were ways of expressing the complete abandonment and surrender of these awakened individuals to God's mercy and kindness. They knew that, of themselves, they could do nothing to merit mercy. They could only call on God for mercy. But this penitential prayer would be heard. It led to a third stage in the spiritual journey, described as a time of grace and comfort: in the midst of the despair of penance and surrender, in the midst of tears and sorrow, God offers forgiveness and new life through Jesus Christ. The "good news" the penitent sinner receives is that God has already forgiven all disobedient and thoughtless sinners by sending his son Jesus – and continues forgiving into the present. For the penitent sinner, in the depths of sorrow and despair, this is good news of the very best kind: Christ's sacrifice on the cross turned God's judgment and condemnation into love and acceptance, for those who believe and who accept God's offer of grace and forgiveness.

The fourth stage in the journey is grateful self-surrender to God. The word our parents used was the same one used by the medieval Catholic mystics: *Gelassenheit*. Gelassenheit means yielding, surrender, or abandonment to the power of God. In our tradition, faith is not just about believing in a cognitive way; more fundamentally, it is an absolute trust in God, placing one's life entirely in God's hands in complete surrender. The good news of God's forgiveness and acceptance in Christ is a gift and an invitation. Faith is the acceptance of this gift in a total sense of acceptance – accepting that God's goodness is real, that God is trustworthy, and that one is ready to place one's entire life into God's hands. Those who abandon themselves into God's hands manifest a true faith. They truly "believe," and so they trust.

Connected with this trusting and absolute surrender to God comes the most important event in the spiritual life of our tradition, which we can call a fifth stage on the inward journey: spiritual rebirth. When the genuinely penitent sinner surrenders entirely to God, God's Spirit and power begin to re-make and re-shape the old human nature into a new nature. It is this birth of God's Spirit in the heart of penitent believers that is the central interior and divine event in our tradition. It makes possible what will occur in the outward spiritual practice of believers.

Although we have sometimes forgotten this fact, our faith tradition is based on the understanding that the living God becomes present in human lives, transforming them with the power of the divine Spirit, and so creating new beings. These new beings can be called "children of God" because they are like branches grafted onto the heavenly vine. These children of God produce divine fruit, not because they are heroes but because they have yielded to God and so allow the power of divine love to flow through them.

If faith is genuine, said our forebears, then it is a faith that trusts in God, surrenders to God, and is willing and ready to follow God's will and God's commandments. It is not enough simply to "believe." One must believe and obey. And it is the spiritual rebirth that provides the power and the means to obey, because natural human beings do not have the strength or the natural inclination to follow God's will. God not only forgave sinners through Christ's sacrifice on the cross; God also produces righteous, obedient children and followers by the power of the living Spirit – the same living Spirit that was present in Christ.

Persons who have been awakened by the presence of the living God, empowered by the living Spirit, and surrendered to God's power, desire to live in the presence of God. Our spiritual tradition held that following these inward stages of awakening, repentance, believing, surrender, and rebirth, a believer would have an overwhelming desire to unite with other believers. Together these re-born children of God would form one body – the body of Christ on earth, sometimes called the church. The experience of passing from darkness to light was inward, a progression or development that would take place in the hearts of individuals. But the spirituality of our tradition said that true belief does not remain inward, exclusively within the hearts of individuals. If faith is real, it will, it *must* express itself outwardly and become visible, tangible, concrete in the midst of life itself.

Here our tradition turned to the Scriptures for guidance. It was true that the living Word of God wrote on the believers' hearts and transformed their beings; but it was the written Word of God that provided truth, guidance, and wisdom for the journey that remained on earth. Since both the spiritual Word and the written Word were words of the same God, Spirit and Word, inner and outer, would coexist in harmony.

## Outward Practice

Following these five inward stages or steps in the spiritual life, our faith tradition focused on what was believed were the necessary outward expressions of the inward spiritual changes I have just described. Because our faith parents believed that the Spirit of God and the Word of God would be in harmony with one another, they expected the outward practice of their inner spiritual renewal to be described in Scripture. They expected to find the path for the spiritual life in the written Word. In the New Testament they found the basic outlines for their understanding of the church, which they called the Body of Christ, or the Bride of Christ. They found four primary outward marks of the church: baptism, discipline (or mutual accountability), celebration of the Lord's Supper, and sharing of material goods with those in need. Very soon more outward marks were added: washing of each other's feet became a church practice, following Jesus' example of humility; also, suffering at the hands of "the world" seemed to our faith parents to be an inevitable result of trying to live faithfully, and a mark of the church.

Baptism in water was the pivotal act in creating the church. In the Gospels of Matthew and Mark, our forebears found in Jesus' words what they believed was a commandment to be followed: go forth, preach the good news, and when people believe, baptize them and teach them to obey the commandments. From these Scripture passages, they concluded that the baptism of infants was a mistake that had destroyed the true church. Baptism had to be reserved for adult believers, they believed, because it was a covenant, a statement of purpose, a promise before God of one's most serious intentions. They believed that what Jesus was calling for could never be managed by an infant. Baptism was an outward sign, a testimony or a witness, that the inward, spiritual surrender to God had taken place. The water as such had no sacramental or divine power; rather it was a covenant sign to

God that one's heart and intentions were pure.

Baptism was in a primary sense an act of visible commitment to God, but in a secondary and equally important sense water baptism was also a covenant sign and promise to other believers that one was prepared to become a living member of the Body of Christ. This baptism in water formed the visible church, and bound the baptized members to one another in a promise of mutual love, to share possessions, and to admonish one another in matters of faithfulness and obedience. In our tradition, then, baptism in water became the visible sign that linked the inward, spiritual renewal of individuals with the outward, communal spiritual practice of the church, or the Body of Christ.

Those who commit themselves by baptism to faithfulness – both faithfulness to God and to the Body of Christ on earth – also celebrate together Christ's meal or the Lord's Supper, with which they promise again to walk on the narrow way of Christ, with one another; they share material goods with each another and with the needy; and they submit to mutual admonition or discipline from fellow believers if they should happen to stray from the path. These were the primary marks of the church, as our tradition understood them to be described in the New Testament.

Our faith parents believed that the true church stood in opposition to the world, and that the world would necessarily stand in opposition to Christ and the church. In the sixteenth century and for several centuries thereafter, this opposition proved to be true, and the "baptizers" (as they were called) suffered persecution that was sometimes extremely severe. Although very few in number, still one-half of all Christians killed for their faith in the sixteenth century were from the baptizing communities. We do not know the exact number, but there were approximately 3,000 martyrs from our tradition in the space of 100 years.

## Spiritual Disciplines

Again, because our faith parents expected the renewing inner word of the Spirit to be in harmony with the outer word of Scripture, they expected to find all they needed to know about spiritual discipline in the Bible itself. They tested the spiritual practices that had grown up and been used in the Christian church over many centuries against the testimony of Scripture. The monastic tradition, for example, had developed lives of regulated prayer, and different monastic rules specified how the religious were to pray. Our parents found none of this in Scripture, and thus rejected the regulated approach. They prayed often and fervently, and very often prayed the prayer that Jesus taught – the Lord's Prayer. Apart from that prayer, which they repeated from memory, they insisted that prayers should not be read or memorized but should rather "spring from the heart." Some eyewitnesses testified that they prayed with great groans, sighs, and tears.

Letters from Anabaptists in prison speak often about the importance of constant and fervent prayer. In a particularly poignant letter, the condemned Joost de Tollenaer wrote a last testament to his young daughter, Betgen, and advised her: "Going, standing, working, always have the Lord before your eyes, calling upon Him with prayer and supplication." He asked her to pray in the following way:

> O Lord, my Lord, direct me in Thy ways; give me wisdom that comes from the throne of Thy glory, and cleanse me from all my sins, that I may be worthy to become a holy temple. Give me grace that I may be meek and humble of heart, and little in my own eyes, so that Thy Holy Spirit may dwell in me, and that I may grow up in Thy holy divine fear; to the eternal salvation of my soul and to the praise, glory and honour of Thy holy, most worthy, adorable name. O Lord, strengthen me, miserable one, since I am but dust and ashes. O Lord, be merciful unto me, and help me forever. Amen.[2]

As well as praying with great frequency, our faith parents also developed the practice of singing what they called "spiritual songs." They would take common, popular song tunes and compose their own verses to accompany the tunes. We know of many thousands of such songs. The Old Order Amish still sing some of them in their church services today. From the frequency with which they composed hymns and sang them, we conclude that singing spiritual songs formed an important part of their daily spiritual discipline. The songs often were like small sermons on topics like baptism, faithfulness, suffering, hope, love, and so forth. Often they set biblical texts to music, to be sung and remembered.

But undoubtedly the most important spiritual discipline practiced by the baptizing community in the sixteenth century was learning and remembering Scripture. The baptizers became well known for the amount of Scripture they could recite; they would quote Scripture at length to their jailers and interrogators. They would sing Scripture in their prison cells. It didn't seem to matter if the prisoner was old, young, illiterate, literate, man or woman, all alike seemed able to "prove their faith" with the words of Scripture. And this was, in fact, their primary spiritual discipline. It was this biblical grounding, this complete owning of the biblical text and story, that was the true source and foundation of Anabaptist spirituality and the heart of their spiritual discipline. Even though jailers took their Bibles away, they continued to meditate on the words of Scripture – which they carried with them in their memories.

Finally, although it seems obvious to say so, their worship together was a central spiritual discipline for our faith parents. I will quote one small testimony from the year 1526, just to illustrate how one prisoner described meeting with a few fellow believers: When he and his fellow believers gathered, this man testified,

> they prayed a prayer together, that God might strengthen them to be able to carry the cross patiently. After that they interpreted the Scripture according to each one's spiritual understanding, that they do nothing against God and act in love toward their neighbours, give enemies food, drink, and love them, etc. . . . In short, that all things should be held in common and each one should do their work, and if someone were needy, then they should share some of the common good with the needy.[3]

The prisoner's compatriot added that "When they gathered together, they admonished one another to beware of sin and disgraceful behaviour."[4] We hear in these confessions the desire to be faithful to

God's will as revealed in the Bible and the wish to live a life of obedience. The interpretation and understanding of Scripture stood at the centre of these small meetings, as well as biblical consolation, comfort, and prayer.[5]

## Discipleship

Our faith parents soon discovered that Scripture could be, and was, interpreted in many different ways. When contentious issues arose, they adopted the practice of looking for the final word in the words and deeds of Jesus, and the practice of the Apostles. They believed that if they followed Jesus' words and actions, they would not go wrong. This belief led our tradition into three practices that caused great difficulty and still challenge us today: first, a life dedicated to love – especially evident in loving enemies and rejecting violence; second, a life dedicated to speaking and living the truth – a life in which one's "yes" means "yes" and one's "no" means "no"; third, they believed that Jesus had shown that earthly possessions were to be shared with all and not accumulated for individual benefit. God's treasure is spiritual and heavenly, not earthly wealth.

And so the baptizers generated much suspicion: they would neither swear the loyalty oaths required of citizens nor promise to defend territory with weapons, and property owners were threatened by what they said about sharing possessions.

I believe others will say more about the nonviolence of our tradition, and perhaps also about the truthfulness to which we are called, and – very difficult for us materialistic Mennonites today – the call to generosity with earthly goods. I will only say here that our spiritual tradition came to focus very strongly on Jesus and on following after him in life. Our tradition has thus been called a tradition of discipleship. Jesus was both saviour and example. Furthermore, the living Spirit made it possible for reborn children of God to follow after him in life.

As 21st-century Mennonites, we struggle with faithfulness, and we are tempted by violence, materialism, and a wide assortment of lies and half-truths. Still, we have not forgotten our spiritual inheritance, which is the call and the vocation to follow after Jesus in life. This call challenges us daily.

## Conclusion

Let me conclude with four brief observations or points of summary about our spiritual tradition:

1. First, one of the marks of our tradition is the desire to integrate the interior life of the Spirit with the external witness of a life that has been shaped by the living God. Both must be present.

2. Secondly, our tradition is dependent on the presence and work of the living God, who invites the rebellious and the alienated into a new life in Christ. The reborn make up the Body of Christ on earth, and live out the life of Christ in the world – that is, a life dedicated to love, truth, and generosity. Connected to this is a passion for justice in human relationships, which our tradition believes is the will of God for all humanity.

3. Third, our tradition places the community of believers at the centre of the spiritual life. The spiritual life is to be lived in community, not in isolation.

4. And finally, our tradition places the life and witness of Christ at the centre of the community's life. It is Christ who is the head, believers who are Christ's members.

In our spiritual tradition we aspire to follow in the footsteps of Christ. We have failed often; we fall short constantly; but our desire to be faithful disciples continues to define our spirituality.

## Endnotes

1   Thieleman J. van Braght, *Martyrs Mirror* (Scottdale, PA: Herald Press, 1972), 646.
2   Ibid., 1076.
3   M. Krebs and H.G. Rott, *Quellen zur Geschichte der Täufer*, VII Band, Elsaß, I. Teil (Gütersloh: Gerd Mohn, 1959), 63. Translation mine.
4   Ibid.
5   In 1557 officials in Stuttgart described the Anabaptist view as follows: "Earlier, when they still loved the world, with excessive eating and drinking etc., they

were loved by the world. But now that they began to die to the world, they are persecuted. Therefore they are forced to come together in secret, just as in the early church, and to comfort one another out of God's Word." Gustav Bossert, *Quellen zur Geschichte der Wiedertäufer, I. Band, Herzogtum Württemberg* (Leipzig: Nachfolger, 1930; New York: Johnson Reprint, 1971), 157. Translation mine. Endris Fecklin was seen preaching to two tables full of people, a Bible in front of him from which he read to the assembled. Ibid., 540.

# Trinitarian Foundations for Christian Spirituality

## A. James Reimer

In this, the third dialogue between Iranian Shi'a Muslims and Mennonite Christians, we celebrate our common humanity and the numerous more particular commonalities that I have identified elsewhere.[1] One of the strengths of our dialogue has been our mutual respect for each other's faith traditions. We both come to the dialogue in a common search for truth that is greater than ourselves, without attempting to reduce our commonalities to a lowest common denominator. This is not a generic dialogue between Christianity and Islam, but a very specific dialogue between two particular traditions within Christianity and Islam. We both come to the table with strong faith convictions that do have some things in common. But there are also differences, which we have no desire to erase. One of these is our respective understanding of God. Muslims are insistent on protecting the transcendent singularity and unity of the one all-merciful God, Allah. The many different names for God in Islam are just that: names, not different manifestations or incarnations of God. Muhammad is an ordinary human being to whom the great truths of God were revealed as recorded in the Qur'an, but in no way an incarnation of the divine.

Christians are one of the three Abrahamic religions (the other two are Judaism and Islam); that is, they are monotheistic, rejecting all forms of polytheism, even though Muslims sometimes sense tri-theistic temptations within Christianity. This tri-theism is admittedly a danger in our tradition. But in its classical theological formulation, it was precisely the unity of God that was a concern in affirming the three historical manifestations of God (the Trinity): God as the one transcendent, creator God of the Hebrews (JHWH, Adonai, Elohim), who acted in Jewish history; God as taking on historical, human flesh

in the event of Jesus the Christ; and God as immanent power in the
Holy Spirit. There were, of course, differences between Eastern and
Western understandings of the Trinity. Mennonite theologian Thomas
Finger states:

> Against modalism, the Eastern solution stresses distinctions
> among the persons (*hypostaseis*), though still by means of
> actions; only the Father begets and *spirates*, only the Son is
> begotten, only the Spirit proceeds. In the East, divine unity
> was conceived as operating within and among the persons
> as the continual flowing back and forth of love, energy and
> delight, or *perichoresis*.... Moreover, the divine essence (*ousia*)
> exists only in each of the persons. *Ousia* does not designate
> some ontological category or thing subsisting apart from
> each. Further, whatever this *ousia*, or essence, is, humans will
> neither know it nor participate in it, now or in eternity. This is
> why divinization can only be participation in divine energies,
> not the divine essence (*ousia*), and can only be transformation
> by God, not into God.
>
> Western theologians, in contrast, tended to locate divine
> unity in a divine essence, or substance, common to the persons.
> Heaven will involve direct contemplation, or a beatific vision,
> of this essence. This enables Westerners to stress the equality
> of the persons, for each share fully in this substance. Moreover,
> each divine person participates in every divine action. This
> tends, however, to underplay the distinctness of each.[2]

In time a distinction was made between the Immanent Trinity
– the threefoldness within God himself – and the Economic Trinity
– the threefoldness of God as expressed outwardly in salvation history
(*Heilsgeschichte).* While some modern theologians such as Karl Rahner
have collapsed the two,[3] I have argued for a distinction so as protect the
transcendence of God.[4] It is true that within the Christian doctrine of
God there is a plurality within God that stands in tension with his unity,
in a way that is not the case in Islam. This is so even though one might
argue that in Islam too there is a kind of threefoldness: the transcendent

singular essence of God, whose will and being is historically revealed through Gabriel to Muhammad the prophet and the Qur'an, and who is spiritually present to individual believers existentially.

In an age when Spirituality is *au courant*, as a Christian I believe it is especially important to remember that Christian spirituality is rooted in an understanding of God as three- in-one, the Trinity. For more than two decades my theological work has centred on the need for Christian theology to ground itself in a classical, trinitarian doctrine of God. This, I have argued, is the core doctrine that is the foundation for all other Christian doctrines.[5] In particular I have repeatedly maintained that the Mennonite concern for Christian ethics and morality, especially the witness to peace and nonviolent love that Mennonites hold so dear, must be rooted in a notion of God as triune (Father, Son, and Holy Spirit), if it is not to deteriorate into pure human agency. Only as the nonviolent love ethic is grounded outside ourselves, in the divine agency of God as transcendent mystery and creator of the world, as historically incarnated in Jesus the Christ, and made present to us and empowering us in the Holy Spirit, will it be sustained over time and history.

Spirituality, in the Christian sense, does not celebrate the human spirit as such, but the human spirit as the divine Spirit, which is itself the Spirit of Jesus Christ and God the Creator, grasps it. The Eastern tradition, as well as the Western mystical tradition, stresses the *unio mystica* – the mystical union of the individual human spirit with God via the divine spirit. The Holy Spirit lifts us up into the very life of the Trinity. In the less mystical mainstream of the Western tradition, what some scholars like Werner Packull have identified as the spiritualist tradition, there is a great divide between God and humanity (due to sin and the fall), and the Holy Spirit functions as a mediation between the divine and the human initiated by God. The Anabaptists of the 16th century, progenitors of Mennonites, tended toward the Eastern notion of deification.

In this essay I assume the Christian doctrine of God as three-in-one simultaneously, and I look at how Anabaptist-Mennonites appropriate that doctrine. Except for a small group of Polish Anabaptists who were either di-theists or unitarians, all the Anabaptists assumed that the

Father, Son, and Holy Spirit played significant roles in the coming of a new creation, and believed that all three were fully divine.

Menno Simons, the Dutch leader who lent his name to the whole Mennonite movement, wrote a treatise, "A Solemn Confession of the Triune, Eternal, and True God, Father, Son, and Holy Ghost,"[6] against another Anabaptist, Adam Pastor, who denied the doctrine of the Trinity. For Simons the doctrine of the Trinity was not to be understood in a carnal and literal sense, but as a spiritual reality:

1. *Father*. The eternal and true God is to be understood as Spirit. About the Father, Simons says: "This one and only eternal, omnipotent, incomprehensible, invisible, ineffable, and indescribable God, we believe and confess with the Scriptures to be the eternal, incomprehensible Father with His eternal, incomprehensible Son, and with His eternal, incomprehensible Holy Spirit" (Simons, 491).

The Son of the Father before the incarnation is not to be understood as a literal word, but as "the eternal, wise, Almighty, holy, true, living, and incomprehensible Word, which in the beginning was with God, and was God, by whom all things were made, and without whom not anything was made that was made, and who will endure forever" (Simons, 492). According to Simons, "His [the Father's] wisdom, His power, His light, His truth, His life, His Word, Christ Jesus, has been eternally with Him, in Him and by Him; yea, that He is the alpha and the Omega" (Simons, 492). In his theology of God the Father as "eternal, omnipotent, incomprehensible, invisible, ineffable, and indescribable" Word and Spirit, Menno remained true to the orthodox tradition.

2. *Son*. In Menno's words, "this same eternal, wise, Almighty, holy, true, living, and incomprehensible Word, Christ Jesus, which was in the beginning with God and which was God, incomprehensible – born of the incomprehensible Father, before every creature – did in the fullness of time become, according to the unchangeable purpose and faithful promise of the Father, a true, visible, suffering, hungry, thirsty, and mortal man in Mary, the pure virgin, through the operation and overshadowing of the Holy Spirit, and so was born of her" (Simons, 492). Menno adds: "To go on, beloved brethren, we believe and confess Christ Jesus to be the true God with the Father" (Simons, 493). Although there is some question about whether he adequately

emphasized Christ's human nature, in accordance with the formulation
of Chalcedon (451 CE) – he seemed to claim Christ had a "celestial
flesh" rather than an earthly, human flesh received from the Virgin
Mary – he did not question Christ's full deity.

3. *Holy Spirit.* According to Menno: "We believe and confess the
Holy Ghost to be a true, real, and personal Holy Ghost, as the fathers
called Him; and that in a divine fashion, even as the Father is a true
Father and the Son a true Son" (Simons, 495). Leaning toward an
Eastern Orthodox understanding, Simons refers to the Holy Spirit as
"proceeding from the Father *through* [my emphasis] the Son, although
He ever remains with God and in God, and is never separated from the
being of the Father and the Son" (Simons, 496). What is the role of the
Holy Spirit for Menno? "He [the Holy Spirit] guides us into all truth;
He justifies us. He cleanses, sanctifies, reconciles, comforts, reproves,
cheers, and assures us. He testifies with our spirit that we are the children
of God. This Spirit all they receive who believe on Christ" (Simons,
496). In other words, the Holy Spirit is the subjective appropriation
of what the Son has done objectively for us. The Holy Spirit gives us
gifts: "we believe the Holy Spirit to be the true, essential Holy Spirit of
God, who adorns us with His heavenly and divine gifts, and through
His influence, according to the good pleasure of the Father, frees us
from sin, gives us boldness, and makes us cheerful, peaceful, pious, and
holy" (Simons, 496). The Holy Spirit is responsible for the regeneration
of believers, empowering them to live a spiritual and ethical life.

Menno shies away from giving ontological status to each of the
three divine realities. Rather he describes them as follows: "these
three names, activities, and powers, namely, the Father, the Son, and
the Holy Ghost (which the fathers called three persons, by which
they meant the three, true, divine beings) are one incomprehensible,
indescribable, Almighty, holy, only, eternal, and sovereign God. As
John says, there are three that bear record in heaven, the Father, the
Word, and the Holy Ghost; and these three are one" (Simons, 496).
These three, although three in some sense, "in deity, will, power, and
works . . . are one, and can no more be separated from each other than
the sun, brightness, and warmth. For the one cannot exist without the
other. Yet all is incomprehensible from the incomprehensible Father,

even as the brightness and heat of the sun" (Simons, 496).

Menno Simons and his colleague Dirk Philips, somewhat like ancient Alexandrians, understood salvation as "christomorphic divinization" (Finger, 383), a concept common to many early Anabaptists and centrally important for their view of spirituality. Through God's salvation believers participate in the divine nature itself (2 Pet. 1:4). This empowers them to live like Jesus lived. Spirituality is always directly related to the ethical life, empowering it. Because of the strong purist strain in early Anabaptist thought, some like Melchior Hoffman and Menno parted company with classical Chalcedonian Christology – because of the corruption of the flesh, Jesus did not take on the flesh of Mary. Similarly, those who participate in the nature of Christ are transformed and overcome the corruption of the flesh as members of the church without spot and wrinkle. In Menno and Dirk, there was a tendency to "overprioritizing" Christ's deity (Finger, 387) and, we might add, human divinity through regeneration as well.

There were some early Anabaptists who rejected the doctrine of the Trinity. Finger has given us a fine treatment of these Italian and Polish Anabaptists (Finger, 387-96), who were not trinitarian in the classical sense but either di-theists (de-emphasizing the Spirit) or unitarian (emphasizing the Father as sole eternal deity). They tended toward an adoptionist view of Christ's deity foregrounding the ethical features of his life, involving "rationalistic, humanistic assumptions different from those that other Anabaptists generally shared" (Finger, 394). Consequently, Polish Anabaptism "lacked the spiritually transformative notion of salvation found in the other three branches [Swiss, Dutch, and Austrian] and the mystical orientation in all but the Swiss" (Finger, 394). For the other Anabaptists, "Jesus' life formed the outward pattern of a present salvation that was also vibrantly inward and spiritual – and directed, of course, toward future culmination" (Finger, 394). Polish Anabaptist themes pointed forward toward modernity, while other Anabaptists referred "back toward features of medieval mysticism and communalism, and ultimately the New Testament" (Finger, 394).

Virtually all Anabaptists, other than Polish di-theists and unitarians, thought of Father, Son, and Spirit as personal agents. In classical Eastern trinitarianism the "divine substance (essence or nature) exists nowhere but in the persons themselves. They are united through their ceaseless giving and receiving of love, glory, energy, joy and praise among themselves." Numerous Anabaptists also saw the energies and activities of the Father, Son, and Spirit as working through each (Finger, 445).

For all the trinitarian Anabaptists, trinitarian language is linked to moral-ethical concerns. Spirituality cannot be separated from personal, moral integrity. Possibly the clearest example of this is found in Peter Riedemann's *Account of Our Religion, Doctrine and Faith*. Ethical concerns are not tacked on to the end of a list of theological doctrines but are incorporated into the very doctrine of the Trinity from the beginning. To confess the first article of the creed – that God is almighty Father, creator of heaven and earth – is itself a moral act for "every sinner who remaineth and continueth in sin, and yet nameth God father, speaketh what is not true. . . ." Further, the whole purpose of confessing the second and third article of the creed – belief in Jesus Christ as the only begotten son of God, and the Holy Spirit as proceeding from the Father and the Son – is to acknowledge that through them we are "grafted . . . into the divine character and nature." This phrase or various versions of it like "participation in the nature of Christ (or God)" appears repeatedly in many of the Anabaptist writers and suggests, as we have already seen, the deification of human nature in a way quite foreign to Luther and Calvin. Concern for genuine moral regeneration is present in the *Account of Our Religion* from the start, and the Hutterite commitment to Christian communalism is linked to the very immanent plurality within God himself. Community, says Riedemann, "is naught else than that those who have fellowship have all things in common together, none having aught for himself, but each having all things with the others, even as the Father hath nothing for himself, but all that he hath, he hath with the Son, and again, the Son hath nothing for himself, but all that he hath, he hath with the Father and all who have fellowship with him."[7]

For the Anabaptists, trinitarian theology is important not for its own sake but as a necessary framework for, and ground of, the regenerated life. Christ and more particularly the Spirit of Christ, the Holy Spirit, is that which unites the Christian with the character and nature of God.

This participation in the character of Christ, and through him in the very nature of God, is one of the most repeated themes in someone like Menno Simons; it is a form of sanctification (or even deification) that can occur only in the context of the believing community: the church.

## Endnotes

1   A. James Reimer, "Introduction" to Revelation and Authority: Shi'ah Muslim – Mennonite Christian Dialogue II in *The Conrad Grebel Review* 24.1 (Winter 2006): 4-11.

2   Thomas N. Finger, *A Contemporary Anabaptist Theology: Biblical, Historical, Constructive* (Downers Grove, IL: InterVarsity Press, 2004), 422-23.

3   See Karl Rahner, *The Trinity* (New York: The Crossroad Publishing Company, 1999). Rahner says: "The 'economic' Trinity is the 'immanent' Trinity and the 'immanent' Trinity is the 'economic' Trinity" (22).

4   See my *Mennonites and Classical Theology: Dogmatic Foundations for Christian Ethics* (Kitchener, ON: Pandora Press, 2001), 487.

5   Reimer, "Introduction," *Mennonites and Classical Theology*, 13-17.

6   *The Complete Writings of Menno Simons* (Scottdale, PA: Herald Press, 1956), 489-98. Here I note page numbers for specific citations to this work, and to Thomas Finger's *A Contemporary Anabaptist Theology,* in the essay itself.

7   Peter Riedemann, *Account of Our Religion, Doctrine and Faith* (London: Hodder and Stroughton, in conjunction with Plough Publishing House, 1938, 1970), 43. Cf. Reimer, *Mennonites and Classical Theology*, 398. The Holy Spirit is what makes this possible within and among us.

In the name of Allah

# From Knowing God to Loving God: Spirituality and Submission

## Ali Mesbah

*In the Creation of the heavens and the earth, and the recurrence of night and day, are signs (of His sovereignty) for wise people; those who remember Allah while standing, sitting, and reclining, and deliberate on the creation of the heavens and the earth, (and say:) our Lord! Thou created not this in vain;*
*Holy You are; so preserve us from the doom of Fire!*

After a long period of relative neglect, and prophecies about the inevitable dominance of modern materialism over any kind of spirituality, the spiritual quest has again become a burning issue in most parts of the modern world. Spirituality and religion share much in their destiny. Max Weber believed that the disenchantment of the world and human life will be the unavoidable consequences of modernity. He called the modern society an "iron cage," void of freedom and meaning. If some secular thinkers spoke of the privatization of religion, others envisaged the evaporation of spirituality altogether. David Griffin speaks of "the archmodernists" regarding religion until quite recently "as an 'opiate' or an 'illusion' with inevitably regressive effects." They considered "religion, to the extent it is opposed to the Baconian world-image of science, [as] an open or potential threat to any modern polity."

Meanwhile, Griffin sees religious spirituality to be emerging as "the only hope for positive social change as well as for conserving truly important values." John Esposito also writes, "The global resurgence of religions in the last decades of the twentieth century, the Islamic reawakening in particular, [has] challenged, some might say discredited, the belief, indeed dogma, of the prophets of modernity. Some critics talk of the collapse or bankruptcy of secularism and the need to replace it with religiously based states," and Griffin suggests that secularism itself is "a spirituality that is not neutral toward historic religious spiritualities."

## What is Spirituality?

In a discussion about spirituality, we have to answer several questions such as the following: What do we mean by spirituality? Is spirituality something radically distinct from the natural world? What is its relation to religion? Are they the same? Does spirituality include religion, or is it included in the latter? And how does spirituality relate to ethics? Diverse and contradictory answers have been proposed for these questions.

"Spirituality" is a term with no historical background in the original Islamic sources, namely the Qur'an and Hadith. However, it has gained currency in the later Muslim literature in the Arabic and Persian form of ma'nawīyat. In order to have a clear understanding of what this term means, we need to examine its literal as well as its technical use. It seems that spirituality was originally connected to "the spiritual meaning that Christians, in the light of revelation, detected under the original, literal meaning of the scriptures. Eventually the idea of a meaning hidden underneath surface appearances was extended to all spiritual reality (the sacraments, especially the Eucharist, even nature itself as expressive of God's majesty)." Today, however, spirituality has gained a wide range of definitions: from the highest human affair, to a quest for an existential meaning, to the transcendental dimension of human being. Some writers have proposed genetic and innate bases for spirituality, and still others suggest that it is an outcome of major life events and challenges that unveil human limits.

## Spirituality and Meaning

Spirituality is a universal human demand. As its diverse uses reveal, it has something to do with "meaning," and its corresponding Arabic (and Persian) term ma'nawīyat reflects the same relation. It comes from the root ma'nā that corresponds to the word "meaning." Meaning refers to a situation in which there are at least two levels of phenomena: a surface appearance that refers to, and reveals, a deeper fact. For instance, we speak of a meaningful text if its words and phrases refer to some facts, either in the objective world or in the subjective world of its author. A text that fails to initiate such a connection would be judged as meaningless, since an expression is an instrument to refer to the more essential fact that is its referent. If it were not the case that one wanted to reveal some meaning, one would not bother uttering a phrase. The same holds true for meaningful actions as the subject matter for the social sciences. A social agent acts in a certain way because he or she wants to achieve a specific goal, without which that action would be meaningless and foolish.

Some philosophers and social scientists looked for the meaning of an action in the objective context of society. Adam Smith's "unseen hand," Hegel's "ruse of the idea," and Marx's "objective logic of dynamic institutions that work themselves out behind the backs of the actors" are examples of this kind of mentality. Peter Winch considered social conventions, and not individual intentions, as the main factor in determining the meaning of particular bodily movements and converting them to meaningful actions. Max Weber's account of meaning, however, ran counter to such objective versions. He took the intention of an actor into account, and wrote that we "understand what a person is doing when he tries to achieve certain ends by choosing appropriate means on the basis of facts of the situation." In this way, Weber related subjective meaning to belief system, values, motivation, and the ultimate ends toward which a certain action is consciously oriented. Therefore, he did not believe in a "normatively 'correct' or a metaphysically 'true' meaning," and considered merely traditional imitations or purely emotional reactions as meaningless actions. Despite their opposing differences, all the above-mentioned theorists shared two ideas: first, that meaning is somehow coupled with the belief system and the goals associated with an action, and second, that meaning is something to be found beneath the surface of an expression or action.

Meaning is a multi-level phenomenon, and relating to any of its levels reveals the existential, as well as cognitive, stage at which a person stands. Each stage involves certain needs, concerns, and joys different from others. However, higher stages incorporate what belongs to the lower ones, and acquiring superior needs and joys fulfills the subordinate ones as well. Some materialist thinkers look for such tangible feelings as hope, tranquility, and liveliness as the only layer in spirituality, suggesting that engaging in activities such as playing music, arts, sports, and relaxation techniques are means for attaining spiritual pleasure. The problem with this approach is that it stops short of getting at the root of the problem. These suggestions may reduce the side-effects of living a nihilistic life, take the resulting pains to the unconscious level of one's self, and give a person provisional energy and optimism, but they fail to answer the human quest for ultimate meaning.

There are others who search for meaning but restrict this search within the limits of the material world. Some spiritual writers suggest that a material goal or even an illusive meaning might suffice for natural spirituality. Of course, material goals might provide meaning for certain actions for a limited period of time, that is, until the goal is attained, but this view falls short of offering meaning to human life in general, and fails to liberate one from the disturbing feeling of emptiness. Illusive meaning is the worst possible answer to the human spiritual pursuit. Such a pseudo-meaning is useless, unless one is unaware of its illusiveness. Suggesting false meaning as the basis for responding to human spiritual need is a regressive move to an age of magic and superstition, relying on sheer pragmatism. The moment one acknowledges its illusiveness, its positive effect evaporates.

## Spirituality and Religion

As John Hick points out, our understanding of the essence of the world resonates in how we live our lives. Therefore, the meaning of our lives depends on the nature of the world and the state of our life as one of its components. One can anticipate a meaningful human life if all one's actions are meaningfully directed at one goal. The meaning of human action depends on one's deliberately chosen goals. Choosing a goal that is not concomitant with the reality of the world and of our capacity for perfection would lead to illusive meaning and therefore to meaninglessness. Robert Neville understands the goal of the spiritual life to be perfection. One's life goal will be real and lasting, if, and only if, it is harmonious with one's position in the world, and can lead to attaining the ultimate perfection that is set for the human being to accomplish. When we speak of "spirituality," we mean exactly this quest for meaning, the finding of such meaning, and the joy associated with it. Spiritual life requires a spiritual dimension of the world and an esoteric layer of human life, and as 'Allamah Tabataba'i said:

> Spiritual life is based on the principle that human esoteric perfections and spiritual stages are factual realities outside the borders of natural reality and material world, and the principle that the esoteric world, as the place for spiritual life, is by far more essential, more real, and more extensive than the corporeal and sensible world. Spiritual ranks are realities and crucially essential situations for the human being, and not ceremonial concepts, or socially stipulated titles.... The relation between human actions and those feelings and characters they bring forth in one's soul, the relation between such feelings and characters to the esoteric stages through which one travels, and also the relation between theses esoteric stages and the world encompassing them, all are realistic relations that exist outside the kingdom of matter and nature. In sum, spiritual life and eschatology (in all its shapes) are based on the essentiality of the spiritual world.

Murta ā Mutahari speaks of a human being's multi-dimensional self: one dimension is the animal self, associated with corporeal needs and pleasures, and the other is the human self, related to higher needs and joys. The deeper that one is acquainted with the reality of the world and the human being, the clearer and more perfect becomes one's understanding of the meaning of the world and of human life. Religion is one of the main sources for providing human beings with the deepest understanding of the realities of the world, its goal and meaning. Muhammad Taqi Misbāh explains that "human attention to spiritual virtues and perfections has its roots in religion and revealed teachings, and is considered one of their results." The relation between religion and spirituality is so close that psychologists of religion have traditionally equated one with another. Others like K. I. Pargmanet think of religion as a more general concept that includes spirituality as its major element, while P. S. Richards and A. E. Bergin consider religion as a subset of spirituality, and still others like David Griffin consider spirituality to imply a more general notion in which religiosity may or may not be a part. One of the important issues to consider is that both religion and spirituality are multi-dimensional and multi-layered phenomena. As W. R. Miller and C. E. Thoresen have mentioned, some of these facets are easily recognized, while others are more hidden and hence may not be noticed without some effort. The deeper the facet goes, the more hidden it becomes, and the harder to be noted or even appreciated.

Divine religions, including Islam, provide us with a comprehensive perspective and a multi-faceted picture of the world, in which the corporeal world is only a minute portion, the tip of the iceberg, so to speak. The main and essential part of being is concealed from the senses. The visible world is an expression of the concealed meaning of being; the perceptible world can be regarded as a text that refers to its veiled meaning. One can access the meaning by contemplating the word (world). According to Mutahari, the relation of this world and human life to their meanings is the same as the relation of the shell to the nucleus of nuts. As a nucleus is preserved within, and hidden by, the shell, the interior reality of the world is maintained by its surface appearance. He also refers to the fact that the life after death is the real meaning of our worldly life, and only true religions unveil this connection, revealing the essence of the world and the truth of human life: "Islam preserves meaning in matter, interiority within an appearance, the Hereafter in this world, and finally, the nucleus within the shell."

But what is this meaning? Within the framework of a religious worldview, the world stems from one source, God, and at the end it returns to him: "He is the beginning and the end, the exterior and the interior."

The natural world and human life expose the esoteric hidden meaning and aim. God created the world as a first step towards creating the human being, and created the human being in order for one to develop one's perfection and to come closer to God, the absolute perfection. Knowing God is the first step in a meaningful life and the first move in the spiritual direction. Understanding God is gradational, and as this appreciation deepens the meaning of life also becomes stronger and clearer. Knowledge comes with knowledge of one's ignorance. As we come to know God, we know that there is more to learn and more that we don't know about him. So, curiosity and the love of knowing more lead us to expand and deepen our understanding of God.

In Islamic philosophy, knowledge is classified into knowledge by representation (*'ilm-e husuli*), which is conceptual and through the medium of mental images, and knowledge by presence, or presentational knowledge (*'ilm-e huduri*), which is immediate and experiential by direct existential connection between the subject and the object of knowledge. One's knowledge about God can be merely conceptual and theoretical. Such an understanding could vary in depth too. One can merely recognize God's existence through philosophical proofs and therefore have a mental concept of what God can be. But one can go through subsequent steps to find out about God's attributes and actions. Deeper theoretical knowledge can involve knowing God's relation to human life and perfection, God's love for us, God's commands, and the consequences of our obedience and defiance. Because God is the most perfect being, and human beings are innately attracted toward perfection, any level of knowing God brings with it a proportionate level of love for him. It begins with a simple attraction toward the referent of the concept of God, and it can grow deeper and deeper as one's knowledge of God and his attributes intensifies.

Presentational knowledge of God can also develop by multiple levels of conscious awareness, depending on a range of elements, including one's existential and cognitive abilities. Such an immediate knowledge of God, as found in presentational knowledge, is more powerful and results in a more intensive love and attraction towards him. There are interactions between knowledge by presence and knowledge by representation, since different levels of knowledge by presence are reflected in various attempts to describe and theorize about them in the form of conceptual knowledge. And interactions also exist between knowledge and love; therefore, levels of love are also developed.

As one level of knowledge prompts love, love may trigger the acquisition of more knowledge about the object of love, and we are led to progress further on the path. We desire to know more about God and what he desires for us, and we may call this cognitive craving an "intellectual love." One person might have some degree of the feeling of love for God because of some vague glimmer of knowledge by presence of him. Another person might love God not just by attraction and feeling but by undertaking to serve God. We learn about what God has commanded for us and how he wants to perfect us, and we yearn to fulfill those commands, desiring to be perfect for God, to please God as he wants us to be. One may evolve to a higher level when one loves God by a total dedication of life, so that nothing can stand in one's way when wanting to fulfill the desire of God. At perhaps the highest degree of knowledge and love, there is the love of the Prophet for God, a level in which one's own personality is obliterated in God and all one's desire and action are absorbed into the desire and the act of God. He acts in such a way that it is not he who throws, but God who throws!

An acquaintance with this fact makes one aware of the meaning of life, and helps one to get to the spiritual dimension of the world, which brings with it real peace of mind: "The hearts settle down/achieve serenity only by remembering Allah." This serenity is also acquired by levels and layers too. By understanding the real nature of the world and human life, their various dimensions, and that their wise creator has his macro-plan, factual hope and lasting vivacity are developed. The deeper such an understanding and love goes, the more lasting and the more real their effects become.

# Spiritual Formation and the Requisites of Faith

## David W. Shenk

## Introduction

Islamic approaches to spirituality, including the Sufi streams within Sunni Islam and the Irfan movements within Shi'a Islam, interest me greatly. In the mid-1970s, when I was living in East Africa, I wrote a substantial essay that explored Sufism as a bridge between Christian spirituality and Muslim devotion.[1] This essay was published in a couple of journals and was intended to explore dialogue centered in Muslim and Christian spirituality. The theological concerns that revolve around discussions of spirituality are significant, both within the Muslim community and the church.

In this essay I seek to describe "biblical spirituality."[2] Although this is an academic paper, I also write experientially, for the biblical spirituality I describe is also a description of my own journey. My years of living and serving with Muslims, especially in Somalia, have also influenced me, especially the pervasive commitment to bring all areas of life under the authority of God. However, this essay is not a comparison of Islamic and Christian spirituality; my focus is the requisites of faith for Christian spirituality.

Christian spirituality is the formation of character that happens as a person believes in and follows Jesus the Messiah.[3] As a person follows the Messiah, there is spiritual growth, for the disciples of the Messiah "are being transformed into his likeness with ever-increasing glory, which comes from the Lord, who is the Spirit" (2 Cor. 3:18).

## Testing Spiritualities

Spiritualities are like streams of water from which we drink. These streams might provide refreshment and life-giving spiritual formation and blessing. However, some streams are polluted and destructive. The apostle John, one of Jesus' disciples, admonished in a letter to the early Christian congregations, "Dear friends, do not believe every spirit, but test the spirits to see whether they are from God" (1 John 4:1). He commends Jesus as the criterion for testing the spirits. We all have observed persons or congregations of believers who might be earnestly seeking to acquire higher levels of spiritual development, but who are drinking from spiritual streams that are not life-giving.

Consider the following examples of questionable or destructive spiritual streams. Several years ago, there was an intense spiritual development at a church near the Toronto airport. People believed they were baptized with the Holy Spirit when they fell down and were overcome with laughter; some roared in ecstasy like lions. For some, these experiences of spiritual ecstasy lasted for many hours or even days. Since this church was near the airport, Christians from around the world flew to Toronto to receive a similar baptism of spiritual ecstasy and power. This spiritual ecstasy was nicknamed "The Toronto Blessing."

However, many Christians asked whether this was really the Spirit of God or whether it represented a spirituality that focused on experience rather than on knowing and serving God. On one occasion I heard a pastor in Germany describe how he went to Toronto and received this incredible "Toronto Blessing." I wrote to him later and said, "You spoke for a long time about the blessing of spiritual ecstasy that you received in Toronto, but you never mentioned Jesus the Messiah once." I asked him, "Isn't the Messiah the ultimate test of all Christian spirituality?" As mentioned above, the apostle John commands, "Test the spirits."

In the Anabaptist-Mennonite spiritual journey, there have been some destructive turns by communities and leaders who sincerely sought to acquire higher levels of spirituality. One such movement occurred in the city of Münster in north Germany in 1534-35. At that time there was much suffering because of floods, wars, and the persecution of Anabaptists. Consequently, many of the faithful yearned for the second coming of Christ to free them from their sufferings. In Münster leaders emerged who taught that the Anabaptists should prepare to welcome Christ when he returns to establish his eternal kingdom. They urged their followers to get weapons, and forced residents of the city to be baptized. By force they intended to establish their vision of the kingdom of God, and thereby acquire an advanced spirituality that would be a preparation for the Messiah's return. They initiated an insurrection. Consequently the regional governing authorities attacked the city, and these misguided Anabaptists were killed. This tragic development gave Anabaptists a bad name, for people equated them with visionary and destructive spirituality. This development has given Anabaptist-Mennonites a spirit of caution when it comes to visionary movements that promise believers utopia.[4]

Three-and-a-half centuries later, a small group of Anabaptist-Mennonites in Russia embraced a similar vision of the immediate second coming of the Messiah. But this time the vision was that he would return and establish heaven on earth for the Mennonites in Central Asia. So, to escape their sufferings in Russia, a small group found their way to Almaty, Kazakhstan. They anticipated the Messiah's second coming when they would be transformed spiritually and enter heaven eternally. They waited in vain, and suffered incredible hardships.[5]

Each of these examples of spiritualities was embraced by sincere believers. They were deeply devout and earnestly sought to obey God. How can such spiritualities be evaluated and guided? What is the test?

## Messiah-Centered Spirituality

We have observed that the Apostle John counsels the churches: test the spirits! That is good advice. He goes on to say that the test of the spirits is Jesus the Messiah. Probably it is the misguided movements in the past that has helped form the central conviction of Anabaptist Mennonites to evaluate all spiritualities in the light of Jesus the Messiah. For example, Jesus taught against running here or there to seek for his second coming (Matt. 24:23-27). He also made it clear that his kingdom is not established by the sword (Matt. 26:50-54). From the biblical accounts of Jesus' life and teachings, it is evident that the intense spiritual yearnings and visions that inspired both Münster and the disastrous trek into Central Asia were distortions of spirituality centered in Jesus.

One of the early Mennonite leaders, Menno Simons, began his teaching ministry among Anabaptists in the context of the Münster tragedy. He insisted that Jesus of the biblical scriptures needs to be the central figure of Christian devotion and commitment. He believed that the horrors of Munster demonstrated a spiritual quest and a vision of Jesus that was contrary to the Bible. He wrote vigorously as he sought to clarify the full-orbed meaning of the Bible and the centrality of Jesus as revealed in the Scriptures. He taught the Bible as the written Word of God and Jesus the Messiah as the living personal Word of God in human form.

Jesus admonished the crowds who followed him, "You diligently study the Scriptures, because you think that by them you possess eternal life. These are the Scriptures that testify about me...." (John 5:39). Menno built upon such teachings of Jesus. His writings have significantly formed Mennonite spirituality with his emphasis on a right and loving relationship with Jesus as the soul of genuine biblical spirituality.[6] This is not to say that Menno Simons always got it right. None of us does. "Now we see but a poor reflection as in a mirror .... Now I know in part," writes the apostle Paul (1 Cor. 13:12). For example, many of us feel that Menno was too strict and used church discipline without enough grace and forgiveness. The church needs to counsel and find the way together, discerning how to apply the Bible and the teachings of Christ in our context, and we confess that we only "know in part."

## Personal Spiritual Journey

My own journey as a disciple of Jesus the Messiah and my spiritual formation have been significantly formed by two expressions of spirituality in two very different contexts. One stream is the Anabaptist story that emerged in 16th-century Central Europe within traditional churches that had a thousand-year history. The other stream is the East Africa Revival Fellowship that emerged in 20th-century Africa within newly emerging churches in a context where the Christian faith was being heard for the first time. I will comment on both movements, because the enormous cultural and historical diversity of these contexts helps to clarify the essential nature of Messiah-centered spirituality.

Although the East Africa Revival Fellowship had no historical connections with the Anabaptist movement, there are similarities in the two movements. This is to say that the Anabaptist movement is not an isolated spiritual movement; the Spirit of God is at work around the world. A description of these two movements demonstrates that reality for both of them developed in radically different cultures and different eras.

## The East Africa Revival Fellowship (Balokole)

My parents were pioneer Mennonite missionaries among the Zanaki people of Tanzania (Tanganyika), which is where I was born and grew up. In the 1930s a powerful movement of spiritual renewal began to transform the young churches throughout East Africa, a movement that continues today and is referred to as the East Africa Revival Fellowship. This movement touched all churches and denominations, including the newly emerging Mennonite churches. From whence did this renewal come? Jesus says there is a mystery about the ministry of the Spirit of God: "The wind blows wherever it pleases. You hear its sound, but you cannot tell where it comes from or where it is going" (John 3:8).

Yet, spiritual renewal comes only as people submit to God. In East Africa it was a Church of Uganda (Anglican) teacher, Blasio Kigozi, in Ruanda, who was one of the people through whom spiritual renewal began. He was discouraged about the difficulties in the school for church leaders where he taught, and so he went to his room and sought God for a week in prayer and fasting. When he left his solitary retreat, he went first to his wife and in repentance made things right with her. Then he called a convocation of the students, and proclaimed that God was calling on them to repent of their sins. Deep conviction of sin fell upon them and in tears they repented before God. Thereafter Blasio and a small team of brothers traveled to different regions preaching and calling on people to repent of their sins. The fire of conviction accompanied their preaching as many turned to God. Those who repented were nicknamed by their communities *"Balokole,"* meaning people on fire. Within six weeks Blasio took ill and died. Yet his short ministry had ignited a fire of spiritual renewal and transformation that continues in East Africa even today.[7]

## The Anabaptist Movement

The Anabaptist movement of spiritual renewal began in a Bible study fellowship in Zurich, Switzerland in 1525. As they studied the Bible together, these brothers and sisters were transformed by the Spirit of God and committed to following Jesus whatever the cost. Although baptized as babies in the Reformed or Catholic traditions of the churches they came from, in that Zurich fellowship they decided to baptize one another as adults upon their confession of faith in Jesus the Messiah. That was the beginning of the 16th-century spiritual renewal movement known as Anabaptism. This movement gave birth to several denominations, including the Mennonite Church that got its name from the leader and teacher I have referred to, Menno Simons.

The Messiah-centered spirituality of the Anabaptists has enabled that movement to absorb a remarkable diversity of spiritual streams. In our modern day, we discern that some Anabaptist-Mennonite congregations or individuals strongly emphasize the peace and justice dimensions of Jesus the Messiah. Others are more at home with quiet spiritual retreats where they contemplate. Some are very tuned into pietism or evangelical expressions of spirituality. In recent decades the charismatic movement, which sometimes encourages ecstatic speaking in tongues, has influenced many of our people and congregations; this movement brings joyous exuberant spirituality into many congregations. It is therefore not surprising that the Mennonites in East Africa became enthusiastic participants in the Balokole movement, for their Anabaptist heritage was open to spiritual renewal movements.

## Comparing Anabaptist and Balokole Spirituality

Mennonite missionaries from North America who were serving in East Africa were among the first westerners to embrace the Balokole renewal movement. One reason for this was that there was considerable similarity between the East Africa Revival Fellowship of the 20th century and the Anabaptist renewal movement of the 16th century.[8] A missionary serving in East Africa, Donald R. Jacobs, wrote to the North American Mennonite theologian John Howard Yoder, "I have met the Anabaptists, and they are Africans!"[9] By this he meant that the spirituality of the Balokole and of the Anabaptists was essentially similar.

The East Africa Balokole movement emphasized commitment to, and love for, Jesus the Messiah; as noted above, the same was true of the Anabaptist movement. Both movements stressed genuine repentance and believed that the fruit of repentance is a life transformed by the Holy Spirit. Jesus described this transformed life as "new birth" (John 3:3-8). Both emphasized following Jesus in all of life whatever the cost, even martyrdom.

In East Africa, as was also true of the Anabaptists, there was the abiding conviction that taking the sword and engaging in violence against one's enemies is contrary to the life and teachings of Jesus. In the 1950s in Kenya, there was a vicious war against British colonialism. The freedom fighters were called Mau Mau. The Balokole sympathized with the desire for independence from Britain, but refused to bear arms or be involved in the violence in any way. That conviction cost them dearly. Many were martyred for refusing to join the violent struggle for independence. The funerals were filled with songs of joy, as the brothers and sisters praised God that another of their fellowship had been counted worthy to die for the sake of Jesus the Messiah whom they loved. Never was a spirit of revenge or hatred expressed in these funerals; rather love and forgiveness for those who were involved.

The Balokole movement was authentically African. These fellowships represented a truly African expression of Christian spirituality. They infused new life into the structures of the traditional churches, but it was an authentically African spirituality that they embraced. Likewise, the Anabaptist movement was a spirituality expressed in the local languages of Europe, in contrast to the Latinized traditional Catholic Church. The Bibles the Anabaptists read were translated into the languages of the people. (This was also true of the mainstream of the

Protestant Reformation.)

Both movements emphasized regular meeting together for fellowship, Bible study, confession, and prayer. The Balokole often said, "One piece of charcoal cannot burn, but coals together burn well." These regular gatherings of small group fellowships were essential for spiritual growth. Then they would plan for regional, national, and occasionally international gatherings where thousands came together for fellowship and spiritual refreshment. Joy, song, messages, and fellowship permeated these gatherings.

Most spiritual renewal movements can be summarized in a core Biblical text. For the East African revivalists the central text was "If we confess our sins, he is faithful and just and will forgive our sins and cleanse us from all unrighteousness" (1 John 1:9). For the Anabaptist leader Menno Simons, the central theme was "For no one can lay any foundation other than the one already laid, which is Jesus Christ" (1 Cor. 3:11).

Although the Anabaptists and the Balokole thrived in very different contexts, at the core the movements were the same; these fellowships were centered in Jesus the Messiah. They drew life from his life, teachings, crucifixion, resurrection, ascension, and promised return to bring to fulfillment the kingdom of God. Both movements drew their spiritual life from a living and loving relationship with Jesus.

I have described these two movements that emerged in very different cultures and contexts because it is significant that movements of the Spirit of God bring transformation in any culture, and there is a kindred spirit in all such movements. For example, throughout the centuries renewal movements have always been characterized by repentance. The Balokole and Anabaptists are examples of this.

## The Holy Spirit

In Christian experience it is the Holy Spirit who energizes all spiritual renewal and empowers personal spiritual transformation. Both the East Africa Balokole and the European Anabaptists were convinced that the renewals they were participating in were the fruit of the work of the Holy Spirit. The Holy Spirit never functions independently of a commitment to God the Creator as revealed in Jesus the Messiah. Jesus promised his followers before his departure from earth, "When the Counselor comes, whom I will send to you from the Father, the Spirit of truth who goes out from the Father, he will testify of me" (John 16:15). Elsewhere he explained, "But the Counselor, the Holy Spirit, whom the Father will send in my name, will teach you all the things and will remind you of everything I have said to you" (John 14:26).

The Holy Spirit reveals and glorifies Jesus the Messiah. He enlightens the mind and soul so that people can understand and receive the message of the Scriptures. The Holy Spirit convicts of sin, reveals righteousness, and guides into all truth. He brings about the new creation that Jesus described as the new birth. The Holy Spirit dwells within the disciple of Jesus, and brings to pass a life of fruitfulness characterized by "love, joy, peace, patience, kindness, goodness, faithfulness, gentleness, and self control" (Gal. 5:22-23).

Followers of Jesus who have received the grace of forgiveness yearn to be filled with the Holy Spirit, also referred to as the Spirit of God or the Spirit of Jesus. The fullness of the Spirit forms the believer into the likeness of the Messiah. The scripture referred to above describes the fruit of the Holy Spirit. These characteristic fruit of the Spirit are of course a reflection of the life of the Messiah. So disciples of Jesus frequently ask, "How can I be filled with the Holy Spirit?"

A British preacher, Roy Hession, was much influenced by the East Africa Revival Fellowship referred to above. He points out that in the Bible the Holy Spirit is sometimes referred to as water. He observes that the Holy Spirit cannot mix with sin: the pure water of the Spirit can occupy only clean vessels. This is why the biblical writers stress repentance and receiving with gratefulness the forgiveness of sins. As the believer walks in daily repentance and receives the daily gift of grace and forgiveness, then his life is clean and ready to receive the gift of the Holy Spirit. The believer's life is like a cup; the Holy Spirit is like water. When the believer holds out a clean cup, God pours into the cup the water of the Holy Spirit until the cup is overflowing.[10] David writes in the Psalms, "My cup overflows!" (Psalm 23:5).

Authentic spirituality is a right and joyous relationship with God. The Holy Spirit within the believer is the promise that all is well and that the believer does indeed belong to God (Eph. 1:13-14). The Holy Spirit enables the believer to know God as loving heavenly Father (Gal. 4:6). The Holy Spirit abiding within is a very precious gift, and it behooves the believer to live in a way that cherishes this gift.

## Community of Disciples

Jesus the Messiah called and appointed twelve men to be his companions in ministry. He did not minister as an independent individual, but rather as the leader of a community of disciples. These disciples were the beginning of the church, a gathering of people who meet for a particular purpose. The Christian church is a gathering of those who meet in the name of Jesus the Messiah. Anabaptists believe that the church is a community of disciples, and this community is essential for spiritual formation in Christian experience.

However, ever since the third century of the Christian era, there have been those who have sought spiritual maturity through retreat into monasticism. This might be a solitary quest or a community of monks or nuns who together seek spiritual development, through retreat from the world, endless prayer, and personal introspection. Anabaptists went in directions very different from monasticism, for they viewed authentic spirituality as rooted in love for Jesus the Messiah and others. This meant seeking to serve fellow believers and non-believers. Introspection that was so characteristic of monastic spirituality was not the path chosen by the Anabaptists.[11] Rather, they sought to identify with the spiritual directions of the early church, where people were nurtured in spiritual development within the fellowship of believers. It is a covenant community of believers and essential to authentic spiritual formation. Spiritual formation equips the believer to serve compassionately in the world as Jesus served.

Within Anabaptist spirituality baptism is a significant sign of commitment to Jesus and the fellowship and discipline of the church. Some Christian denominations baptize infants; Anabaptists baptize upon confession of faith. For Anabaptists the waters of baptism are a sign of the ministry of the Holy Spirit in bringing about a new creation within the life of the person who has repented and is committed to follow Jesus and become a covenant member of the church. A person's parents cannot make that decision for him. Each person is free before God to choose to reject or believe. This is a personal decision made before God. So the waters of baptism are a public witness and sign that the person has left the old life to enter the new life of the Spirit as a disciple of Jesus and a member of the church. Church historian Cornelius Dyck comments:

> What was important for them was a new self which, by grace, was now able to live and work for the glory of God. *Faith and obedience* belonged together, as did the *individual and community. Baptism* was the seal of the Spirit which then encouraged *witness and ministries.* Anabaptist life was *centered on the Holy Spirit ...*[12]

This new life of the Spirit is expressed and nurtured within the fellowship of believers. The word "saint" does not appear in the singular within the Bible. It is always "saints." Believers who faithfully follow the Messiah in fellowship with other believers become saints.

## Spiritual Formation

For the Anabaptists the evidence of faith in the Messiah and authentic spirituality was a transformed life of obedient discipleship. Menno Simons wrote that:

> For true faith which is acceptable before God cannot be barren; it must bring forth the fruits of life. It works through love, enters willingly into all righteousness, mortifies flesh and blood, crucifies the lusts and desires, rejoices in the cross of Christ, and renews and regenerates.[13]

Anabaptists believed that spiritual formation is not climbing a ladder toward God but receiving the gift of God's grace and obeying God's call. They sometimes referred to Jacob's ladder to explain this reality. In the book of Genesis there is the account of Jacob the son of Isaac and grandson of Abraham, who took a journey from Beersheba where his parents were residing, back to Haran where Abraham had lived previously. Early in his journey he lay down for the night with a stone as his pillow. As he slept, he had a dream in which a ladder reached from heaven to the ground, and the angels of God ascended and descended on it.

The Lord stood at the top of the ladder and said,

> I am the Lord, the God of your father Abraham and the God of Isaac.... All peoples on earth will be blessed through you and your offspring. I am with you and will watch over you wherever you go, and I will bring you back to this land. I will not leave you until I have done what I have promised you. (Gen. 28:13-15)

This dream is a spiritual epiphany that Jacob never forgot. He declared, "This is the house of God!" He made a pillar of stones at that place, and some years later returned to this pile of stones remembering that ladder and God's promise of blessing. However, it is noteworthy that it was God who initiated this epiphany. Jacob was not anticipating this revelation. It was a total surprise. The ladder from heaven to earth was God's initiative; it was God who initiated the promise of blessing. And that promise also meant that Jacob needed to conduct himself in a way that blessed all peoples.

This is the nature of biblical spirituality. God takes the initiative. God comes down and meets us; the Biblical accounts have a number of descriptions of God coming down to meet and save people, and especially so in Jesus the Messiah. We cannot make a ladder of spiritual ascendancy up to God or ascend a ladder of progressive spirituality toward God. Rather, it is God who comes to us, seeks us, meets us, and invites us into a right and joyous relationship with God, and who commissions us to be a blessing to others.

Reflecting on this ladder from heaven, an early Anabaptist writer, Dirk Philips, wrote, "How holy is this place! This is none other than the house of God, and this is the gate of heaven. This ladder signifies Jesus Christ...."[14] Menno Simons commented on the mission of Jesus the Messiah whom God has sent into the world. The world as a whole was not anticipating the Messiah; it was God who took the initiative, just as God sent the ladder from heaven in Jacob's dream. Menno writes:

> Behold, worthy reader, how all those who sincerely believe in this glorious love of God, this abundant, great blessing of grace in Christ Jesus, manifested toward us, are progressively renewed through such faith; their hearts are flooded with joy and peace; they break forth with joyful hearts in all manner of thanksgiving; they praise and glorify God with all their hearts because with a certainty of mind they have grasped it in the spirit, have believed and known that the Father loves us so that He gave us poor, wretched sinners His own and eternal Son with all His merits as a gift, and eternal salvation. As Paul says, "The grace and love of God, our Saviour, appeared not on account of the works of righteousness which we have done, but according to his mercy He saved us by the washing of regeneration and the renewing of the Holy (Spirit) which he shed on us abundantly through Jesus Christ our Savior, that being justified by his grace, we should be made heirs according to the hope of eternal life." (Titus 3:7)[15]

## My Personal Spiritual Formation

What are the spiritual disciplines needed to cherish the gift of the Holy Spirit? What are the disciplines that contribute to authentic spiritual formation? Here I will be autobiographical, describing my own personal journey. Others might embrace other approaches to spiritual formation; however, this is my particular journey.

The regular weekly gathering for worship with other believers is very important for me. Meeting with them for fellowship, to hear the Scriptures read, to join in singing praises to the Lord, to confess sin as a body of believers or individually, to receive together anew the gift of forgiveness, to hear the Word preached, to pray and receive at the conclusion of the worship time the pastor's benedictory blessing, to be commissioned to go forth committed anew to glorify God in all that I think, do, say, and am — all that is important.

Complementing the large weekly gathering is the small group fellowship of believers. Beginning in my college years, I have quite consistently met regularly with a small group for fellowship, prayer, confession, sharing, challenge, study of the Bible, worship, and encouragement. A mini-fellowship is my wife and I. When I am home, we have a daily time of prayer, worship, and fellowship together. If I have grieved her, these regular times of sharing provide space for restoring our relationship. I consider my relationship to God to be very directly related to my relationship to others, and that begins within my family relations.

I enjoy reading quite widely, as I seek to integrate faith with modern realities. Symbolically I carry my Bible in my right hand and my *New York Times* in my left hand. A discipline that means much to me is reading the Bible through from Genesis to Revelation every year. I am blessed year by year reading it through, reliving the amazing drama of God calling forth a people, leading them into discoveries of his grace, and equipping them for his mission in the world.

Several times a week I begin my day with an early run. Physical exercise and seeking to maintain the disciplines of good health is an important dimension of my spiritual commitments. Humor and relishing the jovial dimensions of life is important. I want my body, mind, and spirit to be a temple in which the Holy Spirit dwells in peace, and so I do what I can to maintain a healthy, energetic temple in which the Spirit lives so that God will be glorified in all that I am and do.

Time alone with God and the Scriptures is important in my spiritual formation. That is how I have begun my days for many years. I listen to God, I read the Scriptures, I pray, I intercede, I worship. Have I in some way grieved the Holy Spirit? If I have done so, I confess, repent, and receive the grace of forgiveness. Sometimes in those times of quiet, the Spirit shows me that I need to make something right with another person. I cherish those times to be alone with God and receive anew the fullness of the Holy Spirit. Fasting is also a helpful dimension of spiritual formation, when I lay food aside in order to devote myself to prayer.

I am a sinner and a learner on a journey that leads from grace to grace. The apostle Paul states it well: "For it is by grace you have been saved, through faith – and this not from ourselves, it is the gift of God – not by works so that no one can boast. For we are God's workmanship, created in Christ Jesus to do good works, which God prepared in advance for us to do" (Eph. 2:8-10).

## Conclusion

Many years ago I boarded a train in New York City for the three-hour ride to Lancaster where I live. I was a young man completing a doctoral program at New York University. On the train I met an old man, Orie Miller, a global Mennonite Church leader. I was grateful to have three hours to chat with Orie, for whom I had great respect. He made a comment that has lived with me. "My philosophy of life is not complex," he said, "in fact, it is very simple. My commitment is to follow Jesus each day so that God may be glorified in all that I am and do. That is my philosophy of life and my commitment." In that statement, he summarized the soul of the pilgrimage of Christian spiritual commitment and formation.

## Endnotes

1   David W. Shenk, "The Tariqa: A Meeting Place for Christians and Muslims," *Bulletin on Islam and Christian-Muslim Relations in Africa* 1.3 (1983): 1-31.

2   There are diverse spiritual streams within the Bible, although at the center all authentic Biblical spirituality is grounded in a right, joyous, loving, repentant, obedient relationship with God our creator. This is in contrast to alternative spiritualities such as the worship of nature or ego-centered spirituality.

3   I will generally use the term "Messiah," the Semitic title for Jesus, rather than the Greek derived title, "the Christ." There is some mystery about the meaning of the name, although in essence the meaning of Messiah or Christ is "The Anointed One" whom the Christian church confesses to be Lord and Saviour.

4   Cornelius J. Dyck, *An Introduction to Mennonite History* (Scottdale, PA: Herald Press, 1993), 98-99.

5   Ibid., 181.

6   Abraham Friesen, "Menno and Munster: the Man and the Movement," in Gerald R. Brunk, ed. *Menno Simons: A Reappraisal* (Harrisonburg, VA: Eastern Mennonite College, 1992), 131-62.

7   W. B. Anderson, *The Church in East Africa, 1840-1974* (Dodoma: Central Tanzania Press, 1977), 123-24.

8   Richard K. MacMaster and Donald R. Jacobs, *A Gentle Wind from God: The Influence of the East Africa Revival* (Scottdale, PA: Herald Press, 2006), 164-65.

9   Ibid., 165.

10  Roy Hession, *The Calvary Road* (Fort Washington, PA: CLC, 2004), 25-38.

11  Cornelius J. Dyck, *Spiritual Life in Anabaptism* (Scottdale, PA: Herald Press, 1995), 24.

12  Ibid.

13  Helmut Isaac, "Menno's Vision of the Anticipation of the Kingdom of God in his Early Writings," in Brunk, 66.

14  Dirk Philips, "The Congregation of God," in Cornelius J. Dyck et al. trans. and eds., *The Writings of Dirk Philips* (Scottdale, PA: Herald Press, 1992), 326-27.

15  Walter Klaassen, "The Relevance of Menno Simons: Past and Present," in Brunk, 25.

# Mysticism and Religion: A Shi'a View

## Mohammad Fanaei Eshkevari

There is a close connection between mysticism and religion. However, the nature of their relation is debatable. Is mysticism a religious phenomenon? Can mysticism be found outside of religion? Is mysticism compatible with any worldview? The answer to these questions depends on our definition of mysticism. In my view, mysticism is a religious phenomenon. The heart of mysticism is experiential knowledge of God and love of him, and its three essential elements are belief in God, life after death, and a life according to the will of God.

## What is Religion?

In order to reach a clear opinion on the relation between mysticism and religion, it is necessary to have an adequate understanding of religion and its essential elements. However, there is no consensus about what constitutes the essence of religion. A growing tendency in the modern period looks at religion as a kind of feeling and experience.

According to Friedrich Schleiermacher, it is impossible to identify religion either with metaphysics or morals, or with a mixture of the two. Even though metaphysics and morals have the same subject matter as religion, i.e., the universe and the relationship of humanity to it, they are not identical. Metaphysics categorizes things, explains the existence and necessity of what exists, and seeks to discover the general laws of the world. Morality deals with our duties as human beings and our relationship to the universe. Religion must not do these tasks; it is not the highest philosophy in which metaphysics and morals are subordinate divisions.[1]

For Schleiermacher, religion is a kind of feeling, though his concept of feeling is ambiguous. Sometimes he uses the term "sense," by which he means sensibility. Sensibility for the Infinite is to have a feeling for the Infinite. The problem is that sensibility for the Infinite cannot be prior to knowledge of the Infinite; it is impossible to like something without having some kind of awareness of it. We cannot have a feeling for the Infinite without having the idea of the Infinite in our mind. Thus human nature as an intelligent reality is the true seat of religion. Another difficulty with this theory is that since feeling is only a subjective element in experience, it cannot be the basis for religion. This view negates any objective value for religion. It is on the basis of this theory that Ludwig Feuerbach concludes that since you perceive God by feeling, he is only in your feeling.

Paul Tillich thinks that "feeling" as understood by psychologists is a psychological function, and therefore the word "feeling" implies that faith is a matter of merely subjective emotions. But "feeling" according to Schleiermacher "is the impact of the universe upon us in the depths of our being which transcends subject and object."[2] A feeling of "unconditional dependence" is different from the subjective feeling of the individual, for all subjective feelings are conditioned. Tillich suggests that it would be better for Schleiermacher to speak of the intuition of the universe. The more proper term is "religious experience," which indicates "the presence of something unconditional beyond the knowing and acting of which we are aware."[3]

William James, like Schleiermacher, sees feeling as the deeper source of religion. James says that dogmas, creeds, and metaphysical theologies are provoked by religious experience. He defines religion as "the feelings, acts and experiences of individual men in their solitude, so far as they apprehend themselves to stand in relation to whatever they may consider the divine."[4]

However, religion is not equal to religious feeling or experience. An essential element in religion is belief – in the unseen, in the supernatural ground of being, in the ultimate reality, God. But religious belief is different from philosophical and scientific belief. It is associated with devotion, commitment, and practice. Charles Peirce says that religious belief is a living belief, "a thing to be lived rather than said or thought."[5]

Wilfred Cantwell Smith asserts that the modern Western notion of religion as a system of beliefs and practices is a product of the eighteenth century. In the past, it was used in the sense of proper piety, holy affections, the relationship between human beings and God, monastic life, and the like.[6] However, all these are based on a system of belief. Therefore we can identify three dimensions of religion as cognition, affection, and volition; or belief, emotions, and conduct.[7]

Religion (at least in its Western theistic, prophetic notion) is a system of belief and practice revealed by God and announced by a prophet. Religious experience is a state or event in the inner life of a believer. The essence of religion is revelation of God's word, and religiosity must contain at least three elements: belief in God and life after death, and obedience to God. Of course, this kind of characterization excludes many belief systems and ways of life from being defined as religion, such as Marxism and humanism. A tradition such as Buddhism is controversial in this regard, since it is not easy to decide about the idea of deity in this tradition. According to some, Hinayana Buddhism does not recognize a God.[8]

## Is Mysticism a Religious Phenomenon?

Sometimes mystical experience and religious experience are treated as a single reality. But usually scholars distinguish religious experience from mystical experience and religion from mysticism, though they are closely connected. What distinguishes mystical experience from mere religious experience is that the former is involved in unitary vision, a deeper, more advanced and rare state of consciousness. Religious experience depends less on preparation and training, and therefore is more common than mystical experience.

Frits Staal rejects the idea that mysticism is a religious phenomenon. In his view, mysticism has nothing to do with God or gods. He argues that some religions, such as Theravada Buddhism and Jainism, are atheistic.[9] According to Walter Stace, there is no single answer to the question posed above. If "religion" is understood as "one or other of the recognized world religions," mysticism is not essentially a religious phenomenon. However, if "religion" is understood as "the feelings of the holy," mysticism does involve religious feeling.[10] Stace is inclined to say that mystical experience is not a religious experience; mysticism essentially is not a religious phenomenon though it may be associated with a religion. The connection of mysticism with religion is subsequent.

Some assume mysticism is a religious phenomenon, and define mystical awareness as "union with God." Stace insists that "union with God" is no more than one interpretation among many. The essence of introvertive mysticism, he claims, is "the undifferentiated unity" that has no religious content. A Buddhist, for example, interprets it non-theistically. Though a mystic, Plotinus (204/5-270) did not belong to any recognized religion. Stace rejects the necessary connection of mysticism and religion as a system of belief; however, he admits the idea that mysticism involves the feeling of the holy, the divine. This feeling may be regarded as a religious feeling. To Stace, mysticism is independent of all organized religions, though they are linked together because "both look beyond earthly horizons to the Infinite and Eternal, and because both share the emotions appropriate to the sacred and holy."[11]

However, another view is that mysticism is the vital core of religion. William James considers mysticism as "the root and center of religion." In his view, "One may say truly . . . that personal religious experience has its root and center in mystical state of consciousness."[12] According to J. B. Pratt, "While it would indeed be untrue to assert that only the mystical are genuinely religious, it is safe to say that all intensely religious people have at least a touch of mysticism."[13] For Evelyn Underhill, religion and mysticism are so connected that "no deeply religious man is without a touch of mysticism; and no mystic can be other than religious, in the psychological if not in the theological sense of the word."[14] Tillich also admits that mystical experience and rational interpretation are in all religions.[15]

As Tillich suggests, faith and mysticism do not contradict each other; they are compatible and even interdependent. If one of them is considered as an element of the other, they will be compatible. In mystical experience a finite being experiences the presence of the infinite. Faith, which is the experience of the spiritual presence, the divine, is mystical, for it goes beyond the subject-object distinction.

According to Tillich, mystical experience contains faith, for in both cases the person is "grasped by the Spiritual presence." However, they must not be taken as identical.[16]

S. S. Radhakrishnan also insists on the close connection of mysticism and religion. For him, "Spirituality is the core of religion and its inward essence, and mysticism emphasizes this side of religion."[17] Both mysticism and religion are "the admission of mystery in the universe."[18] Contrary to Stace, he believes that "Mysticism is opposed to the naturalism which categorically denies the existence of God and the dogmatism which talks as if it knew all about Him. Both agree in abolishing all mystery in the world."[19] In fact, mysticism is considered as a form of religion that stresses the personal experience of God.

Mysticism is the essence and root of religion and provides a sound ground for the unity of all religions, says W. R. Inge:

> Mysticism is singularly uniform in all times and places. The communion of the soul with God has found much the same expression whether the mystic is a Neo-platonic philosopher like Plotinus, a Mohammadan Sufi, a Catholic monk or a Quaker. Mysticism, which is the living heart of religion, springs from a deeper level than the differences which divide the Churches, the cultural changes which divide the ages of history.[20]

## The Tension between Mysticism and Religion

To Stace, mysticism is not essentially a religious phenomenon; it can combine even with atheism. In response, one can say that although interpretation is not identical with experience, and different people may interpret the same experience differently, this does not mean that all interpretations are equally valid. How can the experience of transcendence and the divine be combined with materialistic metaphysics? Mysticism and religious beliefs, particularly belief in God, are so connected that T. M. McFadden says, "Strictly speaking, there are no mystics among the Buddhists since they do not acknowledge an Absolute."[21] Mysticism has to do with the experience of divine, so it cannot be consistent with atheism, a theory that rejects the divine. It is true that mysticism is not restricted to one specific religious tradition; however, it cannot be combined with just any metaphysics. Mystics emerge out of religious communities, though they sometimes challenge the established religious authorities. Challenging a specific religion or a specific understanding of a religion is not the same as challenging the religion as such.

Some scholars have restricted mysticism to organized religions. Gershom Scholem remarks that "There is no mysticism as such, there is only mysticism of a particular religious system, Christian, Islamic, Jewish mysticism and so on."[22] This implies that people such as Plotinus, who do not belong to any organized religion, cannot be considered as mystics.

Stace claims that mysticism is not genuine in Christianity, and Jesus was not a mystic; otherwise he would have set mystical consciousness at the center of Christianity. It is only a minor strand, which "comes into later Christianity as a result of influences which had their sources in Greece, not in Palestine."[23]

What we should notice in this regard is that mysticism is a universal phenomenon found almost everywhere inside organized religions as well as outside of them. Christian mystics frequently refer to the Bible to support their ideas; Sufis in Islam insist that their sole source is the Qur'an and the teaching and example of the Prophet Mohammad. In formulating mysticism as a theoretical science like any science, mystics learn from the human heritage, regardless of differences in worldview. Moreover, influence by paganism does not give mysticism a pagan identity. While it may be true that mystics are influenced by non-religious worldviews, historical influence is not the only factor in defining the nature of mysticism. If a religion does not have the ground of mysticism in itself, foreign elements cannot enter into it so deeply. Mysticism in religious traditions has its root within the religion, even though it may be influenced by others in the formulation of its doctrine or in its path. Mystics do not borrow their ideas from pagans uncritically. They try not to adopt elements that are against their religious teaching. The same thing happened when Christian and Muslim theologians faced Greek philosophy. Christian and Islamic theologies are influenced by

Greek philosophy and Neoplatonism in their specific argumentation and systematization and in some philosophical theories, but not in their essential religious beliefs, such as belief in God.

Furthermore, this is not the only theory on the origin of mysticism. Some like W. R. Inge and Nicolas Berdyaev hold that mystical union is the essence of Christianity. Although some may think that the Bible contains no mysticism, Christian mysticism nevertheless sees its origins in the teachings of Jesus, in St. John's Gospel, in experiences mentioned in Revelation, in St. Paul, and in the Psalms. Christian mystics' beliefs are what they learned and grew up with from their childhood. And those few mystics who departed from orthodox beliefs have done so as a result of philosophical or theological speculations, not as a result of mystical experience.[24]

In Christianity, scriptures have an undeniable influence on the mystics' language, both in its content and form. The same is true with regard to Jewish mysticism. Many passages in the Old Testament are powerful enough to inspire a mystical tendency; for example, the verse that says "Moses, Moses! Do not come near; put off your shoes from your feet, for the place on which you are standing is holy ground" (Ex. 3:5). Another example is "Before I formed you in the womb I knew you" (Jer.1:5). The source of Islamic mysticism, as mentioned before, is the Qur'an and the tradition of the Prophet and Imams. As Louis Massignon says, the Qur'an is the main textbook of Sufi sciences and the key for their *Weltanschauung*.[25] Most, if not all, of the mystical ethical concepts of Sufism are derived from basic Islamic teachings.

As we saw, Stace insists on the independence of mysticism from religion. Some orthodox from inside the religions and some seculars from outside the religions go further, and think that mysticism and religion are incompatible. David Knowles says that "The mystics' vision and the normal Christian adherence to precise dogma have often been contrasted or declared incompatible."[26]

There are various grounds for orthodox believers to view mysticism skeptically. Mystics' paradoxes, their dubious and semi-heretical utterances, carelessness of some Sufis with regard to *shari'a*, their esoteric interpretation of the Qur'an, and their incorporation of unfamiliar customs such as dance are some of the grounds. Chief among these reasons is the status of God in mysticism and religion. The core of mysticism is union with the Ultimate, or *fana'* in Allah, whereas in theology there is an unbridgeable gulf between the Creator and creatures. Therefore religious experience is considered numinous, which is different from mystical. As Ninian Smart says, "The mystic goal is non-dual," whereas "dualism between God and man is the very essence of numinous discourse."[27]

However, union with God can be interpreted in a way that is compatible with the religious conception. Many mystics interpret unity as the unity of love and will, not ontological unity. Meister Eckhart cites Augustine, who said, "Whatever a person loves a person is. If he loves a stone, he is a stone; if he loves a human being, he is a human being. If he loves God — I dare speak no further."[28] In this interpretation the distinction between the Creator and creatures remains untouched.

Another source of alleged incompatibility between mysticism and religion is thought to be the mystics' distinct approach to life and ethics. Mysticism "ignores the moral requirements that are part of the very fabric of their religious traditions."[29] It is also said that mystical ethics is derived from mystical experience and has no necessary relation to revelation, historical incarnation, and atonement.[30] In sum, it is argued that mysticism stands in clear opposition to religion in view of fundamental issues such as world, life, morality, God, and revelation. Some theologians such as Emil Brunner and Reinhold Niebuhr think that mysticism is anti-Christian and closer to pagan *gnosis*, while others such as J. W. Oman and P. E. More see in it the danger of pantheism.

However, one can claim that genuine mysticism reinforces morality and a positive attitude toward life. While there have been individual mystics whose life and teachings with regard to morality and life are open to criticism, this is not a necessary concomitant of mysticism; rather, it is a deviation from it. As for pantheism, it is not the only or even the predominant interpretation of mystical unitary vision.

The mystics' different approaches to religion should not always be understood as deviations from religion; religion can be understood in different ways, one of which is mystical. The mystics' personal revelation is not always in agreement with the orthodox understanding of religion. Their new ideas sometimes disturb orthodox believers.

Mystics are more concerned with the inner dimension of religion while respecting its outer and apparent dimension. Deviation from orthodox interpretation does not make mysticism heretical. Mystical experience, according to many scholars, is a subclass of religious experience. Even those mystics such as Plotinus who are outside of a specific organized religion are not irreligious; they believe in God and the realm of transcendence, a spiritual life, and a presence in the world. This belief is the heart of religion. Mysticism may also have different forms and aspects. Rejection of some form or aspect of mysticism does not imply the rejection of mysticism. The difference between religious experience and mystical experience is a matter of degree. "The religious experience of the ordinary believer," says Geoffrey Parrinder, "is in the same class as that of the mystic, the difference is one of degree but not of kind."[31]

## Mysticism and Religious Teachings

No doubt mystics in all religions, particularly Abrahamic religions, follow the teachings of their own religions, though they may have different interpretations. For example, belief in God and life after death are two basic principles in these religions – and also basic in mystical trends within them. The ultimate goal of mystics is meeting, proximity, or union with God, which implies a happy life after death. Moral principles are also elemental in the mystical path. Sufis are also careful to follow religious canon law and rituals or the ways of worshipping (*shari'a*/*fiqh*/jurisprudence). *Shari'a*, or revealed law, is an essential part of the religious life in Islam, without which the religiosity of one's life is under question. In Judaism also, religious law is fundamental.

Sufism made the distinction between *shari'a*, the Islamic law; *tariqa*, the Sufi path; and *haqiqa*, the truth. Truth is the end of the spiritual journey which goes through shari'a and tariqa. Shari'a is the broad path all people are obliged to take as the minimum requirement for salvation. Tariqa is a narrow path only for those who are capable and willing to take it. All great Sufis emphasized the importance of shari'a and announced that those who do not observe it are wrong. Mysticism is seeking the truth through observing shari'a and tariqa. Tariqa alone is not enough for salvation and attaining the truth. "No path can exist without a main road from which it branches out; no mystical experience can be realized if the binding injunctions of the shari'a are not followed faithfully first."[32] According to Muslim mystics, Sufism is the true knowledge of the divine law both in its external and internal aspects. In their view, religious law (shari'a) is a candle on the path (tariqa) through which one can attain truth (haqiqa). A Sufi must conform to shari'a, "Since his individual human nature will always remain passive in relation to Divine Reality."[33] In this system, mysticism is a deeper understanding of religion.

The ultimate end of both religion and mysticism is nearness to God, which is the ultimate happiness. It is not reasonable that their ways toward God be in the opposite direction. Observance of shari'a is so important in Sufism that a criterion for distinguishing the righteous guide (*murshid*) from a false claimant in the path of mysticism is "the degree to which murshid observes, in all affairs that concern him, the relevant ordinances of the shari'a. If there is even the slight deviation from the shari'a, then clearly the individual in question is a false claimant."[34]

## Endnotes

1   See Friedrich Schleiermacher, *On Religion: Speeches to its Cultured Despisers* (New York: Harper & Row, 1965).

2   Paul Tillich, *A History of Christian Thought* (New York: Simon & Schuster, 1968), 392.

3   Ibid., 396.

4   William James, *The Varieties of Religious Experience* (New York: Penguin Books, 1982), 31.

5   Charles S. Peirce, *Collected Papers of Charles Sanders Pierce,* eds. Charles Hartshorne and Paul Weiss (Cambridge, MA: Harvard University Press, 1935), Vol. 6, 306.

6   See Wilfred Cantwell Smith, *The Meaning and End of Religion: A New Approach to the Religious Traditions of Mankind* (New York: Macmillan, 1962), chapter 2.

7   Troy Organ, "The Language of Mysticism" in *The Monist* 47 (1963): 417-43 at 417.

8   W. T. Stace, *Mysticism and Philosophy* (London: Macmillan & Co. 1961), 43.

9   J. Frits Staal, *Exploring Mysticism* (Berkeley, CA: University of California Press, 1975), 185.

10  Stace, *Mysticism and Philosophy*, 341.

11  Ibid., 343.

12  James, *The Varieties of Religious Experience*, 379.

13  J. B. Pratt, *The Religious Consciousness* (New York: Macmillan, 1920), 14.

14  Evelyn Underhill, *Mysticism* (New York: Doubleday, 1990), 70.

15  Paul.Tillich, *Systematic Theology* (Chicago, IL: University of Chicago Press, 1951), Vol. 1, 9.

16  Tillich, *Systematic Theology*, Vol. 3, 242.

17  S. Sarvepalli Radhakrishnan, *Eastern Religions and Western Thought* (London: Humphrey Milford, 1940), 61.

18  Ibid., 61-62.

19  Ibid., 62.

20  W. R. Inge, *Freedom, Love, and Truth* (London: Green and Co., 1936), 25-26.

21  T. M. McFadden, "Mysticism," *Encyclopedic Dictionary of Religion*, eds. Paul Kevin Meagher et al. (Washington, DC: Corpus Publications, 1979), Vol. 2, 2476-77.

22  Gershom Scholem, *Major Trends in Jewish Mysticism* (New York: Schocken Books, 1954), 6.

23  Stace, 343.

24  David Knowles, *What is Mysticism?* (London: Burns and Oates, 1967), 73.

25  Louis Massignon, *Essai sur les origines du lexique technique de la mystique musulmane* (Paris: Vrin, 1954), 45.

26  Knowles, *What is Mysticism?*, 72.

27  Ninian Smart, "The Criteria of Religious Identity," *Philosophical Quarterly* 8 (1958): 328-41, at 340.

28  *Meister Eckhart, Teacher and Preacher* (The Classics of Western Spirituality), ed. Bernard McGinn (New York: Paulist Press, 1995), 302.

29  James Horne, *The Moral Mystic* (Waterloo, ON: Wilfrid Laurier University Press, 1983), 26.

30  William J. Wainwright, *Mysticism: A Study of its Nature, Cognitive Value and Moral Implications* (Madison, WI: University of Wisconsin Press, 1981), 223.

31  Geoffrey Parrinder, *Mysticism in the World Religions* (London: Sheldon Press, 1976), 191.

32  Annamarie Schimmel, *Mystical Dimensions of Islam* (Chapel Hill, NC: The University of North Carolina Press, 1975), 98.

33  Titus Burckhardt, *An Introduction to Sufism* (San Francisco, CA: [Thorsens], 1976), 22.

34  Hamid Algar, *Sufism:Principles and Practice* (Oneonta, NY: Islamic Publications International, 1999), 29.

# The Lord's Prayer: A Mennonite View

## Jon Hoover

### Introduction

In the middle of his Sermon on the Mount in the Gospel according to Matthew, Jesus instructs his disciples how to pray. He says,

> Pray then in this way:
>> Our Father in heaven,
>> Hallowed be your name.
>> Your kingdom come.
>>> Your will be done,
>> on earth as it is in heaven.
>> Give us this day our daily bread.
>>> And forgive us our debts,
>> as we also have forgiven our debtors.
>>> And do not bring us to the time of trial,
>>> but rescue us from the evil one.
>
> (Matt. 6:9-13, NRSV)

Throughout the history of the Christian church, this prayer, commonly called the Lord's Prayer, has been used in catechetical instruction, daily prayer, the ritual of baptism, and celebration of the Lord's Supper, that is, the Eucharist.[1] Among North American Mennonites, there are no normative guidelines concerning when it should be prayed, and practice varies widely. In Sunday worship, some Mennonites pray the Lord's Prayer every week while others rarely employ it. The Lord's Prayer is taught in Christian education programs for children and youth,[2] and it is prayed at times in youth group meetings and retreats. Its use is increasing among Mennonites working on liturgical and spiritual renewal. In this regard, the *Anabaptist Prayer Book* produced by the

Institute of Mennonite Studies includes the Lord's Prayer twice a day in the course of morning and evening prayer.[3] Mennonite churches generally do not prescribe fixed texts for prayers. Thus, among Mennonites, the Lord's Prayer is probably prayed more often than any other one text.[4]

Mennonites and their forebears, the 16th-century Anabaptists, have written modestly on the Lord's Prayer. The 1529 court confession of South German Anabaptist Hans Nadler explains what he taught his followers about the Prayer.[5] This is important evidence that the Anabaptists taught the Prayer as basic catechism alongside the Ten Commandments and the Apostles' Creed.[6] We also have a short 1526 meditation on the Lord's Prayer from Moravian Anabaptist Balthasar Hubmaier.[7] A similar paraphrase of the Prayer was written about 1912 by the Mennonite Samuel K. Landis from Lancaster, Pennsylvania.[8]

Instruction on prayer in an early 20th-century handbook of Mennonite doctrine edited by Bishop Daniel Kaufmann cites the Lord's Prayer as a model "of simplicity and directness," and it contrasts this with the "vain repetitions" that Jesus forbade (see Matt. 6:7).[9] Elsewhere in the book, the Lord's Prayer is used to outline the doctrine of God the Father. This unusual way of expositing the doctrine of God may reflect a traditional Mennonite predilection for employing biblical paradigms wherever possible.[10] In 1992, Mennonite pastor and professor Arthur Boers published *Lord, Teach Us to Pray: A New Look at the Lord's Prayer*. This book was written for a popular audience and provides extensive ethical reflection and pastoral admonition.[11]

Using these sources and the writings of various biblical commentators, I will now provide a line-by-line exposition of the Lord's Prayer. My aim is to ascertain what in fact we are praying when we pray this prayer.

## Our Father in Heaven

The Lord's Prayer begins with the invocation, "Our Father in heaven." As Arthur Boers and others note, invoking "Our Father" instead of "My Father" indicates the communal and social character of this prayer. We do not pray it only for ourselves but for others as well. We pray together for our common good. This undermines modern individualism, and encourages us to be attentive to the need around us.[12]

Interpreters generally agree that the "Father" in "Our Father" denotes two things. First, "Father" means that God is the creator, lord, and sustainer of heaven and earth (cf. Matt. 6:26, 32; Matt. 11:25; Luke 11:13). God has brought all things into being, and we are completely dependent upon God for our existence. We are not our own creators.

Second, "Father" denotes that God is personal. God relates to us in a caring and familial way as parents do to their children (Matt. 6:8; Luke 6:36). With the help of Pauline theology in Galatians 4:1-7, we see that God as Father also involves his unique relationship with the Son Jesus Christ and our adoption as sons and daughters of God through the mediation of the Son and the Spirit. As Paul writes, "And because you are children, God has sent the Spirit of his Son into our hearts, crying, 'Abba! Father!' So you are no longer a slave but a child, and if a child then also an heir, through God" (Gal. 4:6-7; cf. Matt. 11:27).

Some interpreters link God's fatherhood to the parable of the lost son in Luke 15:11-32. In this story, a son asks for his inheritance before his father has died and spends it all in licentious living. The son returns in shame, but his father welcomes him back with open arms. The son in the story symbolizes our waywardness, sin, and shame. The father symbolizes God who forgives us and accepts us nevertheless.

The phrase "in heaven" in "Our Father in heaven" indicates God's transcendence and distinguishes God the Father from human fathers. Even if God relates to us personally and as his children, God the Father is still different from us. God's fatherhood cannot be equated to human fatherhood.[13]

What this entails may be seen by addressing two objections against calling God "Father." On the one hand is the Muslim concern that "Father" compromises God's unity, transcendence, and self-sufficiency by implying that God has a son. It is sometimes thought as well that God had sexual relations with Mary, who then gave birth to Jesus. On the other hand is the Christian feminist critique that "Father" is a patriarchal term that reinforces patriarchal social structures and marginalizes women from their humanity and their rightful roles in the church and society. Additionally, negative images of fatherhood distort one's relationship with God, and those who have suffered from abusive fathers may find it painful to call God "Father." For these reasons, it is argued, "Father" is better substituted with another form of address, perhaps "Creator" or simply "God."

It cannot be denied that Jesus carried out his ministry in a patriarchal society and that the term "Father" easily conveys patriarchal values. Yet, the theological significance of God as "Father" makes it difficult to replace. At the least, the Muslim and feminist critiques afford an opportunity to clarify what calling God "Father" does and does not mean. God is not a man, and the fatherhood of God does not constitute an ideal type of what it means to be a male over against a female, or a man over against a woman. Male and female were equally created in God's image (Gen. 1:27), and God is not sexed or gendered male or female. Rather, the love and mutuality in God as Father, Son, and Holy Spirit might serve as a cue for how we interact with each other, whether male or female. Most important, God's fatherhood indicates that God is personal and interacts intimately with his creatures.[14] In prayer, we approach a God who cares about our every need and knows our every action and thought.

## Hallowed be your name. Your kingdom come. Your will be done, on earth as it is in heaven.

After "Our Father in heaven," the Lord's Prayer provides three supplications pertaining to God. These three are identical in grammatical form. Each contains a passive imperative verb in the third person: "Let your name be hallowed. Let your kingdom be made to come. Let your will be done." Because each verb is in the passive voice, it is not clear who is to hallow the name, make the kingdom come, and do the will of God. Is it God or human beings? If God, the supplications presume that God has not yet completed everything that he has promised to do, and they call upon God to hallow his name, bring in his kingdom, and do his will. If humans are the implied agents, these supplications call upon God to allow or bring humans to do these things. In this case, the prayer reminds us to hallow God's name and align ourselves with his kingdom and will.

Modern interpretation usually makes God the primary agent. As Richard Gardner puts it, "We are saying to God: 'Do what is important to you. Make yourself central in our world.'"[15] The world as it now stands does not fully reflect the glory of God. His name is blasphemed and taken in vain. His reign does not extend over all, and his will is not always carried out. These supplications call upon God to finish what he began in the ministry of Jesus and to establish his kingdom in all its fullness.[16] As Gardner and others point out, these supplications do not exclude human response. If in fact God brings his rule to fullness, humans will respond in perfect obedience and praise. Gardner notes that "Hallowed be your name" calls on both God and humans to act. It is saying, "Act in such a way, O God, that the world sees your greatness and praises you for who you are!"[17]

Much of the Christian tradition has understood the hallowing of the name to refer primarily to human response. Commentators like Jerome (d. 420) and Martin Luther (d. 1546) argue that God is already perfect and completely holy as he is. Thus, God has no need to do anything for the sake of his holiness.[18] Rather, "Hallowed be your name" reminds us that we humans should hallow God's name by worshiping and glorifying him and by not blaspheming and taking God's name in vain.

This ethical interpretation of "Hallowed be your name" is readily apparent in the Anabaptist-Mennonite tradition. The Anabaptist Hans Nadler exhorts, "Look, my brother or sister, why have you slandered the name of God? You are to make it holy, and you slander it." Look at your prayer. How did you pray? You have chattered a great deal but have not considered in your heart where it goes."[19] The Mennonite Samuel Landis writes, "[God] would have us know that He is high and holy, wise and good, powerful and mighty. We should regard Him with godly fear mingled with affection, and strive to honor and glorify Him in all things."[20]

Contemporary Mennonite Arthur Boers criticizes the misuse of God's name in swearing and profanity, as well as the casual way some persons speak of God to justify their decisions or their frivolous lifestyles. Boers is especially concerned with institutional and governmental abuse of God's name. He maintains that the motto "In God we trust" found on American money is blasphemous. He also calls asking God to bless military operations blasphemy. Commenting on the 1991 war in the Persian Gulf, Boers writes, "One thing that made this war noteworthy was the fact that the two major personalities of this conflict, George Bush [the father] and Saddam Hussein, both claimed to have God on their side."[21] Boers adds that hallowing God's name is not just about how we speak but also about how we live: "God's name is to be hallowed and glorified in our lives."[22]

In medieval Christianity, the term "kingdom" in the second supplication "Your kingdom come" was equated with the church itself.[23] Reformation and modern interpreters broke down this simple equation, with some going to the opposite extreme and placing the kingdom entirely in the future at the second coming of Christ. While there is some truth in both extremes, the "already" and the "not yet" are best kept in tension. God's kingdom, or rather God's reign, has already partially come in Jesus, among his followers in the church, and anywhere God's rule of justice, peace, and wholeness are found. However, God's reign has not yet been realized in full because injustice, brokenness, and evil continue to plague our world.[24] Praying "Your kingdom come" calls on God to finish the job. The words of the Anabaptist Balthasar Hubmaier well express this: "Gracious Father, we know that we are captives to sin, the devil, hell and eternal death. But Father, we cry out and call to you as our loving Father to come quickly with your kingdom of grace, peace, joy and eternal salvation. Come to our aid, gracious Father, for without you we are totally miserable, afflicted and lost."[25]

For many interpreters, "Your kingdom come" also has implications for human response. The Anabaptist Hans Nadler says that God's kingdom comes with a cross of suffering to each individual: "If God comes with his kingdom and wants to come to you, he does not come to his own unless he brings the cross, to each one his own cross."[26] Arthur Boers links this supplication to Matt. 6:33, "But strive first for the kingdom of God and his righteousness, and all these things will be given to you as well" (NRSV), and points to the priority that God's reign should have in our lives. This precludes, for example, hanging the national flag inside a church. The supplication, "Your kingdom come" also displays and nurtures hope that God will eventually reign in full. As Boers puts it, "We long for the time when Jesus Christ, King of kings and Lord of the universe, is completely obeyed."[27]

The third supplication of the Lord's Prayer is "Your will be done on earth as it is in heaven." The 16th-century Protestant Reformer John Calvin observed that God's will is of two kinds: God's secret will that pertains to his providential governance of all things, and God's will that we should obey. The first will has to do with ontology, with what God brings into existence in his good purposes. The second will deals with ethics, with what God want us to do.[28] In reciting this supplication, we need not feel compelled to choose one over the other. In the end, the two wills will coincide as all creation submits to God's will in its entirety.

Anabaptist-Mennonite interpretation of "Your will be done" often focuses on the ethical aspect. We are to obey God in all things and be willing to suffer in doing that.[29] Boers mentions here the Anabaptist notion of *Gelassenheit* or yieldedness, which is expressed in saying to God, "Your will be done." He elaborates with two quotations from the Anabaptist Hans Denck: "There is no other way to blessedness than to lose one's self will" and "If man [sic] shall become one with God, he has to suffer what God intends to work in him."[30]

With respect to "on earth as it is in heaven," one strand of interpretation going back to Origen in the third century links it to all three supplications in the first half of the prayer: the hallowing of the name, the coming of the kingdom, and the doing of the will. However, the more common interpretation applies it only to the third supplication: "Your will be done on earth as it is in heaven."[31] The term "heaven" may refer literally to the sky or more generally to the physical universe where everything conforms to God's dictates.[32] Or "heaven" may be understood figuratively as the realm in which God's will is carried out fully, whether in the human world or the natural world.[33] Either way, "on earth" denotes the human realm where God's will is still resisted and sin and brokenness have not yet been overcome.[34] Heaven is where everything is complete, perfect, and in accord with God's will. Earth is where God's perfect will has not yet been fully realized. We pray that the reign of God be extended to earth, to all of existence, and we work within God's purposes to bring that to pass.

For Boers, "On earth as it is in heaven" marks the transition from the first half of the prayer to the latter half. He writes, "It is as if we say, 'If God's name were hallowed, if God's kingdom came, if God's will were done, *then* we on earth would all receive our daily bread, our debts would be forgiven, we would resist temptation, we would be saved from evil.'"[35] God's will would then be done "on earth as it is in heaven."

### Give us this day our daily bread.

"Give us this day our daily bread" is the first of three petitions that make up the second half of the Lord's Prayer. The Greek word *epiousios*, which English translations usually render "daily," is extremely rare, and its meaning has been contested from the early church to the present. Meanings suggested include our bread for the following day, bread for a future messianic banquet, our necessary bread, or simply our daily bread. The Catholic tradition has understood *epiousios* to refer to the bread at the Eucharist that is transubstantiated into the body of Christ. This then led to the notion that the Eucharist should be celebrated daily. Catholic interpreters now give more attention to bread as our physical need than they used to. While still linking this petition to daily celebration of the Eucharist, the current *Catechism of the Catholic Church* focuses extensively on bread in its literal sense. Protestant and Anabaptist-Mennonite interpreters do not link this petition to the Eucharist, and they tie it more literally to our daily human need for bread and other material and social sustenance. In this petition, we stand before the God upon whom we depend for our existence, and we ask him to supply our most basic needs to survive. [36]

Sometimes bread is understood to include spiritual need as well, as when Hans Nadler speaks of our "daily bread, of body and soul."[37] Balthasar Hubmaier gives it a wholly spiritual sense as the heavenly bread of God's holy word.[38] Arthur Boers takes *epiousios* to mean "sufficient" or "enough," so that this petition asks God for sufficient bread but not excess bread. On this basis, Boers talks about the snares and temptations of possessing too much, and he notes the importance of being content with only what we need and learning to control our desires. He also highlights the social aspect of the petition. It does not ask God for only "my" bread but for "our" bread, that is, bread enough for everyone so that no one goes hungry. This also directs us to give compassionately and generously in order to meet the needs of those who do not have enough.[39]

## And forgive us our debts, as we also have forgiven our debtors.

Mennonite theologian John Howard Yoder and others tie the term "debts" in this petition to the Torah ordinance of Jubilee found in Leviticus 25. Every fiftieth year, the year of the Jubilee, debts are to be cancelled, slaves freed, and society restored to its original justice. On Yoder's reading, this petition presumes that we have practiced Jubilee justice before going to God seeking forgiveness for our own debts. He explains as well that Jesus extends debts to include offenses or trespasses in general in the verses immediately following the prayer. Here, Jesus clarifies, "For if you forgive others their trespasses, your heavenly Father will also forgive you; but if you do not forgive others, neither will your Father forgive your trespasses" (Matt. 6:14-15, cf. Luke 11:4).[40]

Interpreters from the early Church Father Tertullian down to the present have elucidated this petition with the parable Jesus tells in Matt. 18:21-35.[41] Jesus compares the kingdom of heaven to a king who took pity on one of his slaves and forgave him a great debt. However, this slave then went out to another man who owed the slave a much smaller amount and threw him into prison because he could not pay. The king was angered at his slave's lack of mercy, and in punishment the king had him tortured. Jesus concludes, "So my heavenly Father will also do to every one of you, if you do not forgive your brother or sister from your heart" (Matt. 18:35).

This parable teaches that we should forgive because God has forgiven us, and many interpreters have given the same sense to "Forgive us our debts..." in the Lord's Prayer.[42] This fits with a theology of human sinfulness that is powerless to forgive on its own apart from the grace of God. However, there is no escaping that the petition "And forgive us our debts, as we also have forgiven our debtors," reverses the order. It is not that we forgive because God has forgiven us. Instead, God forgives us after we have forgiven others (cf. Mark 11:25). Thus, as one scholar notes, the time to forgive is before praying the Lord's Prayer, not afterwards.[43]

Another scholar, New Testament exegete Hans Dieter Betz, explains that this is simply a matter of justice. Before we turn to God for mercy, we should do everything that we can to extend forgiveness and mercy to others. Otherwise God would be condoning injustice in us. We dare not ask mercy from God for ourselves while denying it to others.[44] Samuel Landis conveys the full force of the petition when he writes, "God has made it a condition that man must forgive to be forgiven. If any man who has an unforgiving spirit makes use of this prayer with hatred in his heart he condemns himself, for he asks God to do with him as he does with his fellow men."[45]

## And do not bring us to the time of trial, but rescue us from the evil one.

In the New Revised Standard Version of the Bible, this last petition in the Lord's Prayer is translated, "And do not bring us to the time of trial, but rescue us from the evil one." The first part of this petition is more adequately translated by the older Revised Standard Version: "And lead us not into temptation." However, this implies that God himself leads us into temptation, and commentators from the early church down to the present have tried to say this is not what the petition truly means, especially since the New Testament letter of James states explicitly that God does not tempt anyone (James 1:13). Rather, the argument goes, this petition is asking that God not allow us to be tempted by the devil or to suffer testing and trial that will threaten our faith.[46] While this interpretation clears God of leading us into temptation and evil, it unfortunately does not make adequate sense of the text.

Arthur Boers acknowledges this difficulty but does not propose a solution. Rather, he moves on to the practical dangers of temptation and how to resist it. In addition to discussing temptations having to do with materialism, sexuality, and alcohol, he takes up what he calls "righteous temptation." This is the temptation to be so convinced of one's cause that any means are justified to attain it. This includes twisting the truth and suppressing information in order to advance one's own political agenda. A further temptation is complacency and acquiescence to the injustice in our world. We are easily tempted to become too comfortable with the way things are, especially if we derive benefit from an exploitative economic and social order.[47]

Boers's ethical reflections are fitting within the context of this petition. They remind us that we have a role in resisting temptation. However, they do not fully illumine the sense of "Lead us not into temptation." Here, the work of Hans Dieter Betz is more helpful. Betz argues that all efforts to soften this petition fail in the face of its obvious meaning. There is no way to evade the fact that the petition assumes that God leads us into temptation. Betz explains that God is not making a pact with the devil, trying to teach us something, or being capricious. Rather, it is that "God leads into temptation by allowing evil to persist."[48] Betz also connects this to the three supplications in the first half of the prayer. If evil and the temptation that it causes were completely eradicated, there would be no need to call upon the Father to hallow his name, bring in his kingdom, and extend the domain of his will. God has not yet completed the task that he has promised to complete – that of triumphing fully over evil – and it thus follows that we need to pray with vigor that he not lead us into temptation.[49]

The second half of the sixth petition, "But rescue us from the evil one," complements and interprets the first half. Commentators are not agreed on whether the petition is for delivery from evil that is impersonal or from the personal "evil one," that is, the devil. Betz argues for impersonal evil, explaining that this is what causes the temptation mentioned in "Lead us not into temptation." We ask first that God not tempt us, and then we ask God to rescue us from the evil that entangles us and leads to our demise. Only an act of God can free us from evil.[50]

Betz also asks whether this petition "is not an expression of human presumption and arrogance."[51] What right do human beings have to imply that God is responsible for evil, to call upon God to act righteously, and to rescue them from the quandary that he has put them in? For Betz, the answer is found in the invocation "Our Father," which sets us directly before God as the sole source of our existence and the only one who can secure our rights and our future. We are nothing without God. Yet, we are entangled in evil; and there is nowhere to turn but to God. Thus, in praying the Lord's Prayer, we act to inform God of this circumstance, and we call upon him to rescue us from our predicament.[52]

## For the kingdom, the power, and the glory are yours now and forever. Amen.

Christians praying the Lord's Prayer often close with the acclamation "For the kingdom, the power, and the glory are yours now and forever. Amen." This acclamation does not appear in the earliest manuscripts of Matthew's gospel, but it does appear in some manuscripts of the gospel in the fourth century. Praying the Lord's Prayer with this acclamation affirms that all things belong to God and brings the prayer to a natural close.[53]

## Conclusion

The Lord's Prayer situates us before our almighty Creator who loves us dearly. God our Father is both transcendent in heaven and immanent among us, intimately concerned with our daily affairs, even our bread, which he wants us to ask him for each day. We pray to a God who is fully God but whose mission is not yet complete. In response, we call out boldly to our Father to finish what he has promised to do, to hallow his name, to bring his kingdom in full, and to make his will prevail. At the same time, we recognize that we have a role to play in making all of these things come to pass. In response, we too seek to hallow God's name, live in the light of his kingdom, and do his will. And as we seek these things, we also turn to God to fulfill our own needs for bread, forgiveness, and protection from evil. Praying the Lord's Prayer wraps us up in God's purposes, and throws us completely upon his mercy and grace to find our strength and freedom.[54]

## Endnotes

1   For a survey of the journey of the Lord's Prayer through history, see Kenneth W. Stevenson, *The Lord's Prayer: A Text in Tradition* (Minneapolis, MN: Fortress Press, 2004). The prayer appears in different versions in the Gospel according to Luke (11:2-4) and the early Christian instructional text called the *Didache* (the pertinent section is found in J. Stevenson, ed., *A New Eusebius: Documents Illustrating the History of the Church to AD 337*, rev. by W.H.C. Frend [London: SPCK, 1987], 10). The *Didache* specifies that the Lord's Prayer should be prayed three times a day. While Protestants, including Mennonites, call it the "Lord's Prayer," Catholics call it the "Our Father."

2   In this regard, see Glaphré Gilliland, *Praying the Lord's Prayer* (Newton, KS: Faith and Life Press, 1995). This Mennonite Sunday School instructional booklet uses the Lord's Prayer as a model for teaching young people at the junior high level (about ages 12-14) how to pray. It is most concerned to draw them into the experience of praying. The text highlights the personal and practical quality of the Prayer, and discusses forgiveness and God's protection, but it does not carefully interpret the prayer line by line.

3   Arthur Paul Boers, et al., eds., *Take Our Moments and Our Days: An Anabaptist Prayer Book* (Elkhart, IN: Institute of Mennonite Studies, 2005).

4   I am grateful to Warren Tyson, Mervin Stoltzfus, Alan Kreider, and Irma Fast-Dueck for their observations on Mennonite use of the Lord's Prayer.

5   Russel Snyder-Penner, "Hans Nadler's Oral Exposition of the Lord's Prayer," *Mennonite Quarterly Review* 65.4 (Oct. 1991): 393-406.

6   Russel Snyder-Penner, "The Ten Commandments, the Lord's Prayer, and the Apostles' Creed as Early Anabaptist Texts," *Mennonite Quarterly Review* 68.3 (July 1994): 318-35.

7   Daniel Liechty, trans. and ed., *Early Anabaptist Spirituality: Selected Writings* (New York: Paulist Press, 1994), 38-40.

8   Samuel K. Landis, "The Lord's Prayer," in *Readings from Mennonite Writings New and Old*, ed. J. Craig Haas (Intercourse, PA: Good Books, 1992), 299-300.

9   Daniel Kauffmann, ed., *Doctrines of the Bible: A Brief Discussion of the Teachings of God's Word* (Scottdale, PA: Mennonite Publishing House, 1928), 463. It is to avoid "vain repetition" that Mennonites have often hesitated to pray the Lord's Prayer too frequently, preferring instead extemporaneous prayers.

10  Kauffman, 55-57.

11  Arthur Paul Boers, *Lord, Teach Us to Pray: A New Look at the Lord's Prayer* (Scottdale, PA: Herald Press, 1992). All references to Boers hereafter are to this book.

12  Boers, 28-33. See also William H. Willimon and Stanley Hauerwas, *Lord, Teach Us: The Lord's Prayer and the Christian Life* (Nashville, TN: Abingdon Press, 1996), 28-29; Michael H. Crosby, *The Prayer that Jesus Taught* (Maryknoll, NY: Orbis Books, 2002), 36-38; and the *Catechism of the Catholic Church* (New

York: Doubleday, 1995 [1994]), 735-36.

13  Hans Dieter Betz, *The Sermon on the Mount* (Minneapolis, MN: Fortress Press, 1995), 386-89; Ulrich Luz, *Matthew 1-7: A Commentary*, trans. Wilhelm C. Linss (Edinburgh: T & T Clark, 1989), 375-77; Kauffman, 56; Boers, 32-35, 50-55.

14  Here I follow Miroslav Volf, *Exclusion and Embrace: A Theological Exploration of Identity, Otherness, and Reconciliation* (Nashville, TN: Abingdon Press, 1996), 167-81. See also Boers, 36-43.

15  Richard B. Gardner, *Believers Church Bible Commentary: Matthew* (Scottdale, PA: Herald Press, 1991), 118. The *Believers Church Bible Commentary* series is authored by scholars from various churches in the Mennonite and Brethren traditions (Brethren Church, Church of the Brethren, Brethren in Christ Church, Mennonite Brethren, etc.). At the time of writing this commentary, Gardner was a professor and minister for the Church of the Brethren.

16  Gardner, 119. See also W. D. Davies and Dale C. Allison, Jr., *A Critical and Exegetical Commentary on the Gospel According to Saint Matthew*, Vol. 1 (Edinburgh: T. & T. Clark, 1988), 602-06.

17  Gardner, 119. See also Betz, 391-92.

18  Stevenson, 74, 160. See also Luz, 378-80, a modern interpreter who leans against the eschatological interpretation of this petition.

19  Synder-Penner, "Hans Nadler's Oral Exposition of the Lord's Prayer," 405. All references to Snyder-Penner hereafter are from this article.

20  Landis, 299.

21  Boers, 61.

22  Ibid., 64.

23  Stevenson, 14, 153.

24  See Boers, 66-69; Donald A. Hagner, *Word Biblical Commentary*, Vol. 33A, *Matthew 1-13* (Dallas, TX: Word Books, 1993), 148.

25  In Liechty, 39.

26  Snyder-Penner, 405. Snyder-Penner, 399, explains that Nadler in this petition "was influenced by an element of cross mysticism, which is also evident in other parts of Nadler's confession and was especially prominent in the teachings of his mentor Hans Hut."

27  Boers, 69-72 (quote on 71).

28  Stevenson, 164.

29  Snyder-Penner, 405.

30  Boers, 82; Boers took these quotes from the *Mennonite Encyclopedia* (Scottdale, PA: Herald Press, 1956), 2:448-49.

31  Stevenson, 14, 129, 169, 223. Crosby, 44ff., follows the first line of interpretation.

32  So Betz, 395.

33  So Boers, 85. For discussion of the distinction between literal and figurative

"heaven," see Thomas N. Finger, *Christian Theology: An Eschatological Approach*, 2 vols. (Scottdale, PA: Herald Press, 1985, 1989), 1:157.

34  Boers, 85. See also Betz, 395.

35  Boers, 84.

36  For discussions of *epiousios*, see Luz, 380-83; Betz, 397-99; Gardner, 120 (very brief); and the *Catechism of the Catholic Church*, 745-48. Much material on interpretation of the term through history is found in Stevenson.

37  Snyder-Penner, 405. The Mennonite Landis, 299, speaks likewise.

38  In Liechty, 39.

39  Boers, 91-102. These lines of interpretation are much expanded in Crosby, 119-38.

40  John Howard Yoder, *The Politics of Jesus: Vicit Agnus Noster* (Grand Rapids, MI: Eerdmans, 1972), 66-67. Yoder's interpretation is adopted by Crosby, 152-34. Samuel Tobias Lachs, "On Matthew VI.12," *Novum Testamentum* 17.1 (Jan. 1975): 6-8, links this verse to the release of debts every seven years prescribed in Deuteronomy 15:1-2.

41  Stevenson, 31 (Tertullian); Hagner, 150; Gardner, 120.

42  See, for example, Willimon and Hauerwas, 78-86. See also Hagner, 151-52, who asserts – even when commenting on Matt. 6:14-15 – that "God's forgiveness is always prior" to our forgiveness of others; he includes a reference to the parable in Matt. 18:23-35.

43  Bastiaan Van Elderen, "When Do We Forgive?" *Calvin Theological Journal* 33 (April 1998): 169-75.

44  Betz, 404.

45  Landis, 299.

46  For Tertullian, Cyprian, Ambrose, Luther, and others, see Stevenson, 31, 34, 72, 160, respectively. Recent interpreters following this line include Hagner, 151; Davies and Allison, 612-13; the *Catechism of the Catholic Church*, 751; and Michael P. Knowles, "Once More 'Lead Us Not *Eis Peirasmon*'," *The Expository Times* 115.6 (March 2004): 191-94. Landis, 299, also adopts this interpretation; Nadler implies it (Snyder-Penner, 405); and Gardner, 120, does not broach the problem.

47  Boers, 127-36. While Boers implies the temptation to complacency in the face of economic exploitation, this is brought out more fully by Crosby, 162-71.

48  Betz, 411. More recently and more thoroughly, Joseph A. Fitzmyer, "And Lead Us Not into Temptation," *Biblica* 84 (2003): 259-73 (http://www.bsw.org/?l=71841&a=Ani05.html, accessed 14 May 2007), also argues that the petition must be translated "Lead us not into temptation" and refutes any attempts to mitigate its offense. Fitzmyer includes pastoral considerations, one of which is that this petition need not contradict James 1:13 if, following Augustine, we distinguish being led into temptation, which God does, from tempting, which God does not do (272).

49  Betz, 406-11. Betz, 380-81, elaborates the theology implied in these two verses. There is also a sense in which "Do not lead us into temptation" recognizes that God is in full control of human events. It is not that God could not overtake the forces of temptation should he want to, but that God allows the forces of temptation to continue, and we call upon God to bring this state of affairs to an end.

50  Ibid., 411-13.

51  Ibid., 381.

52  Ibid., 381-82.

53  Ibid., 411; Stevenson, 15-16; Davies and Allison, 615 n. 54; Gardner, 118. A similar acclamation, "For thine is the power and the glory for ever," appears in the *Didache* (see Stevenson, 10).

54  I would like to thank Johnny Awwad and Jacqueline Hoover for their helpful comments on an earlier version of this paper.

In the Name of Allah, The Beneficent and
the Merciful

# Supplication in the Words of the Infallibles[1]

## Aboulhassan Haghani Khaveh

### Introduction

Among the distinctive features that Allah has granted mankind is the ability to achieve perfection. He has assigned to human beings two parallel manifest paths towards this end. The first path is one's intellect, which enables people to distinguish between good and evil and to recognize the real way of perfection. The other path is a set of guidelines presented by the Noble Prophet and infallible Imams. These two manifest paths are invaluable lessons in guidance, as the message of heavenly faith seeks to achieve felicity for mankind in this world and the hereafter. According to the Shi'a, Allah has honoured the Prophet and the Imams with infallibility so that their words and actions may capture people's hearts and minds, and light the way of perfection.

According to the Divine teachings, supplication, exalting, and glorifying Allah represent the main ways of enhancing one's life and path towards achieving perfection. Since it is impossible for one to find this way, or to become well acquainted with it, by relying solely on the intellect, one must refer to the prophets and infallibles and follow their guidelines in order to have a clear idea about the reality of the acts of worship and the ways of performing them.

Supplication is practiced not only by those who belong to the Abrahamic religions, but also by those who follow other schools of thought and who believe in the existence of the Lord of the universe. The Noble Qur'an refers to this fact and states that even polytheists or those in distress take refuge in supplication (7:194).

As I have already stated, all heavenly faiths stress the significant effect of supplication and exalting Allah, though they differ in the way of supplicating. For instance, the ways of supplicating followed by prophets like Adam, Noah, Abraham, Job, Moses, and Jesus (peace be upon them all) were different because the circumstances of their times were each different, and the same is true of the ways of supplication of the Noble Prophet and the infallible Imams whom the Shi'ah follow.

Since supplication and glorifying Allah is an instinctive thing, this characteristic exists in everyone. However, for some people it is a weak instinct, due to heedlessness. Therefore, this instinctive feature thrives best in a climate of awareness and intention.

Now, what is the real meaning of supplication? Technically, it means asking or praying to Allah for the satisfaction of needs, and desiring what is with him. In fact, supplication means turning to the One whom the believers serve, and they consider true supplication as a spiritual ascension. Supplication in its real sense is to devotedly turn to the Lord of the world and express one's submission to him. The strength of one's devotion to Allah depends on the degree of one's knowledge and love for him. Therefore, supplication reflects one's submission and devotion to Allah and strengthens one's spirit of servitude. This spirit is what godly leaders attempt to revive in people. Consequently, supplication is the expression of one's submission to Allah, need for him, and connection to him.

## Supplication in the Qur'an

The Noble Qur'an contains many verses urging people to supplicate or to pray. Allah has commanded his servants to call upon him. For example, he says: "Call upon me, I will answer you" (40:60), and "Call on your Lord humbly and secretly; surely he does not love those who exceed the limits" (7:55). Allah mentions in the Qur'an that it is because of people's supplication that Allah esteems them: "Say: My Lord would not care for you were it not for your prayer" (25:77).

## Supplication in the Narrations[2]

The narrations (*hadith*) on the subject of supplications, narrated from the Prophet of Islam and the Imams whom the Shi'a follow, are great in number. They carry detailed information about the importance of supplication, the conditions that contribute to granting a supplicant's need, the advantages of supplication, and the etiquette of supplication.

I will refer to some of these narrations. Regarding the importance of supplication, the Noble Prophet says, "Supplication is the weapon of the believer, pillar of religion and the brightness of sky and earth." In another narration he says, "The weakest person is the one who is weak in supplication." Someone asked Imam Ali, "What is the best kind of speech in the eyes of Allah? Imam Ali answered, "Remember Allah a lot and supplicate." Imam Sadiq, the sixth Imam, also referring to the importance of supplication, says, "There is no vehicle like supplication to take you nearer to Allah." According to another narration, Imam Sadiq says, "There is a station and position near to Allah that can only be reached through supplication and prayer."

It has been recounted that certain conditions contribute to granting a supplicant's need (answers to prayer). Here I will refer to some instances of granting a need. One condition for a supplication to be answered or responded to is having hope in no one except Allah; thus a supplicant has to seek his or her need only from Allah. It has been recounted that Allah has said to Jesus, "O, Jesus! Call upon Me like the call of one who is drowning, afflicted, for whom there is none to aid." According to another narration, Imam Sadiq has said that "Allah does not answer a supplication that is not from the bottom of one's heart and is only outward and negligently prayed. So when you want to pray, pay attention to your heart and be certain of Allah's answer."

The following is a list of the conditions of supplication presented in the narrations of the Infallibles:

1. Supplication in secret is better than supplications in public. One supplication in secret is worth seventy in public.

2. One should call upon Allah not only in times of distress but also in times of comfort and ease.

3. Supplication and practice should be side by side: "One who asks but does not act is like an archer without an arrow."

4. A supplication should begin with praising and thanking Allah.

5. A supplication ought to be said with meditation and in humility.

6. It is better to include others in one's supplication and not to seek only the accomplishment of one's personal needs.

7. One should seek nearness to Allah through one's good deeds.

## The Objectives of Supplication

When people call upon Allah, their objectives are not the same. These people can be divided into various groups. The first group is those who turn to Allah and call upon him only when they face worldly difficulties or want their financial needs to be met. A large number of supplications are of this kind. They do not remember Allah when they are at ease, but only when they find themselves in a critical situation; then they remember him and turn to him to grant them their needs. Allah says, "And when we show favour to people, he turns aside and withdraws himself; and when evil touches him, he makes lengthy supplications" (41:51). When these people face problems and feel they can do nothing, they come to Allah and ask his help.

The second group is those who turn to Allah and call upon him only with the aim of being delivered from the Fire and being admitted into Paradise. In fact, the supplication of this group is concerned with the next world. For true believers, Allah's forgiveness is one of the main concerns. They constantly ask the Almighty to forgive their misdeeds, to cover over their mistakes, and to preserve their good reputation. It is noteworthy that among the distinguished attributes of Allah to which the Qur'an and narrations have referred are his being All-forgiving and All-covering of misdeeds.

The third group is unique; the aim of their supplications is exceptionally sublime. All they long for through their supplicating is the perfection of the soul, spiritual needs, and nearness to the Almighty. Such people call upon Allah in a constant whisper whether in prosperity or distress, because they find a special joy when they talk to their Lord. When in prosperity they thank him, and when in need or hardship they seem patient and take such difficulties as part of Allah's gentleness. This reminds us of the 'Ashura Day in Karbala; although Imam Hussein was facing appalling hardships on that day, he did not call upon Allah to remove them. Similarly, just before being thrown in the fire, Abraham did not call the Almighty to save him because he had confidence in him. Like Abraham, Allah's friends (*awliya*) have this kind of station and character too. They are at the blessed place "in houses which Allah has permitted to be exalted [so] that his name may be remembered in them; they glorify Him therein in the mornings and the evenings" (24:36). Perhaps the reason this group's supplication is so sublime is that, in spite of the special station they enjoy and the abundant blessing granted them by Allah, they feel they are in need of him and they are his servants.

## Recorded Supplication

In calling upon the Almighty, people can express themselves in the way they want and use the language they want. What is important is the genuineness of the supplication and the sincerity of the supplicant. The more sincere the supplication, the greater its influence on ensuring the response. On the other hand, the prophets are the best exemplars of the way that leads to Allah, and they are the guides of mankind. Therefore, it is good to follow the way of supplication of the prophets and the infallible Imams. The reason their supplication is exceptional is that they know the etiquette of servitude to Allah better than others, and thus obviously have a wider knowledge of him. Since they have a particularly extensive knowledge, their demands are much more excellent than our demands and we can learn supplicating from them.

The subject matter of the supplications recounted from the prophets and the Imams whom the Shi'a follow can be divided into three main groups. In the first group, one usually begins with praising Allah and thanking him. The second group exhibits the mightiness of Allah, and the third group shows the servants' neediness before Allah.

A number of famous supplications are frequently referred to by the Shi'ah because of their invaluable contents. One of them is the supplication of Imam Hussein known as *Du'a 'Arafat*, with which he addressed the Almighty at the time of his departure from Mecca. It has been recounted that Imam Hussein together with many members of his family and followers came to a place at the foot of a mountain, stood facing the *kaba*, and started calling upon Allah with utter humility. He entreated Allah like a famished person in need of food. This supplication is thirty pages long. The first sentence of *Du'a 'Arafah* deals with being acquainted with God through his signs in the world. At the end of the supplication, Imam Hussein looks at the sky and with a loud voice and eyes filled with tears, calls upon the Almighty in meekness and says:

> O, most hearing one of the hearers, O, most seeing of the seers, O, You who are quickest in reckoning. O, most merciful of the merciful, My Lord I beg you to accept my lawful wish, that wish which if you give it to give it to me nothing would hurt me if you missed it, and if you do not give it to me nothing will benefit me. I ask you to keep my neck from the Fire. O, My God! I understand [...] that your purpose for me is to show yourself to me in all things so that I may not be ignorant of you in anything.

We hope that peace will prevail in the world and people will come nearer to Allah.

## Endnotes

1   "Infallibles" is the term used to describe the first twelve Imams. The Shi'a emerged from the beginning of Islam as a group who followed Ali as the

successor to the Prophet Muhammad. The successorship is a Divine position. Those Imams, leaders, who follow in the Prophet's line in "the institution of the Imamah as a continuation of prophethood," are considered the leaders of all the political and religious leadership of the Muslim community to this day. "The Imam is the Representative of God on earth (khalifat-Allah) and the successor of the Prophet." As such, "he must be sinless and possess divine knowledge of both the exoteric and the esoteric meaning of the Qur'an." The majority of Shi'a (Twelver Shi'a) believe that the first twelve Imams succeeded the Prophet. These twelve are known as "the Infallibles" and the Imamate, and are considered to have a universal mission over all the household of the Prophet, *thaqulayn*, *'Itrah* and *Ahlul Bayt*. (See Mohammad Ali Shomali, *Discovering Shi'i Islam* (Qom: Ansariyan Publications, 2002.)

2   The Hadith or narrations from the Imams and followers.

In the Name of Allah

# Spiritual Dimensions of Imam Khomeini and the Islamic Revolution

## Mahmoud Namazi Esfahani

*Part I*
*WHAT IS SPIRITUALITY?*

## Introduction

The third millennium of Christian era is known as "the age of faith and spirituality," but it has also been called "the age of science and information." The most important crisis of the age of modernism and postmodernism is that of spirituality. The terms "spiritual" and "spirituality" are crucial in religious discourse. Spirituality is also a crucial place where science and religion could join together in the modern world. While disciplines like theology, mysticism, philosophy, and history have touched the concept of spirituality, it is still foreign to the physical sciences. However, the concept of spirituality is a key word in inter-religious dialogue, and it enables us to move towards a common language and perhaps a common understanding in the inter-religious and international arena.

## A Word Study

"Spirituality" is the English word derived from the Latin term *spiritus,* meaning "breath" or what makes things living. *Spiritus* can also mean soul, courage, or the incorporeal dimensions of life. It can also refer to knowledge from insensible dimensions. Here it refers mostly to the insensible or metaphysical dimensions of the world and the deepest dimensions of scriptures or sacred books. It also plays an important role in religious concepts such as "the first principle" or God, and can apply to the psychology (spirit, or soul) of the human being. The *Oxford Advanced Learner Dictionary* indicates the following range of meanings for "spirituality": (a) "of the human spirit" or "soul," not of physical things, and (b) "of the Church" or "of religion." The Pope, for example, is the spiritual leader of many Christians. Spirituality can also mean the state or quality of being concerned with spiritual matters.

Spirituality should not be confused with spiritualism, which has a very different meaning and has to do with the belief in the possibility of receiving messages from the spirits of the dead and practices based on this belief. A spiritualist is a person who believes in or practices spiritualism.[1]

## The Idea of Spirituality: Towards a Definition

Having in mind the broad scope and personal nature of "spirituality" as a term with different uses in different contexts, we cannot have a simple, comprehensive, and exhaustive definition. The term includes a wide range of meanings as it relates to ideological, theological, ethical, and scriptural studies. However, in its general meaning it refers to immaterial entities. In its particular usages it has different meanings. Some view "spirituality" as equivalent to "undistorted divine religion," while others give it other meanings.

One can perhaps gain an overview by focusing on the key concepts that arise when people describe what spirituality means to them. One can say that a human being's spiritual life totally depends on undistorted divine religion. This is the meaning we focus on here.

## Spirituality: Reality and Actuality

In understanding spirituality it is important to distinguish material from immaterial entities. Immaterial entities are untouchable by the five senses; they have no dimension, size, or weight, but they do surely exist. Immaterial things include metaphysical entities like God, angels, and the Holy Spirit, as well as liberty, justice, and the good. During their long history, human beings have not restricted worthiness only to material things; they have also always valued immaterial things such as freedom of thought, liberty, and a relationship with the spiritual realm. As well as enjoying material objects, people also enjoy attaining spiritual or immaterial goals. Just as one enjoys eating an orange, an apple, or a pizza, one also enjoys doing a good deed.

Philosophers have differentiated three kinds of pleasures: bodily, emotional, and intellectual. Intellectual pleasures are immaterial pleasures and constitute one important part of the enjoyments of humankind. Pleasures and enjoyments are not limited to material things.

## Spirituality and the Iranian Revolution

We might – surprisingly to some – observe the importance of spirituality if we look back to 1979 Iran. This was when people "with empty hands" (i.e., without weapons) and without any support from foreigners made a great revolution that led to the Shah fleeing the country after fifty years of governing. This is an example of an effective spirituality. The same phenomenon is observable in the history of Islam when the Prophet Muhammad and his followers overcame two important empires, Rome and Iran, with empty hands. The Prophet Muhammad, during his twenty-three years of prophetic mission, spread and propagated his religion, Islam, all over the world.[2]

## Elements Forming an Effective Spirituality

Several elements are crucial to forming an effective spirituality. Self-knowledge is the first of those elements and is the root of ethical and spiritual inspirations. Islam as a divine religion leads people to a higher level of human values, self-knowledge, self-consciousness, and ego-discovery. It invites them to a deep self-consciousness. Islam and the Qur'an maintain that if one discovers himself, his intellectuality, and his real existence, he will then find his honour, nobility, dignity, and moral distinction. A famous prophetic tradition observes that "Everyone who knew himself (surely) knew his Lord." People understand and attain ethical inspiration through self-knowledge. The Qur'an asserts that everyone naturally knows right and wrong, and that the man who truly succeeds is the one who purifies and does not corrupt his nature.

In the Qur'an we encounter nine examples of how the universe and human beings know the ways of Allah by nature. We can see these ways in (1) the sun and his glorious splendor; (2) by the moon as she follows him; (3) by the day as it shows up the sun's glory; (4) by the night as it conceals it; (5) by the firmament and its wonderful structure; (6) by the earth and its wide expanse; (7) by the soul, and the proportion and order given to it; (8) by the enlightenment as to wrong and right; and (9) by seeing that he who truly succeeds purifies his soul, while he who fails corrupts it.[3]

The second element of an effective spirituality is asceticism. Muslim scholars see a clear connection between inner (interior) and outer (exterior) attention. As much as a person's inner attention increases, his outer attention decreases, and vice versa. An ascetic is one who leads a very simple life for religious reasons and does not pursue worldly pleasures and comforts. Accordingly, the more an ascetic increases his attention to religious matters and, correspondingly, decreases his attention to worldly things and entities, the more he will receive a deepened spirituality. This works in the opposite way too. When he decreases his concern for religious matters and increases his attention to the world and worldly things, the more he loses spirituality.

The third factor of an effective spirituality involves correcting and adjusting one's internal relations to immaterial entities rather than to the world and worldly entities. The way that one adjusts his behaviour, reforms his concerns, and improves his views and his sight can change his dependence on the world and worldly entities. This is especially true as one increases his concern and dependence on religious matters and defined immaterial things. This can correct, adjust, and deepen his relations with the external world. Let me give an example that involves this principle in the process of differentiating between possessing wealth and depending on it. The main aim is to overcome an inner dependence on or attachment to wealth; it is not a matter of not having or possessing wealth. According to Islamic teaching, it is not how much wealth one has; rather the issue is inner dependence on wealth.

Wealth should belong to human beings and not the other way round. (This relation is often reversed in capitalism.) Accordingly, one should eliminate one's inner dependence on the world and worldly entities.

Neither should one indiscriminately share wealth between people, as is sometimes seen in communism. Rather, one should reduce his dependence on the material world and try to listen to God and serve him. What, how, how much, when, where, and on whom wealth should be spent and distributed is outlined in the holy Qur'an. It is dependence on limited entities like wealth that is undesirable. It is dependence on the unlimited and ultimate reality – that is, God – which is demanded. For dependence on limited entities limits one, but dependence on unlimited and ultimate reality does not limit one.

This is wonderfully expressed in verses of Hâfid, the great Persian poet.[4] Hâfid insists that the overcoming of one's dependence on external things should begin with freeing himself from himself.[5] This is key to one's internal spirituality. Similarly, Mîr Findiriskî, (970/1560-1050/1640), one of the foremost Iranian Shî'î philosophers, also describes this internal shî'î spirituality in his *Philosophical Ode:*

> *Mîtawânî az rah-i âsân, shudan bar âsmân, Râst bâsh wa râst raw kânjâ nabâshad kâstî.*
> You can reach heaven simply by their means. Be true and walk the straight path for there is no falsehood there.

> *Rah nayâbad bar darî az âsimân dunyâ parast, Dar nabugshâyand bar wiy gar ch-i darhâ wâstî.*
> He who worships the world, the door of heaven will never open to him; the doors will not open even if he stands before them.

> *Har ki fânî shud dar 'û, yâbad ªayât-i jâwdân, war bi khud uftâd, kârash bî shak az mû tâstî.*
> He who is annihilated in Him finds eternal life. He who is busy with himself, his affair is doubtless a failure.

The fourth element of an effective spirituality is the correction and adjustment of external (individual, social, political, ethical etc.)

relations. When we realize the external dependence of mankind, then we can see it is urgent that this external dependence be properly understood and properly formed. For if we do not have the proper social forms – economically, socially, legally, and politically – then the external dependencies will overcome the inner spiritual relations. The question, however, is how humankind's relations with material entities should be formed and adjusted. What role does the human play here? Who is ruling?

The Qur'an clarifies that the only way to achieve external reformation and adjustment is by holding fast, worshiping, and serving only Allah. "Say: 'O people of the Book! Come to common terms between us and you: that we worship none but Allah; that we associate no partners with him; that we erect (construct, set up and establish) not, from among ourselves, lords and patrons other than Allah.' If then they turn back, say ye: 'Bear witness that we (at least) are Muslims (bowing to Allah's Will).'"[6] This verse informs us that according to Islam, inner control and interior purification is not absolutely enough; external reformation and adjustment is also needed. Yet Islam insists that no one has any right to impose himself over others.

Normally, when a person or a nation calls upon another person or a nation for educational, sociological, or political relations, the person or nation expects to export his culture, language, and customs to the invitee. But the Qur'anic invitation is totally different. Regardless of one's sect, group, or race, the Qur'an truly invites people to accept this central idea: "To serve and worship only Allah." According to the Qur'an, the common requirement for all people is the same thing: "People worship and serve none but Allah, [and] associate no partner with him" and, even more important, "erect no lord and no patron from among themselves other than Allah."

Mîr Ahmad Alî in his translation of the holy Qur'an says that Verse 64, 3rd Surah proclaims the main policy of Islam and the Holy Prophet Muhammad in dealing with non-Muslims. It says the policy is to maintain peace and general social harmony while preaching the truth. The original scriptures possessed by both Jews and Christians preached nothing but the Unity of God, the basic principle of the faith of Islam, Christianity, and Judaism. The belief in other man-made gods, priests, and other holy men was a later innovation and a fanciful grafting. This innovation and grafting is referred to in 9:31: "They take their priests and their anchorites to be their Lords in denigration of Allah," and "They take as their Lord, Christ the son of Mary, yet they were commanded to worship but one Allah. There is no god but He. Praise and glory to Him. Far is Allah from having the partners they associate with Him." The verse enjoins us to invite Jews and Christians to embrace faith in one God, the common demand of all three religions. However, some Muslims regard certain Jews and Christians as believing in other than the absolute Unity of God – a belief that is nothing but *Shirk* (i.e., associating others with God). Since *Shirk* is abhorred in Islam, Muslims have been told to dissociate with those Jews and Christians in these elements of their faiths. This is to let them know that Muslims, being monotheists, will have nothing to do with any fanciful fabrications about the status of Moses or Jesus.

From the beginning of this chapter, the Qur'an has laid down such principles to be taken as the common ground for argument between the people of the scriptures to settle disputed questions. Of these principles, Islam's most fundamental teaching and belief is the Unity of God. God is not only the ultimate creative authority but the ultimate and absolute sovereign Lord of the universe before whose legislative will or order all must submit. Everyone must surrender to his will and obey him as the sole object of worship, reverence, and obedience. All beings of the angelical, human, animal, or other spheres, and nature in the heavens, in the earth and in between, though one may be greater than the other, are his created ones, subordinate as slaves and subservient to him. To associate anything in any sphere as a separate authority beside him is *Shirk* or polytheism.[7]

After arguing the case of Jesus being wrongly defied, the Qur'an addresses the people of the Book and warns them to be alive to the fundamental principle common to all who believe in God's absolute authority and sovereignty. Whatever view or doctrine they may hold, it should be based on the divine declaration. Doctrines laid down by any individual or any body of the people as right or wrong should have no value whatsoever, as adherence to such views means holding others as authorities besides God. This principle would free humanity of all the doctrinal controversies which created sects and the various contesting schools after each prophet as the Qur'an says (3:18). If the followers of the prophets had strictly adhered to the Word of God and the sayings of their respective prophets without interference from themselves, and had not allowed an ambitious priesthood to exercise its discretion for its selfish ends, there would not have been any division or dissension among the people of the various scriptures.

Muslims are not exempted from this warning. To adhere to doctrines and follow views not based on the Qur'an and the authentic sayings of the Holy Prophet amounts to obedience to others than God and to hold them as the authority beside him. But to pay respect, regard, or reverence to those who were the embodiment of absolute obedience and submission to God is itself obedience and submission to God himself. Remembrance and commemoration of such godly ones is itself the service and devotion to God ordered by him in Surah 38:48, 49. It is particularly mentioned here so that the two issues might not be confused.

In short, every Muslim should always be on guard against any of his actions being motivated by something other than divine authority and order. To worship God and obey him are to follow the prophets sent by him and those whom they have declared to be their successors and representatives. To consider them as having been declared to be so, and following them, means nothing but obedience and worship. But if they are considered to be more or less than what they have been declared to be, or if people other than they are considered to be of the same status without any divine declaration to that effect, this amounts to admitting the authority of another beside God (9:31, 4:69, 4:80).[8]

Accordingly, we can see that Islam offers guidance concerning humanity's internal and psychological dimension as well as its external, economical, social, and political dimensions.

Now we want to clarify the policy and the political system in Islam in general, and how it works in Imâmî Shî'î doctrine and Imâm Khumainî [Khomeni]. As observed above, Islam addresses both the internal and external dimensions of human beings, particularly their relations with themselves and with their society. Here we are going to clarify Islamic policy and the political system of Islam that maintains external and internal relations. This policy and political system has been carefully, accurately, and precisely formulated.

## Political Authority in Imâmî Shî`î Doctrine

The Qur'an illuminates the hierarchy of political authority in the Imâmî Shî`î doctrine in section 4, verse 63: "O believers, obey God, and obey the Messenger and those in authority among you. If you should quarrel on anything, refer it to God and the Messenger, if you believe in God and the Last day; that is better, and fairer in the issue."[9] To clarify this Qur'anic point, I should elucidate and explain the Islamic system of authority.

A political system is a means established to achieve a goal; that is, to do justice, maintain order, and regulate relations in society.[10] Being a means and not a goal, a government requires justification, and insofar as it involves people's rights it needs specifically defined limitations. Different political schools have diverse, and sometimes antagonistic, opinions in this regard. Here we will examine the Imâmî Shî`î doctrine of political authority, its justification and limitations. However, this does not mean that Shî`î Muslims are completely unique in their approach, for many aspects of their doctrine are shared by all Muslims, and some are also agreed upon by non-Muslims.

The hierarchy of political authority in the Imâmî Shî`î doctrine is as follows: God's sovereignty, the Prophet, the Infallible Imâms, and Just and Pious Faqîh.

## Divine *Wilâyah*

The Qur'an in different verses indicates that the planning of the whole world as a total system as well as all trivial systems is ordered, preserved, and directed by God. Sometimes the word "managed" is used to speak of Allah's governance. We come across many verses in which the words *walî* (Islamic jurisprudential guardian), *wâlî* (governor, ruler) and *mawlâ* (master) are employed and mentioned as names and attributes for Allah. In all such cases, Allah is the manager, ruler, governor of the whole world and particularly of human beings.[11] *Wilâyah* is an Arabic verbal noun derived from the root *wly* and carries the basic meanings of friendship, assistance, and authority.[12] However, in the Imâmî Shî`î doctrine, as in other Muslim schools, God's sovereignty is crystallized in the absolute guardianship of the great prophets who terminated in the Prophet Muhammad. This fact is presented in the Qur'an where God says: "The prophet is closer to the believers than their own selves..." (33:6).

Prophethood and Imamate consist in a comprehensive religious authority that includes political authority. Religious authority gives guidance and informs, while political authority is related to leadership, management, and organizing human resources and relations. The great prophets, Abraham, Moses, Jesus/Isa, and Muhammad held both positions. "And remember that Abraham was tried by His Lord with certain commands, which He fulfilled: He said: 'I will make Thee an Imam to the Nations.' He pleaded: 'And also (Imams) from My offspring!' He answered: 'But My promise is not within the reach of evil-doers'" (2:124). This also explains why the some other prophets lacked the office of Imamate and political authority.[13] After the era of the Prophet Muhammad, the socio-political affairs of the Muslim community and the actualization of the religion's goals required authorities who could do the same job as deputies of the prophet.[14] According to the Imâmî Shî`îs, the Prophet, not neglecting his duty in this regard, declared the twelve infallible Imâms as his successors to accomplish the task. God distinguished them by virtue of their being the most pre-eminent of the people.[15] This is considered a necessary grace (*lutf*) from God manifested in the Qur'an when he commands the faithful, "O ye who believe! Obey Allah, and obey the Messenger, and those charged with authority among you. If ye differ in anything among yourselves, refer it to Allah and His Messenger, if ye do believe in Allah and the Last Day: that is best, and most suitable for final determination"(4:59).

The most important question, however, is whether the Imamate in Shî'î doctrine is considered a worldly kingdom and a function of social factor, or a religious station and divine legislation. According to the Shî'ah, the Prophet Muhammad himself had no independent role in determining his successor; rather he was obliged to determine the successor by the approval of God. "O Messenger, proclaim the (message) which hath been sent to Thee from Thy Lord. If Thou Didst not, Thou wouldst not have fulfilled and proclaimed His mission. and Allah will defend Thee from men (Who mean mischief). for Allah guideth not those who reject Faith" (5:67). "...This Day have I perfected your Religion for you, completed My favour upon you, and have chosen for you Islam as your religion...." (5:3). "Your (real) friends are (no less than) Allah, His Messenger, and the (fellowship of) believers, those who establish regular prayers and regular charity, and They bow down humbly (in worship)" (5:55). Therefore, according to Shî'î doctrine and based on the above-mentioned verses of the holy Qur'an, the Imamate is not considered a worldly kingdom or a function of social factors. Rather, it is a religious position that depends on divine determination, because it requires both an inclusive God-given knowledge and infallibility, neither of which can be achieved by ordinary people, although they can be found in certain prophets.[16]

Although people can test those who might claim a right to the Imamate by virtue of their knowledge, socio-political circumstances are nevertheless essential to actualizing the political aspects of such an authority. Unlike dictatorial systems and militarism, the Imamate is not supposed to win by power or rule by force, and unlike democratic regimes, it cannot be subject to attempts at trickery or manipulation with a view to buying votes.

The political situation of the Muslim community, however, did not allow the Imams to actualize the political dimension of their authority, *al-vilâya,* or to establish their preferred government, save for the final years of Ali ibn Abî Tâlib's Imamate, which was ended by his martyrdom by one of the Khârijite in 40 AH/660 AD. Hassan ibn Ali (the second

Imam) was poisoned by Mu`âwîya, and Hussain ibn Ali (the third Imam) was martyred in 60/679 by Yazîd ibn Mu`âwîya. What is more, social conditions were not ready for the other Imams to establish a just Islamic government; therefore, they put greater emphasis on the intellectual, spiritual, and moral training of people. Meanwhile, they did not neglect encouraging and motivating people to oppose their oppressors, and consequently all of them were poisoned by unjust rulers who claimed the caliphate of the Prophet. This was the case for almost two-and-a-half centuries until the twelfth Imam, Imam Mahdî the promised Imam, was born and the lesser occultation, *al-Ghayba al-Sughrâ*, began. Throughout this period, which lasted sixty-nine years (260-329/873-940), only exclusive deputies who were appointed by him acted as mediators between him and his followers.

These deputies were Abû `Amr `Uthmân ibn Sa`îd al-`Amri, Abû Ja`far Muhammad ibn `Uthmân ibn Sa`îd al-`Amri (d. 305/917), Abû al-Qâsim al-Hussain ibn Rûh Nowbakhtî (d. 326/937), and Abû al-Hassan Ali ibn Muhammad al-Samurî (d. 329/940).[17] Then the greater occultation, *al-Ghayba al-Kubrâ*, began, during which there has been no official contact with the Imam to this day. Some Shî`î scholars began to collect the traditions narrated from the Prophet and the Imams to protect them from being destroyed. For example, Abû Ja`far Muhammad ibn Ya`qûb al-Kulainî (d. 329/940), reportedly compiled and systematized approximately 16,200 authentic traditions in his *al-Kâfî fî Usûl al-Dîn*. Later, Abû Ja`far Muhammad ibn Bâbawayh al-Qumî (d. 381/991) composed his *Man Lâ Yauruh-u al-Faqîh*.

Later, some jurists such as Shaikh Tûsî (d. 468/1075) and Sallâr (d. 481/1088) began to develop the idea of a conditional authority for the *faqîh* in the domain of *al-amr-i bi wa al-nahy `an al-munkar* (or "to command what is right, to forbid what is wrong").[18] During the Safavid empire (1501-1722), Muhaqqiq Ali Karakî (d. 940/1533) was one of the most influential religious leaders, theoretically and empirically. He was Shâh Tahmasib's coequal (931-984/1524-1576) and contributed to the idea and practice of the political authority of *faqîh* in its highest rank.[19] Since then, there have been many writings on the issue of *vilâyat-i Faqîh*, with the result that it has become one of the routine issues of *faqîh*. *Faqîh* in its technical meaning is "reasoned comprehension and inferences from the Islamic divine precepts from authentic sources," that is, the Qur'an, Sunna (tradition), Ijmâ' (consensus of fuqahâ'), and intellect.[20] However, an Islamic government (*vilâyat-i Faqîh*) indeed translates into the sovereignty of the divine law. This criterion demands three major qualifications for the ruler: namely his having a profound knowledge of the divine law, his being capable and skillful enough in executing them, and his observing justice and the equality of people before law in his judgment and political actions.[21]

## Conclusion

The Imâmî Shî'î doctrine is considered a comprehensive system. It includes a worldview with value, political, social, legal, economic, and educational components. This inclusive system, called "religion" (*din*), is designed to meet the worldly, spiritual, social, and individual needs of the human being, as well as to undertake the responsibility of guidance and of executing the divine law. Therefore it is necessary for an inclusive religion to establish its fundamental principles in order for a political system to be able to carry out its injunctions and meet its goals. According to the Shî'a, every legitimate authority, *vilâya*, has its roots in God's sovereignty, which is reflected in the authority of the prophets and Imams appointed by him by virtue of being the most qualified of their era. Given the twelfth Imam's occultation, however, the need for a just socio-political order based on the divine injunctions remains unchanged, so that the most qualified person known to the people, referred to as a *faqîh*, must be given the chance to implement the divine law to establish justice and order in society.

## Endnotes

1    See the *Oxford Advanced Learner Dictionary*.

2    Other Iranian scholars note that this paragraph contains an overstatement. – Editors

3    Qur'an 91, verses 1-10.

4    Khwaja Shams al-Din Mohammad Hafez-e-Shiraz, known by his pen name, Hafez (1315-1390), is a very celebrated Persian mystic known mostly for his mystical poems. *Note: The relevant verses by this poet tend to defy translation into accessible English. The Persian originals are provided below.* – Editors

خلاص حافظ از آن زلف تابدار مباد        ك بستگان كمند تو وت سرگاراندن

Khalâs Hâfid az Ân zulf tâbdâr mabâd, k-i bastigân-i kamand-i to rastgârânand.

غلام همت آنم ك زیر چرخ كبود        ز ره چ رنگ تعلق پذیرد آزاد است

Ghulâm-i himmat-i ânam k-i zîr-i charkh-i kaboud, Z-i har ch-i rang-i ta'alugh pazîrad âzâd ast.

مگر تعلق خاطر به ماه رخساری        ك خاطر از همه عالم به مهر او شاد است

Magar ta'alug-i khât b-i mâh-i rukhsârî, K-i khâtir az hamah 'âlam b-i mihr-i 'uo shâd ast

5　See Murtada Mutahari, *Piiraamoun-I Inqilaabi Islami*, 151-55.

6　See the Qur'an, Section Ali Imraan, verse 64.

7　Some other Shi'a Muslim scholars take exception to this view concerning the beliefs of Jews and Christians, arguing that there are no texts in the Qur'an where the beliefs of Jews or Christians are ever called *shirk*.

8　See Mîr Ahmad Alî translation of the Qur'an, Section Aal-I Imraan, verse 64.

9　See the Qur'an, IV, verse 63.

10　See *Encyclopedia Britannica*, vol. 10, 1970, 616.

11　See Muhammad Taqi Mebâ, *Tawîd* (Qom: Intishârât-i Shafaq, 1994), 45.

12　Hermann Landolt, "Walayah" in *The Encyclopedia of Religion*, ed. Mircea Eliade (New York: Macmillan, 1987), Vol. 15, 316.

13　See Mutaza Mutahharî, *Maqâlât Islamiyyah* (Beirut: Dar al-Irshad al-Islami, 1980), 114-15.

14　See Hassan ibn Yûsuf ibn Mutahhar Hilli, *Mukhtalaf al-Shî`ah Sharîfî Ahkâm al-`ah* (Tehran: Maktabat Naynawa al-Haditha, 1923), 69-71.

15　Ibid., 76; see also `Abd al-Hâdî Hâ'irî, *Tashayyu` wa Mashrûtîyat dar Iran* (Tehran: Intishârât-i Amî Kabîr, 1985), 78.

16　See Muhammad Taqî Mesbah, *Âmûzish-i `Aqâ`d* (Tehran: Sazman-i Tabliqat-i Islami, 2nd Vol., 1988), 175-79.

17　`Abd al-Hâdî Hâ'irî, 78.

18　Hassan ibn Yûsuf ibn Mutahhar Hilli, 339.

19　`Abd al-Hâdî Hâ'irî, 81.

20　Abbas Ali `Amîd Zanjânî, *Fiqh-i Sîyâsî*, Vol. 2 (Tehran: Intishârât-i Amî Kabîr, 1989), 366.

21　S. Rûhallah Imam Khumaini, *Kitâb al-Bai`* (Qum: Matba`at Mihr, 2nd ed., 1980), 466.

# Christian Politics: Reflections from a Mennonite Perspective

## Harry Huebner[1]

*We believe that the church is God's "holy nation," called to give full allegiance to Christ its head and to witness to all nations about God's saving love. The church is the spiritual, social, and political body that gives its allegiance to God alone.[2]*

*The distinction between politics and religion was not discovered but invented.[3]*

## Introduction

The expressions of the profound love of God cannot be relegated to a single facet of life, for such love permeates all. This has been the conviction of the Anabaptist-Mennonite tradition, and this is why we have resisted the separation of spirituality and politics. For the Anabaptists, how Christians live – relationships with neighbour, self and God, protection from enemies, matters of governance, views on freedom and responsibilities, structures of health care, protection from harm-like disasters, e.g., insurance protection – all emanate from the conviction that Jesus is Lord and in him we see both how to love God and how to live in this world. Moreover, it is the political/spiritual body called "church" that concretizes both these loves, making it as the body of Christ a deeply political reality.

The conviction of early Anabaptists that the notion of Christian politics is a redundancy has been seen by some as a convergence with Shi'a Islam. French philosopher Michel Foucault observes that within European history small groups of Christians have played an "oppositional

137

role" to mainline governments because of a clash of political philosophies. He singles out the sixteenth-century Anabaptists, saying that they "rejected the power of the state, government bureaucracy, social and religious hierarchies, everything."[4] In other words, religion as "the opiate of the people" no more characterizes the Anabaptists than it does Shi'a Islam. Both are intent on political and cultural revolution. Yet how revolution is to be understood is another matter. While for some Anabaptists (the Münsterites) revolution was seen to be violent, for most within the movement such revolution, since it was to be embodied Christian politics, was characteristically nonviolent.[5]

The Anabaptists were quite aware that there were other ways than theirs of cutting up the Christian pie, which would affect how one views governance, and that their way of understanding the church's embodiment of its rule was at variance with the mainstream Reformation. This made them acutely conscious of two things: (1) their views on governance, power, and structured social relations were different insofar as they were rooted deeply in their convictions about Jesus; (2) their spirituality produced clashes with political bodies, and these clashes were not just ideological but deeply personal and social, resulting in the martyrdom of many.

Yet how those who today claim historical identification with the sixteenth-century Radical Reformers express their views on Christian politics varies considerably, in regard to how they view the role of the state under God's economy and how they see themselves relating to or participating in political matters. Within our tradition there is not a single unified expression of a Christian politics even though there is a common conviction that Jesus is Lord, which has everything to do with loving God and loving neighbour. While some Mennonites find themselves in political office in high places like Ottawa, others may see this as compromising with evil, which the separatist theology of some Anabaptists would prohibit.

This paper seeks to present a view of Christian politics arising from an Anabaptist-Mennonite way of reading the story of Jesus. This is not an easy assignment, since our politics may well be better expressed by how we have lived and are living. And it has gotten more difficult to discern a Mennonite distinctiveness as we have become more and more like other members of society, especially as we have moved away from Mennonite communities with distinct Mennonite identities and into big cities. As long as we lived in Rhineland in Southern Manitoba or in Menno Colony in Paraguay, we knew that our political theology governed us in ways it no longer can when living in Winnipeg and Waterloo. Hence we too, like Shi'ah Islam, know the reality of both oppositional and constructive politics, even though a "national" construction project is foreign to us.

## The Issue of a Mennonite Political Theology

In contemporary Christian ethical discussions, few topics have produced more ambiguity and debate as to how to state the issue than that of Christian political ethics. This ambiguity often carries forward into Mennonite theological discussions. Too often it gets put in a manner that prevents Christians who wish to follow Jesus from having anything noteworthy to say about politics. Common thought has it that if you are committed to following Jesus, you are thereby excluded from giving ethical advice to the social order. Why? For many reasons: one is the assumption that Jesus spoke only about personal or spiritual matters and not about social and political matters. Details of the debate usually bear out other assumptions as well, like the belief that the nature of the state is force while the nature of Christ is anti-force – turn the other cheek, forgiveness, nonviolence. Hence it is thought that the two realms can have nothing to do with one another. For Mennonites who have avowed pacifism, how to state the issues to begin with is particularly important.

Within Mennonite history one finds, broadly speaking, two kinds of readings on the relevance of Jesus for the political order. One, the separatist option, accepts the simple bifurcation of the politics of Jesus and secular politics, and assumes a missionary posture of witnessing to the state and seeing conversion as the faithful outcome.[6] This approach usually took the form of witnessing at a distance, expecting only minor changes, since God has ordained the state to use the sword to keep evil at bay. The church was to follow Jesus' nonviolent path.

Another approach might be called the integrationist option. It involves rejecting the disjunction itself and argues that the nature of the state is *not* force and the nature of Christ is *not* anti-force. They are far more intermixed than the duality suggests. This approach provides either an alternative model of the state or an altered reading of the biblical story. Those wishing to recast the state lift out its foundations, like peace and justice, and emphasize that its recourse to violence is but an attempt to secure peace and justice, which is after all an interest Christians share. They suggest that, given the advances of human wisdom and goodness, we can construct a political order in ways that may make violence obsolete. On the other hand, those wishing to recast the Christian story often bring other theological convictions to bear and argue that the story of Jesus must be balanced with the theology of creation, for example. After all, Jesus was a particular historical figure; since he was never a leader within a political power structure, he could not understand the nature of making compromising decisions, and hence we must take that into account when addressing the needs of peace and justice that the state is to provide.[7] Such an agenda will no doubt produce a more qualified political ethic.

I identify the issue this way in order to indicate that the debate is really internal to the Mennonite tradition: how we understand the state and how we speak about Jesus have not been settled among us. We may all believe that both church and state are givens for Christians, but how they are to be understood together varies. While Anabaptist-Mennonite political theology can perhaps be characterized by debates between the separatist and integrationist approaches, many contemporary Mennonites find neither convincing. The tradition in which I stand, for example, has sought a somewhat nuanced way of stating how our spirituality and politics mix. Our Confession of Faith, written in 1995, says:

> As Christians we are to respect those in authority and to pray for all people, including those in government, that they also may be saved and come to the knowledge of the truth. We may participate in government or other institutions of society only in ways that do not violate the love and holiness taught by Christ and do not compromise our loyalty to Christ. We witness to

the nations by being that "city on a hill" which demonstrates the way of Christ. We also witness by being ambassadors for Christ, calling the nations (and all persons and institutions) to move toward justice, peace, and compassion for all people.

In so doing, we seek the welfare of the city to which God has sent us. We understand that Christ, by his death and resurrection, has won victory over the powers, including all governments. Because we confess that Jesus Christ has been exalted as Lord of lords, we recognize no other authority's claims as ultimate.[8]

One of the latent fears evident in contemporary Mennonite faith statements is that of Constantinianism, rooted in the fourth century when the Emperor became an authority in the church. The fear is that in our North American society the state in subtle ways has too much power in determining the agenda for the church, and that the church unwittingly gives the state too much significance. At the same time there is a strong conviction that all human institutions are under God's sovereignty and are called to seek justice and peace and to set all people free. So we find within the statement of confession above an effort on the one hand to guard against separation – "we may participate in government or other institutions of society" – and on the other hand against the integrationists with the statement "because we confess that Jesus Christ has been exalted as Lord of lords, we recognize no other authority's claims as ultimate."

The rest of this paper seeks to develop the theology behind the spirituality and politics represented in this statement of faith. It will attempt to answer why Mennonites are the peculiar "political people" they are, that is, with a strong view of politics but a fear of assuming political office.

## Biblical/Theological Reflections

I draw my theological reflections largely from John Howard Yoder's *The Politics of Jesus*, where Yoder develops the approach of Jesus as the "way of the cross."[9] He distinguishes this way from two models called "withdrawal" and "insurrection," meaning that the ready-made options for Jesus were either retreating into the hills and concentrating on personal piety and spiritual purity before God, or getting into the fray and fighting for justice, seeking thereby to gain power to impose his justice on the people. Jesus, argues Yoder, rejected both approaches in favour of another less methodologically precise and more enmeshed in subjective discernment by presenting the peace of God in situations and letting the chips fall where they may. It is this "way" that resulted in his own brutal death, which nevertheless did not deter him from faithfully presenting God's love to the people.

Far from being an arbitrary choice, Jesus' way of the cross embodies a tradition of theological convictions. It is hard to summarize this theology in a few short strokes, but it sought to hold together several major affirmations. These are also the convictions that the Mennonite Confession of Faith seeks to draw on. Briefly stated, they are:

1. God created the world *ex nihilo*, good and peaceful, but it is fallen. We therefore have no immediate access to God's good creation.

2. Even the fallen order is under God's sovereignty, which is not the same as saying that God ordains all that happens.

3. Just as God acted in creation, God continues to act concretely in time and space bringing the fallen order to restoration, that is, back to its original intent.

4. To live on this earth means that we live in structured social relationships with others, and given their fallenness, these structures constantly seek to serve themselves and not God, who nevertheless seeks to redeem the world through them.

5. Jesus Christ is Lord over history and therefore he is, and we are not, in control. In Jesus Christ the sovereignty of all the earthy powers has been broken.

6. The role of all human institutions, including the state, is to serve the larger cause of peace and justice, yet even when they don't God can use their work for redemptive purposes.

7. Disciples of Christ are called to embody the rule of Christ and the expression of this rule is called the body of Christ, the church.

8. Disciples of Christ, like Christ himself, are called, if it comes to this, to face death peacefully rather than take up arms in self-defence, or for the cause of greater justice.[10]

These affirmations frame the issue of spirituality and politics in a particular way. There is in the teaching of Jesus a distinct politics that is alternative to the politics of most of the rulers of the world, and it is marked by servanthood rather than by self-serving power. The politics of Jesus is a way that shows Yahweh worshipers how to live life so that it can embody peace and justice and does not self-destruct. Jesus is not about getting the inner, private spirit right in order to live with the harsh outer social, political world. Jesus is about both the inner and the outer worlds living in peace and justice. While there is a duality here, it is not a duality of body-spirit; nor is it a matter of the body being relegated to the state while the spirit is the purview of Christ or the church. Since both church and state care deeply about both the body and spirit, the clash between church and state is itself one of competing spiritualities and politics. Whatever clash exists between church and state, it is not one of divvying up jurisdictions – you get the body, we get the spirit – but one over the politics rooted in the lordship of Christ and all other politics.[11]

In the teaching of Jesus there is a real political agenda. In developing that agenda I will distinguish between the "what" and the "how" of Christian ethics. Yet I make this somewhat dangerous distinction here only as a heuristic device for purposes of organizing my thoughts in this paper. Really these two should not be broken apart.

## The "What" of Christian Ethics

There is little question that Jesus affirmed the Law of Moses, the Ten Commandments, the prophetic teachings, and much of the Jewish tradition. Yet he was a master at digging deeper than many of his listeners appreciated. When Jesus says in Matthew 5 that he has not come to abolish the law and the prophets but to fulfill them, he is addressing a complacent self-righteousness common among his hearers, for it is much more difficult than it seems to be people who are open to God's kingdom coming. It is not so easy to know what constitutes killing, or truth telling, or marital unfaithfulness, or vengeance, or love of neighbour. Acts are not isolated units of behaviour without antecedents or consequences. For example, it's important to realize that anger leads to violence and violence to murder, and lust to violation and destruction of relationships, and so on. Jesus was interested not in the legalism of keeping enshrined laws but in characters that could reflect the love of God to others.

In Luke's presentation, Jesus begins his ministry through proclamation, not of a new message but an old one from Isaiah 61: "the spirit of the Lord is upon me, because he has anointed me to bring good news to the poor, and release to the captives and recovery of sight to the blind, and to let the oppressed go free" (Luke 4:18-19). Now this is truly good news, unless of course one is interested in hoarding. For the oppressed, release is good news, but for the oppressor, it is not. To announce this good news to all people – both Jews and Gentiles – can indeed be frightening. This fear is demonstrated in the story immediately following this text. After the reading from Isaiah the people were happy, but when Jesus suggested that this good news is also extended to the gentiles, they were filled with rage and sought to kill him. The story reveals an important concern of Jesus, namely to open the covenant under God to all people. This concern had to do with the view of the other, the outsider, and is expressed elsewhere in Jesus' ministry.

An especially powerful example of Jesus' concern for how his hearers see the other is the parable of the Good Samaritan (Luke 10:25-37). Jesus tells this story in response to a lawyer's question, "What must I do to inherit eternal life?" (One might say the spirituality question *par excellence!*) And the answer is, "Love God and neighbour." But when the lawyer asked, "And who is my neighbour?" Jesus tells the parable of a man beaten by robbers and left on the roadside to die. Two Jewish religious leaders, a priest and a Levite, came along but offered no assistance. Then a Samaritan, whom the Jews hated, passed by, stopped, and tended to the man, taking him to the nearest inn and paying for his care. Then Jesus asks, "Which of these three do you think was a neighbour to the man . . .?" Kenneth Bailey, a New Testament scholar, argues that the Samaritan's action is really an example of the way of the cross, for the Samaritan risked his life to show love to the enemy. That is what it means to be neighbour. It is an act that under God embraces the one you most wish to exclude from mutual friendship.[12]

Luke follows this parable with an account of the Mary/Martha story. In medieval exegesis these two stories belonged together: the Good Samaritan parable was an example of love of neighbour, and the Mary/ Martha story an example of love of God. It is also an example of how Jesus related to women (the "other") in openness and respect. Here he lauds Mary who sat in studious devotion at the Lord's feet, and chides Martha who was distracted with the mundane tasks of hospitality. It's not that Jesus is critical of hospitality as such, but rather that loving neighbour and loving God belong together. That is, spirituality and ethics, or spirituality and politics, cannot be broken apart. While Jesus accepted the social and political structures on one level, he was critical of them on another. He was not an anarchist, but neither was he accepting of structures that prevented people from being what they were called to be under God, free, loving, at peace with one another, respectful – as God intended in creation.

When the apostle Paul reflects on how Jesus followers view the Roman state, he expresses the same union of spirituality and ethics. Even a state that is oppressive and at odds with God's created intent ought to be respected. As Christians who obey God and believe that God is in control of the world despite its fallenness, they ought to be subordinate to the governing authorities and pay taxes, yet announce loudly and clearly that in Christ their ultimate sovereignty is broken and therefore they live by another authority. This means that as Christians they have ultimate allegiance to God alone and will not obey when the state calls them to do its killing. They believe that it is not necessary for them to kill in order for God's kingdom to come, and they would rather die making that claim than kill and discredit it. After all, God is in control and we are not. This leads directly to the "how" of Christian ethics.

## The "How" of Christian Ethics

One of the temptations for Christians is to look to Jesus for what we ought to be concerned about — poverty, sickness, economics, other justice issues — and then see it as our task to change, however we can, what does not measure up to these standards. But for Mennonite theology this is problematic, and this is also why there is suspicion about relating to the state. For the biblical story not only shows us what the issues are but invites us into a process of moving from injustice to justice in a particular way. Here too our model is Jesus.

Jesus contrasts his rule with that of others this way: "The kings of this earth lord it over their subjects . . . but I am among you as one who serves" (Luke 22:25-27). The "how" of his mission was not characterized by end results but by speaking and testifying to the truth of God's goodness in the face of injustice. What lay behind his non-strategic plan was his conviction that he was not the only agent bringing about change to greater justice; in fact God was the primary agent of such change. This is why proclamation and witness were Jesus' primary social strategies, for they pointed to what God was already doing. So he invited his followers into a new way of seeing themselves and the world. Here we have a new model of human political agency.

Jesus' approach of proclaiming the gospel of peace and justice, healing those who were sick, and speaking the truth regardless of consequences is instructive. Such non-strategic spirituality of politics is meaningful only if God is at work in the world reconciling all people, and it is this "way" that is made intelligible by the relationship between the cross and resurrection. For Jesus' death may well have testified to the fact that when you speak truth to power, you get yourself into trouble, yet it is the resurrection that testifies to God creating (recreating) in this world. Both are required for this view of politics.

Yoder therefore makes the point that just as the relationship between the cross and the resurrection cannot be understood through the laws of causality, since the faithfulness of Jesus produced the resurrection, so as followers of Jesus we should see our own work for justice in the same way. Our fruits are best understood not as the products of our own labour but as gifts of

God's graciousness and goodness. That is why our most faithful stance towards injustice in the world is proclamation and work for justice and peace in openness to God's blessing.

This conviction is in large measure why Mennonites have believed that nonviolent witness is the faithful response to God. Submitting to God is to accept what God has given, even the enemy, and that in its fallen state the world around us can be redeemed by God through our faithful witness and participation in God's redemptive work. Hence we have Mennonite Central Committee (MCC) offices in Washington and Ottawa that speak up on matters of all kinds arising out of Christ's vision for wholeness and shalom; we are all over the world in places of poverty, disease, illiteracy, powerlessness, political conflict and strife, including, of course, in our own countries. We do not have clearly defined strategic paths that will overcome all of these maladies, but we are there working with the people and doing what we can, and praying that God may bless our efforts.

There is a fine line between hard work and taking matters into our own hands, but that's the struggle. As Christ followers, we believe that taking matters into our own hands is an act of unfaith in God's power to redeem and an exaggerated faith in our own limited abilities and knowledge. Of course, such a stance can imply martyrdom, based on the conviction that even if we are to be killed God will redeem, for God's redemptive power is not dependent on our survival. But this form of martyrdom is different from the sacrificial death of a soldier who dies in battle or for a just cause; Jesus did not die fighting a just cause but was killed because the ruling powers could not tolerate his love of enemies.

## Implications: How Then Shall We Live?

The Mennonite church in North America is often misunderstood in its critical yet distanced relationship to political institutions. Our convictions are such that we can neither live comfortably with them nor live without them. I want to list several ways that attempt to clarify this uneasy relationship, especially within contemporary North American cultural politics.

*1. Suspicion* Mennonites are nervous about uncritical alliances with state politics. History has shown how these alliances can lead the church astray through Constantine and through Hitler's Germany, and we see it today in the uncritical acceptance of the political agenda by both the American Christian Right and the Left, in the culture of security, and in many other even subtler forms. Why is this problematic for us? Because we also have political interests, and they derive from another source. For example, we cannot let the state define for us who our enemies are; with whom we dialogue; the terms in which we see the world or relate to others in it; or even what the issues are. When the culture/state sets the agenda of justice, e.g., abortion, war, slavery, immigration, security, or oil, we raise questions about what's not on the list and how those that make it on are cast. Hence Mennonite organizations like MCC or church bodies may or may not sign on in political support for some causes, depending on their own moral assessments, or they may change the language or the terms of reference.

*2. Cultivating virtues* One of our more important tasks is to cultivate the habits that define us as followers of Jesus. We struggle with how to be loving people in a culture of self-interest; how to show that the deepest understanding of life is as a gift given by God, in a culture that defines everything in terms of cash value and purchasability; how to speak up for and live for peace in a culture of violence, preoccupied with issues of security; and so on. We believe that one of the most powerful acts of moral formation for our communities is worship, gathering together under God, listening to the texts that inform us, opening ourselves regularly to a giving and receiving exchange with the One who sustains us, and being empowered by the One who is in control of the universe despite evidence to the contrary. These acts of worship keep us centered in our conviction that love is stronger than hate, peace stronger than war, and talking more powerful than fighting.

3. *Practicing patience*   A special virtue of note for Christians is patience, and closely associated with it is lament. If we are to be followers of Jesus, we must learn the art of giving up control and waiting, for this is what he did in accepting the way that led to the cross. If the Lamb (Christ) as stated in Revelation is the Lord of history, we must learn to live by patience, since things will not follow our desired path. This is difficult in a culture that celebrates domination, control, and speed. We need to develop capacity and skill in the art of waiting. If God is in control, then we must also learn humility and gentleness. This requires constant reminders. When things are not as they should be, lament, counter-voice, protest – but not violence or capitulation – should be our response. Lament acknowledges that in the vision of Christ we can see how the world ought to be but we cannot get there from where we are. Lament is a necessary virtue for nonviolent followers of Jesus.

4. *Interpreting peace*   A special practice for Mennonite politics is peace. Yet there are real temptations associated with this practice. One is simply the assumption that we know what peace and violence are. Practicing peace is difficult because it is a complex concept, and as members of a violent society we need to remind ourselves of our own complicity with the violence around us. Claiming to be peaceful can easily be mere arrogance and self-righteousness talking. These are qualities Jesus condemns. Our commitment to peace can therefore not be seen as coming only from who we are and what we do and know, but from a humble commitment to the One whom we call the Prince of Peace.

5. *Dialogue*   Dialogue is a form of exchange that flows from gentleness and vulnerability. It acknowledges that we are travelling people and have not reached our ultimate destiny. We too may learn to see more deeply through encounter with the other. Dialogue is the stance that assumes that all people are called together under the Lordship of God. We believe that in Christ we have a special

model of dialogue because he freely engaged people not on the guest lists of his hearers – sinners, lepers, enemies, the powerless, children, women, and so on. And of course the point could be made that dialogue is the form of encounter that is represented in the "Word" becoming human and dwelling among us (John 1). Jesus did not condemn people, he dialogued with them. He was the engaging "word."

6. *Active peacemaking*   Peace- and justice-making are always to be our disposition and action. This is why Mennonites have been active in Christian Peacemaker Teams, whose mandate is to be present in violence situations and in the face of those whose interest is in perpetuating the conflict. Christian Peacemaker Teams speak up for those who get hurt and are disempowered in conflict. There is always a need to create space for peaceful ways of settling disputes, for giving expression to violence that is not heard or seen and takes place under the radar. Also at times we dialogue and even partner with governments that are at work making peace and acting justly, but this partnership is always ad hoc and not a permanent union. We partner for this and for that on the basis of our convictions and not the state's. We partner only when we can do so without sacrificing our identity as people who seek to be followers of Jesus.[13]

## Conclusion

All Christians, and certainly Mennonites, are people who by habit read the Bible or listen to it when it is read to them. We may well quarrel about what we read and hear, how it is understood, and how it gets expressed in life, but the Bible is for us normative text. This is especially important because Christians understand the church as a performance of the text or as staging what the Bible discloses. But precisely because it is a staging, there are different takes on the story. So, however one says it, the truth is that the Christian story is itself a dialogue and even a debate; it is an argument over time, and closing off that argument with a final statement, as is often a temptation, is best avoided. The practice of the two inseparable loves – of God and neighbour – is difficult to discern, and thus the mode of this practice is humility, gentleness, and openness to the future.

And He said to them, you shall love the Lord your God with all your heart, and with all your soul, and with all your mind. This is the greatest and first commandment. And a second is like it: You shall love your neighbour as yourself. On these two commandments hang all the law and the prophets. (Matt. 22:37-40)

## Endnotes

1   An earlier version of this paper was given as an oral presentation at the Shi'a Muslim-Mennonite Dialogue III at Conrad Grebel University College in Waterloo, Ontario, May 27-30, 2007.

2   From *Confession of Faith in a Mennonite Perspective*, 1995 available online at http://www.mcusa-archives.org/library/resolutions/1995/index.html.

3   From Catholic theologian William Cavanaugh, *Torture and Eucharist: Theology, Politics, and the Body of Christ* (Oxford: Blackwell Publisher, 1998), 5.

4   Quoted in Janet Afary and Kevin B. Anderson, eds., *Foucault and the Iranian Revolution: Gender and the Seductions of Islamism* (Chicago, IL: University of Chicago Press, 2005), 186-87.

5   According to Mennonite historian William R. Estep, the Münsterite story has always been a dark blot on Mennonite history. It represents the faith of neither the Swiss Brethren nor the Dutch Anabaptists. The Anabaptists derived their faith from the teachings of Jesus, and the Münsterites did not. Hence they have been the occasion for many misrepresentations of the Anabaptists. Estep suggests that it's important to note that Obbe Philips, an early Anabaptist leader, vigorously opposed the Münsterites and placed them, and all those in loyalty to their views, under the "ban." See Estep, *The Anabaptist Story* (Grand Rapids, MI: Eerdmans, 1975), 17-18.

6   An example of such separation can be seen in the early Swiss confession of faith (1527), the Schleitheim Confession: "From this we should learn that everything which is not united with our God and Christ cannot be other than an abomination which we should shun and flee from. By this is meant all Catholic and Protestant works and church services, meetings and church attendance, drinking houses, civic affairs, the oaths sworn in unbelief and other things of that kind, which are highly regarded by the world and yet are carried on in flat contradiction to the command of God, in accordance with all the unrighteousness which is in the world. From all these things we shall be separated and have no part with them for they are nothing but an abomination, and they are the cause of our being hated before our Christ Jesus, Who has set us free from the slavery of the flesh and fitted us for the service of God through the Spirit Whom He has given us."

One could find similar statements of separatism in the Dutch wing of the Radical Reformation, e.g., the Dortrecht confession a century later. Yet it needs to be said that from the very beginning, within both the Swiss and Dutch wings, Anabaptists found themselves at one and the same time shunning public office and participating in such roles.

7   This view of the state also goes all the way back to the sixteenth century and it is expressed by contemporary theologians as well. J. Lawrence Burkholder says, for example, "Jesus did not run anything. He declared his independence from the religious establishment. He was not responsible for the founding and maintenance of a corporate organization – not even an organized fellowship. He defied authority. He did not report to a board or to a constituency. He disavowed most normal cultural ties. He was responsible only to God...." See Burkholder, "The Limits of Perfection: Autobiographical Reflections," in *The Limits of Perfection: Conversations with J. Lawrence Burkholder*, eds. Rodney J. Sawatsky and Scott Holland (Waterloo, ON: Institute of Anabaptist-Mennonite Studies/Conrad Grebel College, 1993), 18-19.

8   From *Confession of Faith in a Mennonite Perspective*, 1995.

9   My reference to Yoder's work, *The Politics of Jesus* (Grand Rapids, MI: Eerdmans, 2nd edition, 1994) should be properly understood. It is not my suggestion that Yoder's work is significantly different from other Mennonite writings, or indeed from many non-Mennonite authors like Stanley Hauerwas, James Wm. McClendon, or William Cavanaugh (to name only a few). But Yoder is careful in developing the theology underlying this view of Christian politics. Add to that two other factors: I share many of his views personally, and I was asked by organizers of this conference to represent his theology.

10   Each of these assumptions could be defended at length, but this is not the place. For such arguments the reader should see especially Yoder's *The Politics of Jesus*.

11   For an excellent study on the clash of political jurisdictions, see William Cavanaugh, *Torture and Eucharist*, cited above.

12   See Kenneth Bailey, *Poet and Peasant and Through Peasant Eyes: A Literary-Cultural Approach to the Parables in Luke* (Grand Rapids: Eerdmans, 1983).

13   For more comment on the notion of ad hoc partnerships, see my *Echoes of the Word: Theological Ethics as Rhetorical Practice* (Waterloo, ON: Pandora Press, 2005), 104-105.

# Spiritual Poverty:
# A Shi'i Perspective

## Mohammad Ali Shomali

*O God, grant me the riches of poverty*
*for in such largesse lies my power and glory.*
– Hafez[1]

Islam teaches us that we need to strengthen our understanding of and need for God to achieve a sense of complete reliance on God. This is called "spiritual poverty." Spiritual poverty is a cornerstone of Islamic spirituality. In what follows, we will first study different senses in which the concept of poverty or *faqr* is used in Islamic sources. Then we will focus on the concept of spiritual poverty and its significance as illustrated in the Qur'anic verses, Hadiths, and mystical literature.

## Poverty Can Mean "Failure to Generate Wealth"
Poverty in this sense is not good. According to Islam, God asks us to work hard to raise money and generate wealth, to be productive and fruitful for ourselves and for the society.

> He brought you forth from the earth and has asked you to improve it, therefore ask forgiveness of Him, then turn to Him; surely my Lord is Near, Answering. (Qur'an 11:61)

God has asked us to improve the earth, to improve our life situation on the earth. This type of poverty causes serious sufferings and may also prevent spiritual progress. For someone who is starving it would be very difficult to focus on one's spirituality. Certianly this type of poverty is to be abolished. The prophet Mohammad is quoted as saying: Had not mercy of God embraced the poor of my nation, poverty would have led to disbelief.[2]

Sometimes the poor cannot protect their faith; they may lose their patience and commit sins or lose their faith in God. Or, they may be so disturbed with difficulties that they may lose their concentration on remembrance of God and their spiritual journey. Imam Ali says:

> One of the catastrophes that may occur is poverty, but more difficult than poverty is illness. And more difficult than illness of the body is the illness of heart.[3]

## Poverty Can Mean "a Modest Life"

Although people are urged to work and generate wealth and improve conditions of their lives or nature in general, they are not supposed to accumulate money. Sometimes you generate money but you do not keep this money for yourself, you spread your wealth and share it. It is not good to have a very luxurious life, because then we may forget our true nature. We may become the richest people, but we should not keep our earnings just for ourselves. The Qur'an blames people who do not share what God has given them with those who are in need:

> ... Those who treasure up gold and silver, and do not spend it in the way of God,  inform them of a painful punishment on the day when these shall be heated in hellfire  and therewith branded on their foreheads, their sides and their backs [and told]: "This is what you treasured up for yourselves! So taste what you have treasured!" (9:34, 35)

> And miserly when good reaches him. (70:21)

Thus, everyone is recommended to be economically productive, but not for the sake of accumulating wealth or spending extravagantly on oneself. This kind of voluntary poverty or modest life is good for all people, but leaders are especially asked to live a simple life so that the poor can be consoled. Imam Ali said:

> Certainly, God, the Sublime, has made it obligatory on true leaders that they maintain themselves at the level of the humble so that the poor do not cry out over their poverty.[4]

## Poverty Can Mean "a Lack of Good Deeds on the Day of Judgment"

Once the Prophet Muhammad asked people: "Do you know who '*Muflis*' [one who is bankrupt] is?" The people answered that a bankrupt person is one who has no money or property. The Prophet said: "The bankrupt from my nation is the one who comes on the Day of Judgment with some prayer, fasting and almsgiving, but he has said bad things to people or misappropriated money of someone or shed the blood of someone. As a result, his good acts will be transferred to those people [who were harmed] and if his good acts are not sufficient, their bad deeds will be transferred to him and therefore he will be sent to hell."[5] Thus, some people are poor because their record of good deeds is empty or nearly empty. The Qur'an says:

> Those whose measure (of good) will be heavy, will prosper and those whose measure will be light, will dwell in hell. (101:6-9)

## Poverty Can Mean "Humbleness" or "Nothingness"

Reflection on our limits and our absolute need for, and reliance on, God leaves no place for any kind of arrogance or self-admiration. Whatever we have or whatever is at our disposal belongs to God and has been given to us as trust for a short period of time. We will be questioned on the Day of Judgment about the way we have dealt with them. Indeed, we ourselves belong to God in our very existence. René

Guénon writes:

> The contingent being may be defined as one that is not self-sufficient, not containing in himself the point of his existence; it follows that such a being is nothing by himself and he owns nothing of what goes to make him up. Such is the case of the human being in so far as he is individual, just as it is the case of all manifested beings, in whatever state they may be, for however great the difference may be between the degrees of Universal Existence, it is always as nothing in relation to the Principle. These beings, human or others, are therefore, in all that they are, in a state of complete dependence with regard to the Principle "apart from which there is nothing, absolutely nothing that exists"; it is the consciousness of this dependence which makes what several traditions call "spiritual poverty."

> At the same time, for the being who has acquired this consciousness, it has, as its immediate consequence, detachment with regard to all manifested things, for the being knows from then on that these things, like himself, are nothing, and that they have no importance whatsoever compared with the absolute Reality.[6]

Imam Husayn [Hussein] prays to God:

> What can I bring when I want to come to you…. Can I come with my ears, my eyes, my tongue, my hands, my feet? Is not this the case that all of these are gifts that you have given me?[7]

Elsewhere he says:

> O My Lord! I am poor in my richness so how can I not be poor in my poverty?[8]

If whatever I have is a sign of my need, a sign of my dependence, what about those things that I do not have? Suppose that there is a person who has taken a loan, say, of one million dollars from a bank and another person who has taken one hundred thousand dollars. Which one is richer, and which one is not? It seems obvious that the one who has taken more money is more indebted and more responsible, and must have more concerns and worries. Whatever God gives us puts us more in debt. If this is the case about what we have, how can I be proud of things that I do not have? They do not belong to me anyway. Imam Husayn says:

> With respect to my knowledge, I am ignorant. How can I not be very ignorant in respect to what I do not know?[9]

What we know is very limited and surrounded with lots of questions. The more we know, the more questions we will have. This is why those who are more knowledgeable are more careful and cautious in their claims and stay more remote from arrogance. Also, what we know we can easily lose or forget. There are people who cannot remember even their own names or names of their closest relatives. Imam Husayn also says:

> O God! Verily the alteration of your affairs and the speed of progress of your decrees prevent those servants of You who know You to be confident when faced with your favour or to feel despair when challenged with calamities.[10]

Everything changes quickly in this world. Sometimes we are happy, and sometimes sad. Sometimes people respect us, and sometimes no one may respect us. Sometimes our children are good to us and sometimes not. There are lots of ups and downs. What is the reason for this? We need to learn that we cannot trust anything except God. No one knows what will happen and, therefore, we should not trust anything. As the Imam says above, this should help us in understanding that we should not trust anything or anyone other than God and at the same time we should not despair. We should not become hopeless when bad things happen. The key is in the hands of God and he can change our situation to better in any moment. Having said all this, Imam Husayn says:

> I appeal to You with my poverty and need for You. And how can I appeal to You with something which is impossible to reach You? Or how should I mention my complaint to You while it is not hidden to You? O my God! How can I not be poor when You have put me amongst the poor? And how can I be poor when you have made me rich with your generosity. [11]

This shows that the means (*wasilah*) that the Imam uses to get closer to God is his dependence on God and his deep understanding that he is poor and nothing before God. Thus, the valuable means that the Imam finds and wants to use and mention is "poverty." According to the Qur'an, we are all needy:

> O ye men! It is ye that have need of God: But God is the One Free of all wants, worthy of all praise. (35:15)

We are all needy; only God is rich and free of need. Many people do not understand this. But Imam Husayn declares that he understands and admits this, and wants to use it as a means to get nearer to God. Then he says that when he wants to come with his poverty there is a problem, in that poverty does not reach God. This is to emphasize that poverty is only from one side; poverty cannot reach God. It may also mean that the one who goes towards God admitting his poverty will meet God while he is rich. To become rich you must take poverty with you, but those who feel they are the poorest people are, indeed, the richest people in the eyes of God. Whoever is most humble, God will raise him more than anyone else. As we find in a Hadith, "Whoever tries to be humble for God's sake God will elevate him." [12] In a divine saying (*Hadith Qudsi*) we find that God told Moses:

> The reason why I made you a Prophet is that I looked into the hearts of all people and I saw that you are the most humble one before Me. [13]

According to a well-known Hadith, the person who avoids arrogance and chooses to be humble before God and serve Him sincerely is no longer a slave of others or of his own whims. He will achieve some kind of lordship:

> The servitude to God is a substance whose essence (core) is the lordship.[14]

In another Hadith, we read:

> My servant, obey Me. [If you do so] I will make you similar to Myself. I am alive and never die, so I make you alive and never die. I am rich and never become poor, so I make you become rich and never poor. Whatever I want it will be, so I make you in the way that whatever you want it will be there.[15]

Reflecting on his life, one can see in the Prophet Muhammad the perfect example of humbleness. Indeed, the reason the Prophet was chosen by God lies in the fact that he was a true servant of God and the most humble person before God and his people. Muslims at least nine times a day in their prayers "bear witness that the Prophet Muhammad was a servant of God and His Apostle." This means that amongst his qualities these two must be very outstanding: first, he managed to be a servant of God, and second, he was rewarded by being appointed as the Apostle of God.

The Prophet was so humble that he never admired himself. He never felt superior to others; he never separated himself from the masses and always lived a very simple life. Both when he was alone and powerless as well as when he ruled the Arab peninsula and Muslims were whole-heartedly following him, he behaved the same. He lived very simply and was always with the people, especially the poor. He had no palace or guard. When he was sitting with his companions, no one could distinguish him from others by considering his seat or clothes. It was only his words and spirituality that distinguished him from others.

Just before his demise, the Prophet announced in the Mosque: "Whoever among you feels that I have done injustice to him, come forward and do justice. Surely, enacting justice in this world is better in my view than being taken account of in the Hereafter in front of the angels and the Prophets." Those present wept, for they were reminded of all the sacrifices the Prophet had made for them and the troubles he had undergone in order to guide them. They knew he never gave any priority to his own needs or preferred his comfort and convenience to that of others. They therefore responded with statements of deep gratitude and profound respect.

But one among them, Sawadah b. Qays, stood up and said: "May my father and mother be your ransom! O Messenger of God! On your return from Ta'if, I came to welcome you while you were riding your camel. You raised your stick to direct your camel, but the stick struck my stomach. I do not know whether this strike was intentional or unintentional." The Prophet replied: "I seek refuge from God from having done so intentionally."

The Prophet then asked Bilal to go to the house of Fatimah and bring the same stick. After the stick was brought, the Prophet told Sawadah to hit him back. Sawadah said that the stick had struck the skin of his stomach. The Prophet therefore lifted his shirt so that Sawadah could in return strike his skin. At that moment, Sawadah asked: "O Messenger of God! Do you allow me to touch my mouth to your stomach?" The Prophet gave him permission. Sawadah then kissed the stomach of the Prophet and prayed that because of this act of his, God would protect him from fire on the Day of Resurrection. The Prophet said: "O Sawadah! Will you pardon me or do you still wish to retaliate?" He replied: "I pardon you." The Prophet then prayed: "O God! Pardon Sawadah b. Qays as he pardoned Your Prophet, Muhammad!"[16]

Thus, in Islamic spirituality it is very important to feel humble and that we are nothing in front of God, not just as a claim we utter without firm belief but as a deep sense of nothingness. Once a person saw Imam Sajjad in Masjid al-Haram, next to Ka'bah at Hijr of Isma'il. He says: "I went to Hijr Isma'il and saw Ali b. Husayn there saying his prayer. Then he went for Sajdah (prostration). I told myself that this is a pious man from a pious family so let me listen to him while praying to God in his Sajdah." Then he quotes the Imam as praying:

My Lord, your small and little servant has come to your door, your captive has come to your door, the one who is poor has come to your door, the one who begs you has come to your door.[17]

In the Qur'an, God warns the believers that if they turn away from his religion, soon God will bring forward a people who have, among their characteristics, humbleness before the believers:

O you who have faith! Should any of you desert his religion, God will soon bring a people whom He loves and who love Him, [who will be] humble towards the faithful, stern towards the faithless, striving hard in the way of God, not fearing the blame of any blamer. That is God's grace which He grants to whomever He wishes, and God is all-bounteous, all-knowing. (5:54)

In Islamic literature, especially in Persian poets, great emphasis has been put on spiritual poverty. For example, in a long poem in his *Mathnawi,* Rumi illustrates the significance of this feeling of nothingness and humility, and the fatal danger of pride and arrogance. Rumi argues that when people bow in adoration to anyone, they are (really) cramming poison into his soul. If he is not spiritually strong, he may be deceived and feel proud of himself. In this way, he may become arrogant and damage himself and lose his humility. Rumi goes on praising those who are humble in themselves, in contrast to those who are arrogant. The example of someone who has not established humbleness in himself is like the one who drinks a poisonous wine. In the beginning, he may feel happy and joyful, but after a few minutes he will collapse.

Another example is a fight between two kings. When one king wins the battle, he will either imprison the defeated king or kill him, but he will never punish "a fallen wounded man." Indeed, he may help and promote him. Rumi says the reason is that such people are humble and have no ambition of becoming a king, and therefore by no means pose a threat to the new king. Another example is a caravan going from one place to another. When thieves come to rob the caravan, those who have no money will be safe. Or when wolves attack, they may attack anything that comes before them. They may even attack each other; when they want to sleep, they sit in a circle so they can watch each other carefully. But, Rumi says, wolves never attack a dead wolf. And we know that the Prophet Khidr made a breach in a boat, because an unjust ruler in the area used to confiscate every boat or ship passing by. Thus, the only way for that boat to be saved was to be broken. Here Rumi says:

> Since the broken (contrite) one will be saved, be thou broken (contrite). Safety lies in poverty: enter into poverty. [18]

If a mountain or hill has lots of valuable minerals inside, people will excavate all its soils, sand, and minerals. But an ordinary hill or mountain with nothing special inside will remain intact. Another illustration from Rumi goes like this: Someone who is walking is standing on his feet and his neck is straight. Therefore, his enemies may cut off his head with their sword, but no one would cut the head off his shadow. When a ladder is going to collapse, the higher anyone goes up it the more foolish he is, for his bones will be broken more badly. After mentioning these examples, Rumi finally says:

> This is (constitutes) the derivatives (of the subject), and its fundamental principles are that to exalt one's self is (to claim) copartnership with God.

> Unless thou hast died and become living through Him, thou art an enemy seeking to reign in copartnership (with Him).

> When thou hast become living through Him, that (which thou hast become) is in sooth He: it is absolute Unity; how is it copartnership?

> Seek the explanation of this in the mirror of (devotional) works, for thou wilt not gain the understanding of it from speech and discourse. [19]

On the same idea of losing one's self, René Guénon says:

> This "poverty" (in Arabic *al-faqr)* leads, according to Islamic
> esotericism, to *al-fanaa,* that is, to the extinction of the "ego";
> and, by this "extinction" the "divine station" is reached (*al-
> maqaam al-ilaahii*), which is the central point where all the
> distinctions inherent in the more outward points of view are
> surpassed and where all the oppositions have disappeared and
> are resolved in a perfect equilibrium.... This reduction of the
> "distinct ego", which finally disappears by being reabsorbed
> into a single point, is the same thing as *al-fanaa,* and also as
> the "emptiness" mentioned above. [20]

## Conclusion

It has been suggested that poverty means not to possess something
and at the same time desire to possess it. For example, he who feels
in himself a certain lack of human perfection and sincerely desires to
remedy this lack is a *faqir.* Furthermore, it has been suggested that
in Sufism "the longing of love is born of *faqr* ('spiritual poverty')". [21]
I think there are some problems with this understanding of poverty.
First, poverty is much more than not possessing and then desiring to
possess. Poverty is an awareness of our absolute need and dependence
on God. As long as we are what we are, this need cannot be removed.
Second, this sense of poverty is a spiritual gift and virtue that should be
maintained forever. Poverty is not a transient station towards richness
or affluence. Rather, poverty itself is the greatest wealth and fortune
that human beings can ever have. The Prophet Muhammad is quoted
as saying, "Poverty is my honour." [22]

## Endnotes

1  English translation cited from Javad Nurbakhsh, *Spiritual Poverty in Sufism,*
   trans. Leonard Lewisohn (London: Khaniqahi Nimatullahi Publications, 1984),
   4.

2  For example, see Mohammad Baqir Majlesi, *Bihar al-Anwar,* Vol. 69 (Beirut:

al-Wafa, 1983): 48.

3  *Nahj al-Balaghah* [Shi'a sermons], No. 338.

4  Ibid., No. 208.

5  *Bihar al-Anwar,* Vol. 69: 5.

6  René Guénon, "Al-Faqr or Spiritual Poverty" in *Studies in Comparative Religion* (Winter 1973): 16-20.

7  "Du'a of 'Arafah" in Shaykh Abbas Qummi, *Mafatih al-Jinan.*

8  Ibid.

9  "Du'a of 'Arafah" in *Mafatih al-Jinan.*

10  Ibid.

11  Ibid.

12  This hadith is narrated from Jesus (*Bihar al-Anwar,* Vol. 14: 307), the Prophet Mohammad (Vol. 16: 265; Vol. 72: 120), Imam Sadiq (Vol. 72: 121), and Imam Kazim (Vol. 75: 312).

13  Ibid. Vol. 13, 8.

14  Mohammad Rey Shahri, *Mizan al-Hikmah,* Vol. 6:13, No. 11317.

15  Hurr 'Amili, *Al-Jawahir al-Saniyyah fi al-Hadith al-Qudsiyyah,* 284.

16  Shaykh Husayn Nuri, *Mustadrak Wasa'il al-Shi'ah,* Vol. 18: 287, 288.

17  *Bihar al-Anwar,* Vol. 96: 197.

18  Jalal al-Din Rumi, *Mathnawi Ma'nawi,* Book Four, ed. and trans. Reynold Alleyne Nicholson (Tehran: Nashr-e Buteh, 2002).

19  Ibid.

20  René Guénon, "Al-Faqr or Spiritual Poverty," 16.

21  Javad Nurbakhsh, *Spiritual Poverty in Sufism.*

22  *Bihar al-Anwar,* Vol. 69: 32, 55.

# "Spiritual Poverty" in Mennonite Traditions

## Thomas Finger

### Biblical Considerations

Mennonites seek to derive their practices and beliefs as directly as possible from Jesus. Consequently, if we want to know what Mennonites believe about spiritual poverty, we can begin by asking, Did Jesus ever teach anything like this? In this case, we almost immediately hit the jackpot. The best-known collection of Jesus' teachings, the Sermon on the Mount in Matthew 5-7, opens with the words, "Blessed are the poor in spirit, for theirs is the Kingdom of Heaven" (Matt. 5:3). However, much material found in the Sermon on the Mount also appears, in different forms, in Luke 6, sometimes called "the Sermon on the Plain." Here Jesus begins by saying, "Blessed are you poor"– without adding "in Spirit" – "for yours is the Kingdom of God" (Luke 6:20). Soon afterwards Jesus adds, as he does not in Matthew, "Woe to you who are rich, for you have received your consolation!" (Luke 6:24). At first glance, Matthew and Luke seem to refer to two kinds of poverty: spiritual and economic poverty.

Scholars often debate which of these statements is, or is closest to, "*the* original saying" of Jesus. In my view, this question is misplaced. Jesus was an itinerant preacher who conveyed his basic teachings multiple times to different audiences in diverse settings in various ways. He could well have blessed "the poor" in both the forms found in Matthew and Luke, and in other forms too. His followers could well have passed on both of these more or less intact. In any case, his teachings on poverty were not limited to these two sayings. I mention them only as illustrations of something which a fuller investigation of the gospels would show: that Jesus taught a "spiritual poverty" that was often closely related to, though never identical with, economic poverty.

These teachings had deep roots in the Old Testament. Quite often, Hebrew words for "the poor" refer not to the poor as a class, but to God's special people, who are persecuted by wealthy persons, including rulers, in an unjust, oppressive society. Although most of these people are economically poor, some of them, in some settings, are not. All of "the poor," however, manifest a humble, open attitude of complete reliance on God.[1]

When Anabaptism arose in 16th-century Europe, it was very largely a lower class movement. Most of its adherents were economically poor to begin with, and most of the rest became that way due to heavy persecution. Many of these people embraced a profound kind of spiritual poverty which did not originate from their socio-economic circumstances, but which sustained them in the midst of these circumstances. My main claim will be that many early Anabaptists and many later Mennonites practiced a "spiritual poverty," whether or not they gave it that name, which, as in Jesus' teaching and often in the Old Testament, was different from economic poverty yet often closely associated with it.

From a Christian perspective, no kind of poverty is good in and by itself. God ultimately desires not emptiness and poverty, but fullness and a kind of richness, for every person. But since people usually desire the wrong kind of riches, or are oppressed by other people who desire riches, or both, poverty can render us "blessed" and can provide an opportunity to be purged of desires and possessions that will finally destroy us, and open us to receive God's riches instead.

## Spirituality in Mennonite History

I will focus mainly on a spiritual movement, often called "Rhineland Mysticism,"[2] which arose in medieval Catholicism and flowed into early South German/Austrian Anabaptism.[3] I am selecting this small slice of history because it is difficult to generalize about Mennonite spirituality from after the Reformation to the present, for several reasons.

First, Anabaptist-Mennonites, like nearly all Protestants, have been reluctant to describe spiritual experiences or techniques in precise ways. Medieval Catholics often specified these in detail. But Protestants felt that Catholics, by so doing, were focusing too closely on their own works, or "works righteousness," rather than on relating to God through faith. Consequently, although Protestants and Anabaptists value the spiritual dimension, they have said relatively little about it and how it can be pursued.

Second, as we shall see, "spiritual poverty" for Mennonites means something like "humility." "Humility" includes a humble, receptive attitude before God and a non-assertive, servant-like attitude towards other people. Humble Mennonites do not focus on themselves but on God and their neighbours. This has made them reticent to speak of their spiritual experiences, for that would be to focus on themselves. Third, if any one value has primacy for Anabaptists and Mennonites, it probably is obedience – to Jesus and his teachings in all aspects of life. Obedience can be understood as an "outward," ethical category, which indicates what people *do*, or should do, without necessary reference to "inward" experiences or motivations. The Gospels often refer to obedience to Jesus as discipleship. In the mid-20th century, Mennonite historian Harold Bender strongly influenced Anabaptist studies by designating discipleship as "the essence of Anabaptism."[4] Although discipleship, for him, was not simply "outward" action divorced from "inward" spirituality, many of his followers understood it this way and seldom discussed it, like their ancestors.

Fourth, much discussion of post-Reformation Mennonite spirituality concerns its relation to Pietism, which greatly values spiritual experience. Robert Friedmann, a colleague of Harold Bender, acknowledged that Anabaptists and Pietists both stressed inner experience and outward behaviour. Yet Friedmann concluded that the outward, in the forms of community, mission, and suffering in the public world, was distinctive of Anabaptism, while Pietism's "essence" in contrast was "pure subjectivity."[5] Much recent scholarship has questioned this dichotomy. It recognizes that Pietism comes in many varieties, some of which stress "outward," ethical activity, and that "pietist" experiences have often not weakened, but strengthened, Mennonites in their Anabaptist convictions.[6] However, I find Pietist-Anabaptist issues too complex to connect them helpfully with spiritual poverty in this essay.

In sum, because post-Reformation Mennonites said little about their spirituality, and because Anabaptist-Pietist issues would take us too far afield, I will limit consideration to "Rhineland mysticism." I will suggest, however, that some themes that it articulated can be found in the unarticulated spirituality of many Mennonites in other places and times, including today.

## "Rhineland Mysticism"

This spiritual stream is commonly traced back to Meister Eckhart, a Dominican theologian and Vicar General (1260?-1328?). Closer investigation reveals, however, that Rhineland mysticism was fed by many tributaries and branched off into many channels, and perhaps should not be called one stream. For instance, Eckhart and his younger colleague, Johannes Tauler (1300?-1361), preached to and directed many spiritual women. It is highly unlikely that all their main ideas flowed in one direction only, originating from these learned men, and never in the reverse direction, from these devout women to them.[7]

Significant numbers of these women, many of them called "beguines," were not nuns, but lived together independent from ecclesiastical structures, devoting themselves to prayer and serving the poor. During the 14th and 15th centuries Rhineland mysticism attracted numerous lay people. Many Germanic regions where it spread suffered under Papal interdict at various times. Deprived of sacraments and priestly services, lay people and the former monks, nuns, and priests among them had to devise their own forms of spiritual nurture.[8] Detailed directions and exercises for spiritual growth, which were found in monasteries, seldom appeared among these people. The challenges and struggles of everyday life became their spiritual disciplines instead. If we approach Anabaptism from this historical direction, it looks less like a Protestant movement and more like a radical, biblicized form of this lay-oriented medieval spirituality that emerged from the earlier popular and monastic traditions.[9]

The rest of this presentation will outline five themes common to both Rhineland mysticism and early Anabaptism. I will draw mainly on two medieval Catholic sources that clearly influenced Anabaptists: the sermons of Johannes Tauler[10] and the anonymous, widely read German

Theology; and also on three early South German/Austrian Anabaptists – Hans Hut, Hans Denck, and Leonhard Schiemer – and finally, the Hutterite leader Peter Riedemann (1506-1556). I will suggest that themes like these are congenial with the unarticulated spirituality of many Mennonites through the centuries, and I will try to show what these themes can mean today. Since my efforts must be somewhat speculative, I welcome responses from my Mennonite colleagues as well as my Iranian friends.

## The Ground of Our Souls

This was Rhineland mysticism's primary and most novel notion.[11] The Ground (*Grunt*) is the dark, mysterious, and deepest region of the soul where it merges into, or perhaps is identical with, God. Earlier Rhineland mystics like Meister Eckhart sometimes seemed to make this identification. This raised objections that I will soon consider. In any case, God, for Rhineland mystics, was encountered chiefly in the depths, or the Ground, of their souls. God also existed beneath, within, and among all creatures. Consequently, God was to be sought not so much in the heavens, or the heights, as within our world, especially in its depths.

I suggest somewhat speculatively that this kind of awareness of God appealed not only to early Anabaptists but to many of their Mennonite descendants, although they did not usually articulate it this way. This, I contend, is because God's presence, for Mennonites, and their participation in that presence, is closely connected with daily life and its tasks. Most Mennonites, of course, experience God in church and in prayer. But such encounters in special times and places mean little unless God is also felt to be present within, beneath, and around them, throughout the day and night.

Much Mennonite spirituality, I want to suggest, is subliminal. While their active lives are shaped by Jesus' teachings and example, Mennonites often experience God's presence in a more diffuse yet more pervasive way. However, if the deep, dark Ground of our souls where God is experienced *is* Godself, as some Rhineland mystics apparently thought, would this not mean that we, and perhaps all creatures, are actually divine? Does such an orientation not clash with Islam, which insists on God's transcendence over, and utter distinction from, everything else?[12]

Divine transcendence, it would seem, is best expressed by metaphors of height, and is often seriously compromised by metaphors of depth. If Mennonites want to affirm God's transcendence, should we not draw mainly on metaphors of height? On the other hand, height metaphors can suggest that God is not simply *distinct*, but also very *distant*, from creation. In Western society, divine transcendence has often been conceived as distance.[13] This has helped to banish God from the modern world and deliver the world over entirely to human control. I suggest, however, that many Mennonites experience God's *transcendence* precisely through God's presence within and beneath all creatures.[14] Perhaps the largely unarticulated Mennonite spirituality offers clues for expressing transcendence in concepts and metaphors of depth.

For Mennonites, God's manner of presence among creatures is most visible in Jesus, who, while being transcendent over humans as divine, utterly emptied and opened himself to become present among all people, including the lowliest criminals and slaves.[15] Many Mennonites approach God by being open to this One who, while being utterly distinct and different from us, has become accessible to and present with us. But to experience this, we must admit our weaknesses and sins, or our "spiritual poverty" towards God.

Such an apprehension of God provides an alternative to concepts of transcendence that distance God from creation, and to concepts of immanence that tend to identify God with creation. This God is present within, beneath, and among all creatures precisely as the self-giving *Other* who creates, sustains, and renews them. Paradoxically, then, people can enter into this presence only by approaching God precisely as other, as utterly distinct from them.

## Inordinate Creaturely Attachments

Rhineland mysticism abounded with agricultural metaphors, which increased its appeal to rural people during the 14th to 16th centuries.

Since God is found in (or is) the Ground of our souls, humans distance themselves from God when they allow other things to take root in, and to clutter, this Ground. This happens when they become more attached to creatures, by desiring them or possessing them, than to God.

"Creatures" include plants, animals, and things made from them that we need for nourishment, shelter, and other basic necessities. Creatures also include spouses, parents, children, relatives, friends, and the societies and countries where we live. For most people, the realm of desirable creatures expands to include the wealth, status, security, or power which they acquire, or hope to acquire, by possessing more and more creatures, and more elaborate products made from them, than they really need.

Earlier Rhineland mystics, such as Eckhart, sometimes spoke as if creatures, simply by themselves, formed obstacles to union with God. But Tauler made it clear that *attachments* to creatures that supersede devotion to God are the problem.[16] Such attachments, as it were, send down roots into the souls, or Ground, of people who prize creatures. As people become wholly preoccupied with creatures, their Ground becomes cluttered with these roots and weeds and vanishes from their awareness. God, who really moves beneath, within, and around them, becomes far distant from all that matters to them.

To return to this Ground, people must struggle against their desires to fill themselves with worldly possessions, or riches. One's soul must be emptied of these desires, which can only happen if one is willing to give up all worldly riches. This inward process of becoming empty, or the state of being empty, so that one might eventually be filled with God, is, I propose, what spiritual poverty meant for Rhineland mystics and early Anabaptists. It included a humble, receptive attitude before God and a non-assertive, servant-like attitude towards other people – very like what Mennonites call "humility."

For Rhineland mystics, the roots of creaturely attachments had to be painfully torn up. Our three early Anabaptists – Hans Hut,[17] Hans Denck,[18] and Leonhard Schiemer[19] – also underwent such experiences. Due to heavy persecution, they and their converts often had to surrender not only their attachments to things but the things themselves, and became economically as well as spiritually poor. Hut was martyred after only 16 months as an Anabaptist, as was Schiemer after about six months, while Denck succumbed to the plague around two years after his baptism.

As creaturely attachments were extirpated from their Ground (*Grunt*), they felt abandoned by all creatures, sometimes even by God. They descended into the deepest Ground (*Abgrunt*), or into Hell, with Christ. There they could only accept their emptiness, or acute spiritual poverty, and wait patiently for God to raise them to new life with Christ, and fill them with the Holy Spirit. For many early Anabaptists, such intense experiences amounted to a conversion, which they called "the Baptism of the Spirit," and prepared them for baptism in water. Nevertheless, this struggle continued in some sense throughout their lives.[20] It required a continuing attitude of spiritual poverty, often accompanied by its economic counterpart. This uprooting, however, formed only one aspect of their journey.

The three early leaders just mentioned perished too soon to say much about Anabaptist life after baptism. But many converts from South Germany, Austria, and elsewhere fled to Moravia, where the local nobles offered to protect them. Some of these refugees formed religious communities that were also self-sufficient economic units of production and consumption. To explain the continuing Anabaptist experience, Peter Riedemann, a leader of the Hutterite community, employed the ground and related agricultural metaphors somewhat differently. The ground, for him, symbolized not the depths of the soul but a person's overall environment, or world. Roots symbolized not particular attachments within a person but the entire person's attachment to, or embeddedness in, that world. God's Spirit extricated people from the evil world, or ground; but also replanted them into new soil, or grafted them into a new plant, into Christ. God's Spirit "makes them one mind with [Christ], in his very character and nature, so that they become one plant and organism with him. Christ is the root or stem; we are the branches."[21]

People freed from the world and its behaviour patterns were replanted into the living, spiritual Christ, and at the same time into his earthly body, the Christian community, which is inseparable from him. Hutterites began living in a new environment, and according to behaviour patterns that differed greatly from their former, worldly environment, and began the transformation process into the character of Christ, their Root.

Since the Reformation, many Mennonites have grown up in Christian homes, and have experienced conversion gradually, rather than as radical uprooting. But despite these different experiences, I want to suggest that several assumptions about spiritual transformation, first articulated by linking the soul with the Ground, shaped the largely unarticulated Mennonite spirituality through the centuries.

If the soul is a kind of ground and not a detached, purely spiritual entity, many creaturely desires can arise from it and become entangled with it. Such a soul will be profoundly shaped by physical desires, psychological processes, and social influences. Each person's soul, or self, will be significantly configured by that person's body and social context. If many Mennonites apprehend the soul in such a way, even if inarticulately, this may explain why Mennonite spirituality is concerned not simply with a "spiritual" realm but with all of life's dimensions. Most Mennonites sense that a person's deeper self, or soul, is profoundly shaped, and often distorted, by its material and social "world." If so, souls or selves cannot be transformed unless they are released from these influences and re-formed in a very different environment.[22] As this re-forming process transpires in their communities, Mennonites tend to focus on its "outward" aspects, that is, on people's specific behaviours, and sometimes limit their attention to these. Still, I suggest, Mennonites usually sense that these behaviours are prompted by far deeper "inward" inclinations towards or away from God, and that lasting transformation must occur on this level also.

## Economic Poverty

The theme of inordinate attachments can show how spiritual poverty is closely related to economic poverty, and yet different from it, as Jesus and some Old Testament writers taught. According to *The German Theology*, people sin when they turn away from the unchangeable Good (God) towards some creaturely good or some changeable creature, and treat this creature as though it belonged to them or was their property.[23]

Inordinate attachment to creatures, that is, involves *owning* them, or desiring to own them. Indeed, it is by claiming that creatures are their own that people begin the journey towards Hell.[24]

In Reformation times, Thomas Müntzer (1491?-1525), a renegade Catholic priest steeped in Rhineland mysticism, identified this possessive tendency, systemically, as the source of economic and social inequality. The desire to possess things leads people to acquire more and more of them. Different people begin desiring the same goods, and some of these people start taking these goods from others by force. Through this process certain persons and groups accumulate far more goods than others, including means of defending their goods and means of acquiring more goods from the possessions, or through the labour, of others.[25] Inordinate attachments to creaturely goods, then, bring wealth to some people and groups but alienate them from the true Good, or their Ground. The same process, though, plunges many other people and groups into economic poverty. Yet it distances them too from the true Good, for the same desire for possessions dominates them, although it is repeatedly frustrated.

For Rhinelanders and early Anabaptists, I have proposed, spiritual poverty was the process of being emptied, or the state of being empty, of these desires to own things or to acquire worldly riches. Economic poverty is related to spiritual poverty in two ways. First, economic poverty can result from, or accompany, spiritual poverty: to truly renounce one's desires for riches, one may need to renounce riches, or possessions, themselves. And if people who practice spiritual poverty belong to a marginalized or persecuted movement, they may lose their possessions in any case. Second, it may be easier for some people who are economically poor may to practice spiritual poverty than for others. Since poor people have few possessions, they will have less to lose if they cease desiring them. Moreover, living with fewer or no possessions might not be as difficult for some of them as for other persons, since they are quite used to it. In these ways, then, some poor people may be more open to God and God's Kingdom than most other people. This, I believe, is a major reason why Jesus called them "blessed."[26]

The notion that owning things is harmful to their owners carries significant socio-economic implications. Peter Riedemann placed this issue in a comprehensive theological framework. The universe, he proclaimed, was created in order that "God's glory, majesty and divinity might be seen, known, and praised. . . ." All creatures were originally designed "to lead people to God."[27] But because people turned these creatures into objects to be seized, hoarded, and controlled – that is, into possessions – these creatures now lead them away from God.[28] Although Riedemann, like most Anabaptists, defined sin as disobedience to God, he added that "all sin has its source and origin in wrong taking."[29]

This meant that anyone who wishes to return to God "must give up what was previously appropriated wrongly;" that is, "give up acquiring things and holding property."[30] Hutterite converts had to forsake the acquisitive patterns that spawn conflict, inequality, and injustice in worldly societies. But they immediately formed communities that produced and shared creaturely goods together, replacing those worldly patterns with co-operation, peacefulness, and equality.[31] In other words, spiritual poverty as Hutterites practiced it led towards eradicating economic poverty and establishing economic equality and prosperity.

But have most Mennonites since Riedemann's time practiced spiritual poverty, and connected it with economic poverty as he did? My impression is that most Mennonites have practiced *humility*: a humble, receptive attitude before God, and a non-assertive, servant-like attitude towards others. They have also practiced *economic simplicity*: limiting possessions, for the most part, to what they need, and to less elaborate and expensive versions of these things. But humility and simplicity are practiced for two very different reasons.

Some Mennonites practice them simply because God commands them. But if this is their only reason, such people often develop negative self-images. They wonder why they cannot fulfill many of their desires and own nice things. They usually conclude, even if subconsciously, that they must be unworthy and evil. They may acquire a humility and simplicity that seem natural. But these will be forced, and much of their natural spontaneity will be squashed. Other Mennonites find that severing inordinate attachments, despite some pain, brings healing, and that the emptiness that follows is filled by God. Gradually they conclude this process is for their good and happens because they are loved. Eventually – perhaps slowly – serving other people and owning fewer things feel natural and spontaneous and bring joy.

In regard to spiritual poverty, I am not sure which of these two motivations is more common among Mennonites today. But when I consider economic poverty, I notice this: Most Mennonites recognize that when wealthy people and nations gratify their desires and accumulate possessions without limit, most of the world remains poor. Mennonites agree that these drives should be curbed, perhaps even severely reduced, for that reason. But many fewer Mennonites, in my experience, advocate this because such drives hurt them. I wonder how many suppose that genuine humility and simplicity result from simply cutting back a bit on pleasures and possessions, without considering the potential harmfulness of their desires and their deeper spiritual roots.

To conclude this discussion of economic poverty, let me glance back briefly at Thomas Müntzer. Like Riedemann, Müntzer wanted to replace social poverty and inequality with moderate prosperity and equality. But how would God accomplish this? Müntzer's answer paralleled his own severe experience of inward uprooting and spiritual impoverishment. His God was extremely harsh. God hurled Muentzer so far into the *Abgrund* that he lost faith in God altogether for a while.[32] Müntzer's Jesus was the "bitter Christ," whom he experienced in this sort of desolation. He denigrated talk of a "sweet Christ" who bestowed comfort and compassion.[33] Müntzer concluded that much as God had plowed up the ground of his own soul, God would also plough up and extirpate the evil roots which infested society.[34] And who were these? They were the rulers and other classes. But who would provide, or be, the ploughs? In Müntzer's scenario, they would be the peasants. They could do God's work because poverty had already freed them from inordinate creaturely attachments. Müntzer accordingly led these destitute folks to disastrous defeat in the German Peasants' War (1524-1525). Too late, he acknowledged that he had underestimated their degree of spiritual poverty, or detachment.

The difference between Müntzer's version of Rhineland mysticism and most others, and especially its Anabaptist versions, had much to do with his harsh, violent picture of God. For Jesus' peaceful way and character qualified it very little.

## Peace

Many Rhineland mystics connected spiritual poverty and peace in much the way that early Anabaptists and many later Mennonites did and do. The energies that fuel the grasping, seizing, controlling, and hoarding of possessions also fuel aggression. Intense desires to possess things and strong inclinations to dispossess other people and groups often go together.

But as a person's urge to possess and control things is stilled in spiritual poverty, that person not only ceases to harm, or think of harming, other creatures, but begins to "will and wish and do what is best for them."[35] As such persons cease raising themselves up over other creatures, they come to consider themselves as lower than, and as servants to, all of them. According to the *German Theology*, other people can do whatever they want to, and even inflict great harm on, this kind of person. But even if this person were killed a hundred times and "should come to life again, he would still harbour love for his killer, and this despite the injustice, evil, and wickedness committed: he would wish the assailant well. . . ." This, of course, "can be seen, proved and confirmed in Christ's life."[36]

Jesus' way of peace, I suggest, has flourished among Mennonites, past and present, when it was embedded in this kind of deep-seated gentleness and care towards all creatures. When people guided by this way are threatened by enemies, they can remain open and receptive to whatever happens in the situation rather than close themselves off by counter-attacking or fleeing. They can remain alert to God's presence in the situation and perceive positive, nonviolent possibilities for resolving it.

## Participation in Christ

I will tie this essay together by considering Jesus' role in Rhineland and Mennonite spirituality. Meister Eckhart said relatively little about the earthly Jesus but spoke very often about God's eternal Son. God's Son, he said, is perpetually born from the Father and returns to the Father through the Holy Spirit in the Ground of the soul. We can return to our Ground by participating ever more deeply in the return of that Son in that Ground.

Christians, of course, believe that this Son once came from his Father into this sinful world and, empowered by the Spirit, led humankind back to the Father through his life, death, and resurrection. Eckhart, too, could refer to one's return to the Father, or to one's true Ground, as following Jesus' path during one's life. Yet he seldom did this. For Eckhart, this return was primarily an inward, spiritual process. He often seemed to regard the soul in its depths not as a creature distinct from God and inseparably united with a body, but as identical with God. Humans, then, were not finally creatures who should follow the Son to the Father, but, deep down, all were that same Son.[37] Our "outward" physical and social characteristics were not ultimately involved in this process. Only the soul's "inner," uncreated reality could fully reunite with God. Eckhart called this process "divinization," which often, apparently, meant actually becoming God.

Tauler, however, distinguished created, finite humans more clearly from God than Eckhart did. Their union with God was a unity of wills, not of being.[38] According to Tauler, the entire person returned to God. In this process, a person's "outward," physical features, as well as the "inward," spiritual features, played a vital role. "Divinization" for Tauler meant not becoming God but being transformed by God. As we might suppose, the earthly Jesus was far more central for Tauler than for Eckhart. For Jesus was united with God outwardly and physically as well as inwardly and spiritually. Jesus provided the model for *both* inward and outward communion with God.[39] Our way to this communion, then, had to include following his teachings and example, or discipleship.

Early Anabaptists identified even more closely with this Jesus. For when they began to follow him they were severely persecuted; or, as they put it, they experienced the same things Jesus had.[40] This led them to examine his teachings and example even more closely. They began to base their practices even more explicitly on Jesus than Rhineland mystics had, although these practices were much the same. Yet following Jesus' teachings was not simply ethical obedience to his commands. On the contrary, early Anabaptists criticized Protestants for treating Jesus merely as an external, historical figure. Jesus, for them, was also the powerful, living Word who transformed them from within.

Schiemer wrote a meditation on the Apostles' Creed that insisted every article had to be experienced inwardly as well as confessed outwardly. It is true that Christ suffered, and we should confess this; but his "suffering destroys sin, even as he suffers in me. . . . Christ does not keep me from sin unless he suffers in me." It is true that Jesus died and rose again, and we should confess this also; but if Christ does not die in someone, "Christ did not go to heaven for him, and he also will not go to heaven with him."[41]

In short, for these early Anabaptists Jesus was the historical person whose command they obeyed, the one whom they followed as disciples. But also he was also the living, resurrected Christ, so that salvation involved "the conception, birth, death, and resurrection *in us* of Christ who is our righteousness."[42] Through the Holy Spirit, the risen Christ took root in the Ground now cleared, through spiritual poverty, of tangled, choking roots.

If "discipleship" means outward following of Jesus' teachings or example, it denotes an aspect of early Anabaptist experience but not the whole. This experience can better be called inward and outward participation in the life, death, and resurrection of Jesus Christ. And the key to it was spiritual poverty, or opening oneself to be emptied of all attachments that block the way to God in order to be filled with God's renewing energy.

## Endnotes

1   See, e.g., Psalm 18:7, 69:29, 86:1; Isa. 3:15, 25:4, 26:6; Amos 2:7; Zeph. 3:12. The main Hebrew word for the poor "denotes the one who is `wrongfully impoverished or dispossessed'...." The antonym is the word for "violent." (Gerhard Kittel, ed., *Theological Dictionary of the New Testament* Vol. VI (Grand Rapids: Eerdmans, 1968), 888.

2   Some historians question the adequacy of this title, since this stream was fed by many tributaries and branched off into many channels. However, I find

it sufficient to indicate this movement very generally, for purposes of this article.

3 From here on, to avoid cumbersome phrases, "early Anabaptists/Anabaptism" will mean the early South German/Austrian kind, unless otherwise specified.

4 Harold Bender, *The Anabaptist Vision* (Scottdale, PA: Herald Press, 1944), 20. The three components of Bender's "Anabaptist Vision" were discipleship, the church as a voluntary brotherhood (26-31), and an "ethic of love and nonresistance as applied to all human relationships" (31).

5 Robert Friedmann, *Mennonite Piety through the Centuries* (Goshen, IN: The Mennonite Historical Society, 1949), 11, cf. 85-88.

6 E.g., John Roth, "Pietism and the Anabaptist Soul" in Stephen Longenecker, ed., *The Dilemma of Anabaptist Piety* (Bridgewater, VA: Penobscot, 1997), 17-33. Arnold Snyder demonstrates that early Anabaptists were energized by a lively spirituality in *Following in the Footsteps of Christ* (Maryknoll, NY: Orbis Books, 2004).

7 See the articles in Bernard McGinn, ed., *Meister Eckhart and the Beguine Mystics* (New York: Continuum, 1997).

8 See Bengt Hoffman, trans., *The Theologia Germanica of Martin Luther* (New York: Paulist Press, 1980), 2-14; Josef Schmidt in Maria Shrady, trans., *Johannes Tauler: Sermons* (New York: Paulist Press, 1985), 2-9; Bernard McGinn, *The Harvest of Mysticism in Medieval Germany* (New York: Herder & Herder, 2005), 407-31.

9 A major theme of Kenneth Davis, *Anabaptism and Asceticism* (Scottdale, PA: Herald Press, 1974).

10 Twenty-three of Tauler's 80 sermons appear in Shrady, trans., *Johannes Tauler: Sermons*, but much is paraphrased rather than translated. The modern German translation of all 80 sermons is far more accurate. See Georg Hofmann, trans., *Predigten*, 2 Vols. (Einsiedeln: Johannes Verlag, 1987).

11 See McGinn, *The Harvest of Mysticism in Medieval Germany*, 83-93.

12 However, similar tendencies towards identification of God, humans, and creation appear in Sufi mysticism; see William Chittick, *Sufism: A Short Introduction* (Oxford: Oneworld Publications, 2000), 12-15, 35-37, 46-49, 93-96, etc.

13 This can lead to the notion that "... God is in his kingdom – which is not of this earth – and we remain in another place, far from his dwelling.... God is worldless and the world is Godless; the world is empty of God's presence, for it is too lowly to be the royal abode....Whatever one does for the world is not finally important in this model, for its ruler does not inhabit it as his primary residence...." Sallie McFague, *Models of God* (Philadelphia, PA: Fortress Press, 1987), 65.

14 Rhineland mystics, especially Eckhart, suggest a way of conceiving this: precisely because God is utterly distinct and different from all creatures, God

can be equally close to every one of them. Otherwise, if God were more like some creatures, such as rulers and warriors, than others, would not God be more identified with certain social classes and structures than others? On this "distinction of indistinction," see McGinn, Introduction to Edmund Colledge and McGinn, trans., *Meister Eckhart: The Essential Sermons, Commentaries, and Defense* (New York: Paulist Press, 1981), 34.

15  According to a favorite Mennonite text, Jesus Christ "though he was in the form of God ... emptied himself, taking the form of a slave.... And ... humbled himself and became obedient to the point of death – even death on a cross" (Phil. 2:6-8). This text begins with the ethical exhortation: "Let the same mind be in you that was in Christ Jesus..." (2:5).

16  Oliver Davies, *God Within* (New York: Paulist Press, 1988), 86-87, 94. Tauler could call this "spiritual poverty" (86).

17  Hans Hut, "The Mystery of Baptism," in Daniel Liechty, ed., *Early Anabaptist Spirituality* (New York: Paulist Press, 1994), 75-81.

18  Hans Denck, "Whether God is the Cause of Evil" in Clarence Bauman, ed., *The Spiritual Legacy of Hans Denck* (Leiden: E. J. Brill, 1991), 93; "The Order of God" in Bauman, ed., 219-21.

19  Leonhard Schiemer, "Three Kinds of Grace...." in Liechty, 90-93.

20  Ibid., 95-97; Thomas Finger, *A Contemporary Anabaptist Theology* (Downers Grove, IL: InterVarsity, 2004), 163-65.

21  John Friesen, trans., *Peter Riedemann's Hutterite Confession of Faith* (Scottdale, PA: Herald Press, 1999), 97.

22  Thomas Finger, "A Sixteenth-Century Anabaptist Social Spirituality" *The Conrad Grebel Review* 22.3 (Fall 2004): 99-101.

23  *The Theologia Germanica of Martin Luther*, 62.

24  Ibid., 142, cf. 149.

25  "What is the evil brew from which all usury, theft and robbery spring but the assumption of our lords and princes that all creatures are their property." (Müntzer, "Vindication and Refutation" in Peter Matheson, ed., *The Collected Works of Thomas Müntzer* (Edinburgh: T & T Clark, 1988), 335.

26  So understood, Jesus' "preferential option for the poor" differs from backing the aspirations of an entire social class in a revolutionary struggle. For a fuller discussion, see my *A Contemporary Anabaptist Theology*, 245-46, 249-51.

27  *Peter Riedemann's Hutterite Confession of Faith*, 62.

28  Ibid., 120.

29  Peter Rideman, *Confession of Faith* (Rifton, NY: Plough Publishing, 1970), 58-59. Instead of "wrong taking," Friesen translates "embracing what is unrighteous" (94). "Wrong taking," however, is more appropriate for the original "unrechten Annehmen" Peter Rideman, *Rechenschaft unserer Religion, Lehr und Glaubens, von den Bruedern, so man die Hutterischen nennt* (Cotswold-Bruderhof, Ashton Kennes, Wiltshire, UK: Verlag der Hutterischen Brueder, 1938 [reprint of the

original *Rechenschaft* of 1565]), especially since he cites Genesis 3:6 in support (59). Riedemann also characterizes sin, more broadly, as "disobedience" from which "all other wrongs grow as branches from a tree" (Friesen, trans., 92).

30  *Peter Riedemann's Hutterite Confession of Faith*, 94. This was taught earlier by Hut ("The Mystery of Baptism," 72-73) and Schiemer ("Three Kinds of Grace...," 92).

31  *Peter Riedemann's Hutterite Confession of Faith*, 120-22.

32  Müntzer, "Vindication and Refutation," 199, 204-206; "On Counterfeit Faith" in Matheson, 214-18; "Sermon Before the Princes," in George Williams and Angel Mergal, eds., *Spiritual and Anabaptist Writers* (Philadelphia, PA: Westminster Press, 1957), 59-60.

33  Müntzer, "On Counterfeit Faith," 220-23.

34  Müntzer, "Sermon Before the Princes," 68-69.

35  *The Theologia Germanica of Martin Luther*, 104.

36  Ibid., 104-105.

37  Davies, *God Within*, 55-56. Moreover, in the soul's depth, or ground, the Son's birth from the Father transpired "'entirely in the same way as ... in eternity'" (quoted on 57). See McGinn's discussion in Meister Eckhart, 51-57.

38  Davies, *God Within*, 78-80, 83; Josef Schmidt in *Johannes Tauler: Sermons*, 28-34; McGinn, *The Harvest of Mysticism in Medieval Germany*, 263-64, 280-95; for *The Theologia Germanica of Martin Luther*, see 28-34 and Davies, 113-17.

39  Accept "the cross, from whichever direction it comes, *from outside or from within*.... follow your crucified God with a humble spirit, in true abnegation of yourself, *both inner and outer*.... and unite yourself with him" (quoted in Davies, *God Within*, 89 [italics mine]; cf. 96; cf. *Johannes Tauler: Sermons*: "the decisive difference between Tauler and Eckhart ... is the imitation of Christ, placing an emphasis on His humanity never to be abrogated...."(xv); cf. McGinn, *The Harvest of Mysticism in Medieval Germany*, 271-75 (on *The Theologica Germanica*, 398-400).

40  Schiemer, "The Apostles' Creed: an Interpretation" in C. J. Dyck, ed., *Spiritual Life in Anabaptism* (Scottdale, PA: Herald Press, 1995), 33: "as soon as one wants to begin living as a Christian one experiences none other than what Christ experienced...."

41  Ibid., 34, 35.

42  Schiemer, "Three Kinds of Grace...,"90.

# The Roles of Islamic Rituals in Cultivating Morality and Spirituality

## Aboulfazl Sajedi

## Introduction

Is there any relationship between Islamic rituals and the growth of morality and spirituality in the individual and in society? In what follows below, I will try to give a positive answer to this question. By "ritual" I mean what is accepted by true and sound Islamic sources. This does not include those present in some popular superstitions, practices, and even prohibited ceremonies. (An example is the practice of people injuring and blemishing themselves in the name of Islamic ritual.) Therefore, ritual covers all necessary and recommended actions or various ways of God's worship like prayer, fasting, pilgrimage (*hajj*), going to holy shrines and mosques, and other recommended social and individual behaviours.

Moral development depends on three factors: understanding, emotion, and behaviour. The first, understanding, includes anything that refers to the cognitive aspect of the human being such as thinking, reasoning, and imagination. The second includes what refers to the heart – feeling, emotion, stimulation, etc. The last relates to social and individual behaviours. Islamic rituals provide good background for all three factors in moral development.

## Cognitive Aspects

To develop morality and spirituality, we need information about moral principles and details regarding how we reach the goals. Human reason, by itself, is helpful for recognizing the main guideline for perfection, but it is not sufficient for teaching us the way to reach it. Reason, in spite of its benefits and positive aspects, has limitations for guiding and moving us toward absolute perfection. For instance, we do not know what will happen in the hereafter. As another example, we can refer to the Islamic way of worship: we understand the benefit of talking to God and worshiping him, but we do not know the better way. The Qur'an states that rituals like prayer and fasting are better ways of worshiping and it obliges us to do them. Because of the limitations of reason, revelation is needed. In the Qur'an it says:

> God has sent the Book and wisdom down to you and taught you what you did not know; God's bounty towards you has been splendid! (4:113)

The necessity of revelation does not mean that Islamic teachings are not based on reason. This point can be explained as follows: Islamic teachings are divided into two categories, main principles and rules of conduct. The main principles include the existence of God, the necessity of prophecy and receiving revelation, and the existence of the hereafter. The rules of conduct cover teachings such as prayer, fasting, going on the hajj, and tithing from one's extra money and property to the needy and for general benefit (*khums, zakat*). According to Islamic theology, the main principles can be, and even should be, approved by reason. By having such a great God with absolute knowledge and mercy, it is rational that we listen to him and follow his revelation. The rules of conduct also function reasonably for human beings. For example, prayer and fasting are beneficial for spirituality, and giving money to the needy is beneficial for all.

## Reminders

A basic obstacle in the cultivation of morality is our neglect of good individual and social behaviour. Islamic rituals can help us to stay attentive and cultivate this behaviour. Daily prayer is one example. When we pray, it reminds us to do good deeds, so prayer reminds us not to neglect cultivating our morality. Islam prohibits immoral behaviours and improper attributes such as jealousy, selfishness, various forms of annoying others and disrespect of others, and advocates acquiring moral attributes. The prohibitions serve as a guideline that should be respected by all Muslims. Daily prayer helps remind them about the moral attributes and about engaging in regular self-reflection. Good prayer will result in fostering moral attributes and self-control. The Qur'an refers to this when it says "Keep up prayer: prayer restrains one from sexual misconduct and debauchery" (29:45). The self-awareness gained through the practice of ritual prayer serves to cultivate morality and self-control, and guides us to good conduct with other people.

Prayer also promotes our spiritual journey. The weakness in our journey is rooted in our neglect of God and our relationship to him. Prayer can remove this obstacle. The necessity of daily prayer is a very helpful way of talking personally to God and being mindful of our conduct, our relation to God, and our being on a good spiritual journey.

Some elements in prayer that will make it a useful reminder, and helpful in moral and spiritual formation, are as follows:

1. Distributing prayer throughout the day. Muslims should pray five or three times; morning, noon, and night. Good prayer will be like an umbrella that covers all times and actions, and will not allow anyone to be neglectful for a long time; rather, it will bring a continued awareness of God in one's conduct.

2. Great emphasis on deep attention during prayer. Such attention and pondering during prayer awakens the human spirit from neglect and connects the person to God.

3. The content of words and sentences during prayer. The content of prayer is very useful and effective for cultivating morality and spirituality. For instance, we say at one point in our prayer: "You do we worship and you do we call on for help. Guide us along the Straight Road, the road of those whom you have favoured, with whom you are not angry, nor who are lost!" (1:5-7).

Attentively repeating these words gradually changes our personality and our behaviour to others. According to Islamic teaching, worshiping God means applying his commandment in our life. Those who recite these words honestly will try to do their best in relation to others. Such people evaluate their behaviour step-by-step to see whether it is acceptable to God or not, and they achieve strong self-control to avoid evil actions. In prayer we should say several times, "God is the greatest, he is the Mercy-giving, the Merciful, he is the ruler on the Day for Repayment! O, God, glory be to you." Repeating these words regularly, with attention, prepares our soul for daily walking with God, the spiritual journey.

## Motivation

Another barrier or obstacle for cultivating morality and spirituality is the lack of strong motivation for moral living and keeping our hearts dedicated to God. Islamic ritual can help us in this respect as well, for instance in the obligation of daily prayer. When something is not required, many people will not do it because of their conflicting desires or laziness in choosing the right or best thing. However, when something is required, people do it and get used to it and take benefit from it.

There are other prayers that are recommended so that whoever does them will receive a good reward. The more we pray attentively, the more we will develop our spirituality and will draw nearer to God (in Farsi, "will have the journey to God").

Another religious factor regarding motivation is the holiness of God and his commandments. If we receive advice from a holy source, we would have more motivation than when the source is not holy. The above-mentioned benefits of daily prayer are also true with respect to the practice of reciting the Qur'an. This is also a recommended practice, a spiritual discipline, to be done with full pondering. It is essential in cultivating moral and spiritual character because the Qur'an is continually reminding us of God, our relation to him, and God's rules for doing good deeds toward others.

Muslims have much to motivate them to recite the Qur'an. It is highly recommended with great reward, particularly in the month of fasting (Ramadan). Moreover, it has an attractive sound and content. Reading or reciting the Qur'an repeatedly can internalize Islamic moral and spiritual values in us. For example, the Qur'an says in 16: 90-91: "God commands justice, kindness and giving [their due] to near relatives, while He forbids sexual misconduct, debauchery and insolence. He so instructs you (all) so that you may draw attention to it. Fulfill God's agreement once you have pledged to do so, and do not break any oaths once they have been sworn to. You have set God up as a surety for yourselves; God knows whatever you do." The Qur'an beautifully repeats moral values, and thus affects us unconsciously: "We have already spelled out matters in this reading so they will notice it" (103:41).

Following Qur'anic spirituality helps human beings to acquire the best result from their lives and to be very glad at the end of life. Such people will have God's invitation at that time:

"O tranquil soul, return to your Lord well pleased and pleasing [him]! Enter among my servants, and enter my garden" (89: 27-30).

## Conclusion
Islamic rituals, like daily prayer and proper recitation of the Qur'an, can cultivate our morality and spirituality. They can remove our tendency to neglect God and the doing of good deeds. Islamic rituals remind us frequently to keep riding on the right path; they give us strong motivation in our moral conduct, and they lead us to experience a deeper relationship and attachment to God.

# Spirituality, Ritual and Ethics in the Anabaptist-Mennonite Tradition

## Irma Fast Dueck

## Introduction

The conference planners have asked me to describe for our Shi'a colleagues, Mennonite rituals, both corporate and personal, that have shaped Anabaptist-Mennonite identity and self-understanding, and to reflect on their relationship to spiritual formation and Mennonite ethics. Clearly, this is not an easy task to fulfill in a limited time. So I have chosen to focus on rituals connected to corporate worship and the private practices of prayer, to which our Shi'a friends have asked that particular attention be given.

Before I turn to those specific practices, I want to say a few words about Anabaptist-Mennonite spirituality in general. It has already been established by the other papers that describing Anabaptist-Mennonite spirituality is no easy task, as I'm sure it isn't easy to describe Shi'a Muslim spirituality. How do we distinguish Anabaptist-Mennonite spirituality from the popular spiritualities prevalent in our contemporary culture? Much could be said on this point, but I want to highlight the communal nature of the spiritual life in Anabaptist-Mennonite traditions. Christian spirituality is often nurtured in solitude, in the community of faith, and through life in the world. An important theme in Anabaptist-Mennonite theology is the communal nature of the Christian life; Christians are not Christians alone but together with others in the church. A healthy spirituality deepens and fosters life in the church community. For that reason I will begin with the corporate rituals of the church and then move to more personal and private rituals.

## Rituals, Religious Identity, and Spiritual Formation

Before turning to some "theological" descriptions of Mennonite ritual practices, I would like to draw on some insights from anthropology that shed light on the significance of rituals for all religious communities, for people of faith. Anthropologist Mary Douglas has argued convincingly that when members of religious groups distance themselves from their religious rituals by losing sight of the rituals' origins and questioning their relevance, they create conditions for the possible demise of the group. Douglas traces various stages of disenchantment from religious rituals, where the final stage represents the possibility of adaptation to the larger society.[1]

Daniel Smith draws on the work of Douglas when he focuses on the response of the minority Jewish community in the Babylonian exile when threatened by either destruction or assimilation by the dominant Babylonian culture. Smith argues that social groups in minority situations need to develop creative mechanisms to maintain their identity amidst the dominant culture. These mechanisms include the development of particular patterns of social organization and leadership, which help to mediate between the minority culture and the dominant culture in ways that the former does not have to sell out to the latter. However, perhaps most significant for contemporary Anabaptist-Mennonite communities, is Smith's argument that rituals are a significant mechanism for what he calls "boundary maintenance." Rituals and symbols demarcate the minority community by providing a clear vision of its identity, thereby distinguishing it from the symbols and rituals of the dominant culture.[2]

We know that ritual practices are critical not only to the moral formation of any religious community but in the development and preservation of identity and self-understanding (clearly, moral formation and identity are related). Robert Taft, a Christian liturgical theologian, writes that

> Ritual itself is simply a set of conventions, an organized pattern
> of signs and gestures which members of a community use to
> interpret and enact for themselves and to express and transmit
> to others, their relation to reality. It is a way of saying what we

are as a group in the full sense of that are, with our past that made us what we are, our present in which we live what we are, and the future we hope to be.[3]

Our rituals create a perspective from which to make coherent sense of the Christian/Muslim (or any other religious community's) faith and life, and of the world.

However, rituals do much more than simply communicate ideas: rituals are something we *do*. They are formative actions. What makes them formative is that they are something we do, we engage in. Or, as Ronald Grimes claims, "Rituals are deeds; they are not just colourful or oblique ways of 'saying' something."[4] Understanding is developed through participation within the ritual itself. The ritual of worship, for example, trains us to see, "to discern ourselves, the church, and the world – indeed all of life and reality – as formed by the Gospel."[5] Harmon L. Smith summarizes it well:

> Christians are a people whose vision of the moral life is formed by adoration and praise, by penitence and pardon, by thanksgiving and offering, by petition and intercession, by revelation and confession ... and by all of these ascribed and supplicated to the God whom we know through Jesus. When our vision of the moral life is formed in these ways, we Christians will know that we worry about war and sexuality and racism and the rest *soli Deo gloria*."[6]

Simply put, if we are to understand each other as Shi'a Muslim and Mennonite Christian, it would be wise for us to give attention to those rituals we engage in and inquire into what they reveal about who we are and how they shape and form us as people of faith.

## Mennonite Rituals and Spiritual Formation
*Corporate Worship and Moral Formation*
The Anabaptist-Mennonite tradition has taken the unity of worship and life (what might be more commonly called worship and *work*) very

seriously, making it difficult if not impossible to discuss Mennonite worship without somehow giving attention to its relationship to ethics or faithful living. Mennonites have insisted that worship encompass all of life and not be restricted to the practice of particular worship rituals or sacraments. Edward Poling claims in his description of early Anabaptist worship that this was "not to deny the sacred in life but to see that all of life was under God's dominion and thus special."[7] Mennonites rightfully have refused to separate the sacred from the secular. Worship and work are one.

> One of the gifts Anabaptists may offer the larger church body is their stubborn insistence on the integral relationship between what is said in worship and what is done in life, between the encounter with God and the encounter with the world, between the honouring of God with music and words and the honouring of God with obedient lives.[8]

The unity of worship and work recognizes and honours that all life is sacred and under God, and that we are invited to live our lives as sacrament – holy. We are called to worship God through all that we do and not just in our gathering for corporate worship. Next I will describe worship practices and then reflect on their connection to moral formation.

## Mennonite Worship Practices

From their Anabaptist beginnings, Mennonites have consciously sought to distinguish themselves from other traditions, making the development of particular liturgical forms problematic, since traditionally their own worship patterns have been fairly ordered and predictable. Edgar Metzler writes that "at the conservative church in Pennsylvania where I spent boyhood summers working on a farm, the local bishop would have decried the suggestion of a 'liturgy.' But the invariable sequence of 'two songs, a prayer, scripture reading, offering, another song, sermon, announcements, and benediction' was more rigid than the service in a nearby church based on the Book of Common Prayer."[9] While Metzler describes what may have in the past been considered a typical pattern, it would difficult to find such an ordered pattern in Mennonite worship practices today. Only a few decades ago, it was possible to attend worship in most Mennonite congregations on a Sunday morning and know what to expect. Now there is great diversity in worship practices. One pastor who had been attending different Mennonite worship services for the past number of years writes that these services "are not easy to describe: Sorta like a Presbyterian church without the robes ... or maybe a Vineyard but with four-part singing ... kinda like a Baptist church without the altar call."[10]

Mennonite worship covers a wide spectrum from charismatic to traditional, from "seeker-service" to a more high church liturgy. This diversity in practices is not surprising, given Mennonite polity, which allows for great autonomy in congregational practices. This congregational autonomy emerges out of Anabaptist-Mennonite ecclesiology, which emphasizes the authority of the gathered and accountable community of faith. While this great diversity makes it hard to reflect more generally on Mennonite worship practices, it is not impossible. Similar to most congregations in the "free church" tradition, singing, prayer, and preaching are among the primary elements of nearly all Mennonite worship services, despite various cultural influences (expressed primarily through songs and musical styles).

In their worship practices, Mennonites are perhaps best known by their hymn singing. The types and styles of hymns and songs are as diverse as their worship practices, ranging from classical chorales and 19th-century gospel songs to music from various monastic communities, folk songs, and contemporary Christian choruses. In a recent research project on Mennonite singing, Kenneth Nafziger and Marlene Kropf claim that for Mennonites, in the absence of a weekly Eucharistic tradition, singing in many ways fills a sacramental function. The body of Christ is experienced corporately as congregants sing together. Not surprisingly, for many Mennonites, singing is a significant, if not central, part of their worship experience.

For many Mennonites interviewed, there is little in corporate worship that *needs* to be done that cannot be done by singing together. Singing can gather the congregation; it can become the vehicle of praise, confession, and intercession; it can speak the word of God; it can transform and empower a people. It not only carries the actions of worship forward, it is the primary action of worship.[11]

Since congregational singing plays such a significant part in worship, many Mennonite churches use a song leader to lead the singing rather than have the congregation follow the lead of an organ or piano.

While various styles of public prayer have been used in Mennonite worship practices in recent decades, the pastoral prayer is the most popular. The pastor or worship leader prays on behalf of the community, offering statements of thanksgiving, confession, petition, and intercession. Traditionally these prayers were composed extemporaneously and were often quite lengthy. Up until the 20th century it was a custom to kneel during prayer; this practice still continues in a few groups (Amish, Old Colony Mennonites).

Often the pastoral prayer is the main prayer (if not the only prayer) found in the service. Generally, there has been reluctance to pray shorter prayers through the service or to repeat prayers from service to service. In addition, there has been some scepticism about using prayers that are not one's own (for example, prayers from a worship resource or worship book), although this is beginning to change. As a result of the emphasis on the importance of the community of believers, time for people to share concerns and experiences from their lives may be included in the prayer.

Generally, confession of sin and acknowledgement of grace are elements that have not been emphasized in Mennonite worship. For some congregations, preparation sermons and services prior to communion (the "Lord's Supper") serve this purpose. Traditionally, a strong emphasis has been placed on the need for reconciling conflicts, confession of wrongdoing, and subsequent forgiveness before one can participate in communion. For a long time, righteous living and morality have been stressed in worship, but this too is changing.

Preaching is the central element of Mennonite worship; it requires most of the allotted worship time. The sermon is usually the orienting point of the service, influencing the selection of hymns, prayer themes, scripture readings, etc. Again, traditionally, ethical issues and lifestyle concerns have provided the primary themes for sermons. Stories for children are often incorporated into the worship service and frequently draw on the theme of the Scriptures or the sermon.

Increasingly in Mennonite churches, lay people are the primary shapers of congregational worship, through worship leadership, participation on worship committees, and as preachers and song leaders.

Mennonites normally practice two sacraments which they have called "ordinances:" baptism and the Lord's Supper.[12] Some congregations also practice footwashing, often together with the Lord's Supper. Believer's (adult) baptism is usually practiced annually around the time of Pentecost. The Lord's Supper is observed with varying degrees of frequency. Some groups practice it twice a year, while others do so quarterly. In a few congregations, communion is celebrated more than four times a year. I will return to the practices of baptism and communion later, but first a short reflection on the relationship of corporate worship and ethics.

## Worship and Ethics

A number of years ago, John Howard Yoder, a prominent Anabaptist-Mennonite theologian and ethicist, argued for an intrinsic theological connection between worship and ethics, a perspective consistent with the Mennonite emphasis on the unity of worship and work. Yoder was responding to the tendency of theologians and liturgical scholars to reflect upon the relationship of worship and ethics in a way that assumed that worship and ethics were somehow separate from each other. Some perspectives emphasize how worship shapes the moral character of person or community and that character/identity determines the style of moral discernment. Other perspectives stress the "inward" nature of worship (an understanding that presupposes a kind of withdrawal from the world) which serves to empower and energizes Christians for "outward" action in the world.

The problem with most approaches, Yoder argues, is they assume that worship and ethics are indeed separate from each other, that there is a distance between them, and that this distance needs to be bridged. When considering the relationship of worship and ethics, the focus has been primarily on how worship helps us live more ethically or be more faithful and obedient to God as revealed in Jesus Christ. Yoder argues that this separation of ritual and ethics, or the separation of the sacred (life in worship) and profane (life in the world), non-political or political, may actually be part of the problem. In other words, it may be misleading even to question the relation of the performance of worship to the performance of ethics, because it assumes that in some way they are separate.

Yoder, along with a number of Catholic theologians,[13] proposes that Christian worship practices (more specifically, the Lord's Supper and baptism) are themselves ethical. For example, the Lord's Supper is an act of economic ethics; bread eaten together is a paradigm for economic sharing. The practice helps to illuminate social ethics. It becomes a paradigm for how other social groups may function. While still embracing the idea that worship creates a particular identity and character from which a person or community acts, Yoder is cautious about what appears like a "derivative" ethic (that is, an instrumental understanding of practices in which ethics is a kind of by-product) and prefers to take a much more intentional approach to social ethics. He argues that the church has for many years failed to take seriously the discipleship ethics of Jesus Christ as normative. His approach assumes an integral relationship between worship practices and ethics, one rooted in the apostolic tradition and practices of the early church.[14]

Yoder's approach reflects the Mennonite understanding of the unity of worship and work. Worship and ethics are inseparable. Worship is paradigmatic of the Christian's witness in the world; it reveals the nature of our life in the world. When Christians gather to worship, they give witness to, and participate in, the reconciling movement of God in the world. As such, worship actions are testimonies to God and visible signs of God's reconciling mission. Worship is like a reversible jacket: if it is turned inside out, the mission of God is revealed.[15]

## Sacraments/Ordinances

As mentioned, Mennonites normally practice two sacraments that they have called "ordinances"16: baptism and the Lord's Supper. Some congregations also practice footwashing, often together with the Lord's Supper.

For the early Anabaptists, a critical point of departure from the liturgical traditions of medieval Rome was the rejection of a sacrament as *opus operatum* conveying the grace of eternal life. The Anabaptists' strong emphasis on discipleship based upon the life and death of Christ and their subsequent stress on the regenerated and obedient community of believers served as a helpful corrective to the medieval Church and the Protestantism of the time. They concluded that the sacraments had become idols and had to be reinterpreted, and they attempted to interpret the sacraments and rituals in such a way as to emphasize human responsibility, reducing the sacraments (baptism and communion in particular) to "mere symbols" and focusing rather on the human response to divine initiative. Their emphasis was not so much on what God was doing but on the human response to God.

Thus, any Anabaptist theology of the sacraments and of worship was mostly a reaction to the medieval Church and the magisterial Reformation, for both of which the definitive characteristic of a sacrament was God's initiative. The Anabaptists emphasized the human response of faith and love. They were more interested in the nature of the human action within the sacrament than with the nature of the sacrament itself.

The traditional definition of a sacrament is "an outward and visible sign of an inward and spiritual grace." This definition, which finds its roots in Augustine's "the visible sign of an invisible grace," is useful in that it describes how something visible, tangible, from ordinary experience can be used to communicate something that transcends ordinary experience. Originally the definition meant that, while the outward sign was being performed, grace was being infused into the soul. As Christian history attests, this perspective eventually produced a mechanical notion of grace. While the belief in this understanding of grace has waned, the traditional definition has tended to be reinterpreted symbolically. For example, the bread and wine are "only symbols" of the "real" thing, which is an "inward and spiritual" communion with God. Thus, the genius of sacrament that binds the material and the spiritual together has been lost.

Another traditional, more functional definition of sacrament is "a sacrament effects what it signifies."[17] That is, it enables to happen what it points to. Augustine referred to the sacrament as "the visible Word" (*verbum visible*)[18] and Martin Luther called baptism "the Word in the water."[19] This definition preserves the unity of the material and the spiritual (worship and life, worship and ethics, worship and mission, etc.). It links the spiritual and the material in a way analogous to the Incarnation where God is in Christ, "truly God and truly human," one person and one substance and not divided into two.

The early Anabaptists argued for this link between the spiritual and the material when they insisted that the sacrament was the "real presence" of Christ in the church. Christ is what enables the church to be the church. In this way, the sacrament effects what it signifies. Early Anabaptists believed that Christ became incarnated through their corporate actions as the body of Christ. In this way the church became a sacrament. They insisted that there was a physical presence of Christ on earth through the life of the church. Christ became embodied as the community strove to live in a way consistent with the teachings of Jesus.

The belief in the holiness of the church was clearly reflected in Anabaptist-Mennonite practices of baptism and the Lord's Supper. These ordinances had significance in the community not because of the rites themselves or their sacred function but because of their role in the community.

## Baptism and the Lord's Supper

Many of the meanings and understandings of baptism are connected to basic understandings of water. Much that the church believes about baptism is connected to what is more generally believed about water. Obvious meanings embody themes of cleansing, refreshment, nourishment, life, etc. A predominant New Testament way of speaking about baptism and the primary way that the apostle Paul speaks about it is *death*; we drown in the baptismal water:

> You were buried with him in baptism, in which you were also
> raised with him through faith in the working of God, who
> raised him from the dead. And you, who were dead..., God
> made alive together with him.... He disarmed the principalities
> and powers and made a public example of them, triumphing
> over them in him. (Col. 2:12-15)

The context of this passage is that Paul was having a difficult time
bringing together Jews and Gentiles. As a matter of principle he
made them members of the same community, eating and worshiping
together, but the policy was criticized from both sides. In the course
of that argument he wrote to the Corinthians: "If anyone is united
to Christ, there is a new world; everything old has passed away; see,
everything has become new!" (2 Cor. 5:17). The New English Bible
uses the translation "there is a new world" or creation; not merely the
individual (the "creature," as it is often rendered) is new. In Christ, a
new creation is going on: the inherited social definitions of class and
category are no longer basic. In baptism the person "dies" to those
definitions and rises to a new one.

Baptism is that entry into the new people, the new creation, the
new world. For the early church, it was the distinguishing mark of this
people, and it transcends previous definitions. In a similar way Paul
writes to the Galatians: "Baptized in Christ, you are clothed in Christ,
and there is neither slave nor free, neither male nor female; you are
all one in Christ Jesus" (Gal. 3:27, 28). A new creation, a new way of
relating, happens in Christ, and baptism marks that entrance into that
new community, the new humanity. Baptism marks a new kind of social
relationship, a unity that overarches the differences and separations
(Jew/Gentile, male/female, slave/free), a new reconciled community in
Christ.

The Anabaptist-Mennonite tradition has taken very seriously
baptism as a sign of a new kind of community. Baptism signified a
changed life by virtue of Christ's death, but not in an individualistic
sense; it marked the entry into the new community. Repeatedly

Anabaptists argued that baptism included Christ's rule of "binding and loosing" (Matt. 18:15-22). The person who is baptized commits her/himself to the community and is held accountable within it. Through baptism the person commits her/himself to live a new life consistent with the words and life of Christ but, at the same time, also agrees to receive and to give active, deliberate help in doing so through participating in the community.

For the early Anabaptists the practice of the Lord's Supper had little to do with the veneration of the bread or the adoration of the wine. The meal was described from the beginning as the "supper of fellowship." Rooted in their understanding was a strong emphasis on incorporation with Christ and the gathered community, the body of Christ. Conrad Grebel, an early Anabaptist reformer, writes:

> Although it is simply bread, yet if faith and brotherly love precede it, it is to be received with joy, since when it is used in the church, it is to show us that we are truly one bread and one body, and that we are and wish to be true brethren with one another . . . [it is a commitment of willingness] to live and suffer for the sake of Christ and the brethren, of the head and members.[20]

The purpose of the Lord's Supper is to signal, through its expression, the reality of a new community of love, peace, and truth.

The Anabaptists strongly believed that it was God's will that all people should live in harmony. They conceived of the church as the community of those who deliberately resolved to realize, in the present, God's will for the whole of humankind. Peter Riedemann writes:

> The Church of Christ is the basis and ground of truth, a lantern of righteousness, in which the light of grace is borne and held before the whole world, that its darkness unbelief and blindness be thereby seen and made light, and that men may also learn to see and know the way of life. Therefore is the church of Christ in the first place completely filled with the light of Christ as a

lantern is illuminated and made bright by the light, that his light might shine through her to others.[21]

The early Anabaptists argued that a community that does this is holy because it is united with God in God's will and purpose in and through Jesus Christ. Walter Klaassen claims it was this understanding of the sacred that was at the heart of the radical religion of Anabaptism. While it was not a completely new understanding and it existed partially in both Protestantism and Roman Catholicism, he argues that the Anabaptists were practically the only ones who sought to find and express God's will in radically personal and communal terms.[22]

In summary, the Anabaptists essentially agreed with Ulrich Zwingli in their radical rejection of the sacramental mediation of grace. Repeatedly they claimed that the "water is just water," "the bread is just bread," and "the wine is just wine." As mentioned, there is no divine power in the priestly blessing of these physical elements that renders them as sacraments, as "visible signs of invisible grace."

The Anabaptists were, however, very interested in the incarnational question: In what way may God be said to be present here and now to humanity? This was critical for everyone living in the late medieval religious and intellectual world, and to their understanding of the church as sacrament. While they denied that the body of Christ was made physically present to humankind in the elements of the mass, the Anabaptists insisted that there was a physical presence of Christ on earth and this was the true church; Christ was present in Christ's members.

> When we read Anabaptist statements describing the church as the Body of Christ, and individual believers as members or limbs of that Body, we tend to take this as an extended metaphor, not a literal description. There is much evidence to suggest, to the contrary, that for many Anabaptists it was intended as a *literal* description, and not a metaphor at all. As ecclesiology assumed more importance, so too did a sacramental conception of the church.[23]

## Personal Rituals and Spiritual Formation

If Mennonite worship practices are hard to describe, the rituals (spiritual disciplines) practiced personally/privately are nearly impossible. However, in closing I will say a few things on this theme. I'll begin with a description of the family and personal devotional life of Mennonites that nurtured me into the Christian faith. I suspect that these pattern/ rituals sustained the families and generations of Mennonites from which my family came.

Our rituals were for the most part shaped by the meals of the day. At breakfast time, the first meal of the day, my father would read from the Bible and say a prayer for the day that we might be faithful to Christ, or sometimes we would pray a familiar (often rhyming) prayer together in unison. At lunchtime we would pray a memorized prayer/grace in unison. At supper time we would begin with a unison prayer (the same one most of the time), and at the end of the meal, a family member would read from devotional literature prepared by our Mennonite denomination, based on a scripture verse or Biblical passage followed by a longer prayer of petition that brought the needs of our family, our church, the world before God, prayed usually by my father or mother. Sometimes we would sing hymns/choruses together. This was an important time for our family, and I recall my friends knocking on our back door begging for my siblings and me to go outside to play, while my parents ignored them and continued on with the prayers and readings as if they were not even there.

Finally we had a time of prayer and devotion before bedtime. My parents encouraged us to develop personal spiritual disciplines for bedtime: to read contemporary versions of Bible stories to ourselves and of course to end the day in prayer. I know that my parents read the Bible to each other before they slept and prayed together. These were some of the religious rituals that shaped our daily life.

On Sunday, our Sabbath day of rest, other rituals were added including attendance at worship services at church in the morning and evening. But perhaps of greater significance was the expectation that we refrain from particular activities that shaped the weekdays. No work was permitted (though my mother was allowed to prepare the meals), and we frequently spent the day with members of our church or our relatives. Implicitly we were not allowed to play with those outside of our faith tradition on Sundays. When my father's family would gather on Sundays (which seemed often), our gathering frequently included singing hymns of faith together. I imagine that my experience with religious rituals in our home is not much different than what many who were raised in the Mennonite faith tradition experienced. Today I suspect many of these patterns have changed, and family religious practices are more diverse and perhaps not quite as ritualized.

Earlier I claimed that Mennonites rejected elaborate liturgies, rituals, and dogmatic theology in favour of practices and rituals that were simple and "quiet."[24] In the early beginnings, silent prayer appeared to be commonplace in Anabaptist communities. However, late in the 16th century this began to change and audible prayers were more commonly practiced.[25] Soon there were collections of prayers written by Mennonite authors for use in worship or private devotions. By the late 16th and early 17th century, prayers were being collected and became part of a body of devotional literature.[26]

At its beginning, the Anabaptist-Mennonite experience of prayer had been deeply shaped by the ethical imperative to follow Jesus at all costs. It was prayer (both private and corporate) that sustained the persecuted Anabaptists as they were imprisoned and led to their executions. Their prayers embodied their *Gelassenheit*, their "yieldedness" to God in humble trust; they prayed for the strength to remain faithful and to follow the path of Christ.

Mennonite prayer practices were shaped by their understanding of discipleship as following Christ. As Beulah Hostetler claims, prayer was the grateful expression of a trusting heart to the One who enables right living in the Christian community and in the world. Mennonites have reflected an "alternate understanding of the gospel – one that was more lived than spoken, more relational than dogmatic, one seeking peace rather than conquest."[27] At least traditionally, Mennonite prayer was rooted in Mennonite discipleship, where prayer simply invited trust in God's presence and the care of God in all things (this pattern is one that I easily recognized in the prayers of my grandparents and parents).

While the ethical imperative to follow Christ has remained in Mennonite thought and practice, the connection between prayer and ethics has shifted in the past while, primarily as a result of the influence of rationalism and pietism.[28] Robert Friedmann, in his classic work *Mennonite Piety through the Centuries*, has argued that the influence of pietism has challenged Mennonites to all but abandon notions of costly Anabaptist discipleship in favour of a "sweet," more interiorized piety, focusing more on the personal experience of God (frequently with emphasis on emotional encounter with God) than a self-sacrificial ethic rooted in the following after and the suffering of Christ.[29] These changes have often brought about tensions between different Mennonite groups, with some moving more in the direction of Pietism, resulting in more mainline evangelical and charismatic expressions of Anabaptist-Mennonite faith, and others emphasizing more the external expression of faith through discipleship ethics, peacemaking, service, etc.

Today, there is no uniform practice of spiritual disciplines, including prayer, but rather a plethora of expression in various settings and cultures, all of which seek to follow Jesus faithfully in their own particular context. On the whole, non-Western Mennonites experience prayer in particular in much more spontaneous and rigorous ways than do their Western brothers and sisters, though they may engage in more ritualized actions in other areas of Christian life (around the life cycle, worship, etc.).

In the late 20th century, Western Anabaptist-Mennonites began to explore the whole area of Christian spirituality and spiritual disciplines, and to examine more deliberately the relationship between spiritual disciplines and ethics, or what Dennis Martin describes as "the interrelationships between ethics and doctrine and on the mystery of God becoming human so that men and women could know God intimately and ontologically (in being) as well as ethically (in actions)."[30] Some Mennonites in the Western world remain quiet and private in their expressions of faith and spiritual devotion, while others are more emotionally expressive, perhaps influenced by charismatic renewal movements. Still others have been turning to liturgical (Catholic?) forms of prayer and personal worship and to the use of symbolic expressions to aid in their personal devotional life.[31] There is also a renewed interest among North American Mennonites in practices of meditation and reflection as part of prayer, the reading of the Bible, and personal devotions.

Finally, brief consideration needs to be given to the place of small groups (prayer groups, Bible study groups, cell groups, etc.) in helping shaping the spiritual and ethical life of the Anabaptist-Mennonite communities. From its beginnings the Anabaptist-Mennonite tradition has a long history of meeting in homes together with fellow believers for prayer, Bible study, and fellowship. These patterns have continued in various forms: some churches have small groups meeting together for many years (a group in our church has met for over 35 years); some engage in regular rigorous study of the Bible; some meet weekly, others monthly; some share very personally about their spiritual journey of faith; some groups hold each other accountable for their Christian living around a whole host of issues, including how money is spent and the engagement of personal practices of prayer and scripture reading; some groups engage in service projects together; some groups engage in political protest together.

The example of small groups models Anabaptist-Mennonite theology very well, particularly the corporate nature of spirituality. While small groups engage in many ritual practices such as prayer and scripture reading that are also done personally and privately, it is the community that strengthens and nourishes the personal/private and vice versa.

## Conclusions

The idea that authentic faith is necessarily embodied in a life of following the teaching and example of Jesus may seem obvious, although the history of the church and its current context reflects the need to be reminded again and again of this truth. For the early Anabaptists, to be called to follow the path of Jesus is also to be called into community. Being a disciple of Jesus is not something done alone; it is not an individual project to save the world. Rather, discipleship is deeply dependent upon a community, the body of Christ, which is not a theoretical doctrine but a lived community of worship, of corporate and personal spiritual disciplines, mutual love, and accountability. The rituals that the community engages in, both corporate and personal, serve to remind the community of their identity in Christ. A ritual such as baptism is not merely about the forgiveness of individual sins; rather, it is incorporation into the eschatological community of God's people. It is to become part of a new people, a particular kind of people, called to embody a different way of being in the world. To be part of this new society is to engage in rituals and practices that reflect an alternative imagination of the world, rituals rooted in Scripture and shaped by Jesus.

## Endnotes

1  See Mary Douglas, *Natural Symbols* (Harmondsworth: Penguin Books, 1979).

2  Daniel L. Smith, *The Religion of the Landless: The Social Context of the Babylonian Exile* (Bloomington, IN: Meyer-Stone Books, 1989). In this context Smith draws on the work of Mary Douglas in Purity and Danger, where Douglas claims that the purity rituals in the Old Testament grow out of the fear of "pollution" from the dominant culture. These rituals play a significant functional role in the preservation and symbolic resistance of the minority group. See Mary L. Douglas, *Purity and Danger* (New York: Praeger, 1966).

3  Robert Taft, *The Liturgy of the Hours in East and West* (Collegeville, MN: Liturgical Press, 1986), 334-45, as found in Robert Webber, ed., *The Complete Library of Christian Worship*, Vol. 2 (Nashville, TN: Star Song, 1994). 268.

4  Ronald L. Grimes, *Beginnings in Ritual Studies* (Washington, DC: University Press of America, 1982), 60.

5  See Harmon L. Smith, *Where Two or Three are Gathered: Liturgy and the Moral Life* (Eugene, OR: Wipf and Stock Publishers, 2004), 70.

6  Ibid., 2-3.

7  Edward N. Poling, "Worship Life in Sixteenth-Century Anabaptism," *Brethren Life and Thought*, 37 (Spring 1992): 122.

8  Robert R. Miller, "Concerning Coming Together," in *Anabaptist Currents*, Carl F. Bowman and Stephen L. Longenecker, eds. (Bridgewater, VA: Penobscot Press, 1995), 110.

9  See Edgar Metzler, "A Response to John Rempel: Surely the Lord is in This Place," *The Conrad Grebel Review* 6.3 (Fall 1988): 263.

10  Rod Stafford, "The ABCs of Mennonite Worship," *The Mennonite* Vol. 2, No.23 (June 15, 1999), 4.

11  Marlene Kropf and Kenneth Nafziger, *Singing: A Mennonite Voice* (Scottdale, PA: Herald Press, 2001), 27.

12 The term "ordinance" has been used to emphasize that the practices of communion, baptism, and footwashing originate in the ministry and command of Christ. That is, these actions were "ordained" by the Lord. In the latest Mennonite Confession of Faith there is a shift from the language of "ordinances" for describing these ceremonies to calling them "signs." Here the emphasis is on "sign" as both an act of God and the corresponding human action. For example, the commentary following the article on baptism says: "baptism is sign, representing both God's action in delivering us from sin and death and the action of the one who is baptized, who pledges to God to follow Jesus Christ within the context of Christ's body, the church." See *Confession of Faith in a Mennonite Perspective* (Scottdale, PA: Herald Press, 1995), 47.

13 See Tissa Balasuriya, *The Eucharist and Human Liberation* (Maryknoll, NY: Orbis Books, 1979); Geevarghese Osthathios, *Theology of a Classless Society* (Maryknoll, NY: Orbis Books, 1979); Rafael Avila, *Worship and Politics* (Maryknoll, NY: Orbis Books, 1981); Joseph A. Grassi, *Broken Bread and Broken Bodies* (Maryknoll, NY: Orbis Books, 1981); Monika Hellwig, *The Eucharist and the Hunger of the World* (Kansas City, MO: Sheed and Ward, 1992).

14 John Howard Yoder, *Body Politics* (Nashville, TN: Discipleship Resources, 1992); John Howard Yoder, "Sacrament as Social Process: Christ the Transformer of Culture," *Theology Today* 48.1 (April 1991). In *Body Politics*, Yoder is careful to point out that it cannot be assumed that worship will automatically translate into ethical living. He is particularly critical of two perspectives on the relationship of worship and ethics. The first perspective assumes that worship forms the character of the person or community and that character/identity determines the style of moral discernment. A person or community formed on the basis of the Christian narrative will act out faith in a way consistent with the character of Jesus. This view is reflected particularly in the work of Stanley Hauerwas. The second perspective sees worship as creating a foundation or "motivation" for ethical behaviour. This motivation would be based on the love of God. The problem with both approaches, Yoder claims, is that they assume a distance between worship and ethics that needs to be bridged.

15 The relationship of worship and ethics in the Mennonite tradition was the focus of my doctoral dissertation, where I developed further the paradigmatic nature of worship's actions. See Irma Fast Dueck, *A Critical Examination of Mennonite Worship and Ethics: A Praxis Approach* (Toronto, ON: Emmanuel College of Victoria University and the University of Toronto, 2005).

16 See Note 12.

17 Peter Lombard writes, "A sacrament is properly so called, because it is a sign of the grace of God and the expression of invisible grace, so that it bears its image and is its cause." This understanding of sacrament therefore sanctifies as well as signifies. See Elizabeth Frances Rogers, ed., *Peter Lombard and the Sacramental*

*System* (Merrick, NY: Richwood Publishing Co., 1976), 80 as found in James White, *Introduction to Christian Worship* (Nashville: Abingdon, [1980], 156. In *Sacraments as God's Self-Giving* (Nashville, TN: Abingdon, 1983), White highlights the word "signify" in relation to an understanding of sacrament. Sacraments signify God's self-giving to humanity. God relates to humanity through (but not only) the sacraments: "Sacraments are actions through which the power of God is conveyed to us. God not only became human once, but continues to meet us on human terms by divine self-giving, through words and actions" (27).

18  St. Augustine of Hippo, "Tractus on John," LXXX, 3 NPNF, 1st series, VII, 344, as found in White, *Introduction to Christian Worship*, 145. John Calvin repeats Augustine's axiom when he writes, "Add the word to the element and there results a sacrament, as if itself is also a kind of visible word." See *Institutes*, IV, xiv, 4, as found in White, *Introduction to Christian Worship*, 145.

19  See Martin Luther, *The Bondage of the Will*, trans. J. I. Packer, O. R. Johnson (Westwood, NJ: Fleming Revell, 1957), 306.

20  G. H. Williams and A. M. Mergal, eds., *Spiritual and Anabaptist Writers* (Philadelphia, PA: Westminster Press, 1957), 79, as found in Walter Klaassen, *Neither Catholic nor Protestant* (Waterloo, ON: Conrad Press, 1973), 17-18.

21  As found in Walter Klaassen, ed., *Anabaptism in Outline: Selected Primary Sources* (Scottdale, PA: Herald Press, 1981), 30-31.

22  Klaassen, *Neither Catholic nor Protestant*, 18. The church as sacrament has its roots in the Roman Catholic tradition. For Roman Catholics the language of the church as sacrament has been re-appropriated in a fresh way after Vatican II, linking it specifically with the icon of the Trinity. Generally, the notion of the church as sacrament is understood in a threefold sense: (1) as a *symbol, icon,* or *image* that represents God's life and will; (2) as a *sign* that points to God's presence and activity; (3) as an *agent*, an instrument of God's grace and salvation. See Bruno Forte, *The Church: Icon of the Trinity*, trans. Robert Paoluccci (Boston: St. Paul Books, 1991). See also the Lumen Gentium, no. 4 where the church is presented in a sacramental perspective in terms of its relation to Christ as the primordial sacrament. Note also Edward Schillebeeckx, *Christ: The Sacrament of the Encounter with God* (New York: Sheed and Ward, 1963); Robert Kress, *The Church: Communion, Sacrament, Communication* (New York: Paulist Press, 1985); Otto Semmelroth, *Die Kirche als Ursakrament* (Frankfurt: Josef Knecht, 1953), perhaps the most classic statement of the model of church as sacrament from the Roman Catholic point of view; Avery Dulles's classic *Models of the Church* (Garden City, NJ: Doubleday, 1974). For Dulles "the church as sacrament" is described as one typology of a model of the church.

23  C. Arnold Snyder, *Anabaptist History and Theology* (Kitchener, ON: Pandora Press, 1996), 223.

24 I use the word "quiet" because initially Mennonites (Dutch) prayed silently during worship. They knelt to pray as "everyone called upon the Lord without confusion or indecent noise." See Robert Friedmann, *Mennonite Piety through the Centuries* (Goshen, IN: Mennonite Historical Society, 1949), 177. Their prayers were also silent at their homes, before and after meals.

25 Hans De Ries, a Dutch pastor, is said to have initiated audible prayers during worship. Soon others also began praying audibly and no longer kneeling in worship, a change that brought some discord.

26 See for example, *Die ernsthafte Christenflicht* (known in contemporary times as *Prayer Book for Earnest Christians*, trans. Leonard Gross, (Scottdale, PA: Herald Press, 1996)), published in 1739 and followed by at least ten more editions in Europe to 1852 and at least twenty-four in North America to 1940, where it became the prayer book of the Amish.

27 Beulah S. Hostetler, *American Mennonites and Protestant Movements* (Scottdale, PA: Herald Press, 1987), 327.

28 Pietism was a movement within Lutheranism from the late-17th century to the mid-18th century. It proved very influential throughout Protestantism and Anabaptism, inspiring not only Anglican priest John Welsey to begin the Methodist movement but also Alexander Mack to begin the Brethren movement. The Pietist movement combined the Lutheran emphasis on Biblical doctrine with the Reformed, and especially Puritan, emphasis on individual piety and a vigorous Christian life. Pietism had its greatest strength by the mid-18th century; its individualism helped prepare the way for the Enlightenment, which would take the church in an altogether different direction. Yet some would claim that Pietism contributed largely to the revival of Biblical studies in Germany and to making religion once more an affair of the heart and life and not merely the intellect. It likewise gave a new emphasis on the role of the laity in the church.

29 Robert Friedmann, *Mennonite Piety through the Centuries*. Friedmann has a more negative view of the influence of pietism on Anabaptist-Mennonites. This negative image of Pietism has been challenged by a number of scholars, notably Dale Brown from within the Believers Church tradition. Whether Pietism is viewed as a negative or positive development, most interpreters have used Anabaptism and Pietism as the two poles for analyzing Mennonite spirituality, with "interiorizing" Pietism being continued in revivalism and the charismatic and evangelical movements, and "externalizing" Anabaptism being reborn in the 20th century "recovery of the Anabaptist vision," the Concern movement, house churches, and the Eberhard Arnold Hutterian Brethren, to name a few examples. Another variation on this dominant framework has been offered by Joseph Liechty, Theron Schlabach, and others. In this view, humility, in part under Pietist influence, replaced the original Anabaptist understanding of suffering discipleship. Dennis Martin argues that because Mennonite scholars,

with a few exceptions, have not explored the pre-Reformation tradition of humility in depth, humility is portrayed as inwardness rather than as a comprehensive attitude related to ascetic discipline, martyrdom (both literal and figurative), and crossbearing, as understood in the early and medieval church. See Dennis D. Martin (1989), "Spiritual Life," in *Global Anabaptist Mennonite Encyclopedia Online*. Retrieved 23 May 2007 http://www.gameo.org/encyclopedia/contents/S687ME.html.

30  Martin, "Spiritual Life." Martin claims this is not to say that Mennonites have not had their own spiritualities but that they have not reflected on the character of those spiritualities in a sustained, systematic way. Much research remains to be carried out in this field.

31  See Arthur Paul Boers, Barbara Nelson Gingerich, Eleanor Kreider, John D. Rempel, and Mary H. Schertz, *Take Our Moments and Our Days: An Anabaptist Prayer Book* (Scottdale, PA: Herald Press, 2007), which includes liturgical prayer forms from the earliest Christian centuries but shaped by Anabaptist-Mennonite theology.

# Dialogue of Life: Recalling the Living Exchange in 2007

## Susan Kennel Harrison

*The dialogue of life is the exchange of religious information by means of observation in the context of everyday life.*[1]
– J. Mark Hensman

*If we cannot talk with those who oppose us, how can we ever find opportunities for improved relationship and pave the road to peace? Coming to the table does not mean that we agree on all or even fundamental issues. Dialogue is not a reward or validation of someone's position. It is a means to begin the process of reconciliation....*[2]
– Mary Ellen McNish

The "dialogue of life" is where our beliefs are embodied before one another in a common context. It implies a shared geographical place that we coexist in, even if for a short period of time. The dialogue of life is a time when our experiences of each other become shared experiences, where we encounter one another as real persons, often one-on-one; where we see one another in situ, how we conduct our lives with our peers and within our cultural milieu. Attention to fostering a dialogue of life presumes that knowledge production is not limited to speeches, presentations, or book knowledge, but values the non-verbal communication that is most fully noticed when other opportunities are provided.

As James Reimer points out in the preface, and Darrol Bryant reflects on in "A View from Outside" later in this volume, the Shi'a Muslim – Mennonite Christian Dialogue III was an academic conference which developed out of a larger context of a series of relationships that expanded over a long period, beginning with the relationship started by Mennonite Central Committee (MCC) and the Iranian Red Crescent Society when they began working together on earthquake relief in the early 1990s. From that experience grew the idea of a student exchange, which was entered into by the Imam Khomeini Education and Research Institute (IKERI) and by MCC which, while not being an academic institution itself, facilitated enrolling Shi'ite students at the Toronto School of Theology (TST), Regis College.[3] Mennonite exchange students who lived in Qom and studied with IKERI teachers regularly spoke and wrote to North American Christian audiences about their experience and what they were learning about Iran and her people. Additional relationships with Iranian institutions and a series of learning tours also provided encounter opportunities between Iranians and the North American Mennonite community, complementing the series of scholarly cross-cultural and inter-theological conferences that have developed between IKERI and North American Mennonite scholars.

All these varieties of encounters and more have fostered a sustained conversation and interaction between the scholarly cross-cultural and inter-theological dialogue and the general experiences of shared daily life. The Mennonites learned a great deal about hospitality when in Iran, and sought to be gracious hosts in return, recognizing the importance of learning that takes place in the dialogue of life and time spent together. Mennonites typically understand the rationale for this exchange of relationships and sustained conversation across religious and other differences to be rooted in their ethic of bridge-building for peacemaking. To be sure, the exchange and its offspring provide a modest opportunity for mutuality between people whose governments are perpetually escalating the tensions between one another.

This essay will reflect on the dialogue of life that went on before, during, and after the Dialogue III conference. Dialogue III was a long time in planning, and came about through a give-and-take of conversations between IKERI and the planning committee, resulting in the two sides agreeing to discuss the topic of spirituality. Seeking a dialogical process, scholars from each community were invited to submit the questions they had about the other religion's spirituality. After collating the questions, the planning committee created several categories and assigned presentation topics on that basis. The committee intended to develop a conference that modeled and fostered mutual learning both on the level of academic interchange and in a more personal way of learning, through the dialogue of life. The hope for fostering a significant dialogue was shaped around a pre- and post-conference itinerary called the *Interreligious Hospitality Project*.[4] Some aspects of this project included attending a significant Mennonite community event together, the New Hamburg, Ontario MCC relief sale, and visiting "The Mennonite Story" museum in St. Jacobs, Ontario. In reality, most of the careful planning was set aside, after delayed flights and schedule changes required nearly a full revamping of all that was planned.[5]

During the conference itself, these parallel levels of learning were planned for by extending personal invitations to both Mennonite and Shi'ite members of our geographic community to observe and be present for the scholarly papers and discussions;[6] having multiple scheduled break-out groups for both the observer circles and the scholar circles; positioning a listening committee to solicit and report on break-out conversations; scheduling several public sessions, including background lectures to introduce basic Mennonite and Shi'ite beliefs about spirituality, a public panel, "Two People, Two Faiths in Dialogue," intended to focus on what the exchange students had learned from their sustained experience; and a follow-up panel discussion at TST about what we learned during the conference.[7] Meal times were also designed to offer further opportunity for academics and observers from both religious communities to exchange conversation and share in their learning together. Notable, although not planned for, ongoing dialogue ensued after the Shi'ite scholars returned to Qom, on account of post-conference media reports that needed clarification. This itemization does not do justice to the amount of learning each community achieved, nor what each learned about their own faith community during the process of holding this conference. Suffice it to say that the dialogue of life was at least as important as the content of the essays presented in the main sessions for what we learned about one another.

The notion of theological dialogue being substantially important for better understanding and for facilitating better political relations between our nations is a big stretch for many. It might help the reader to consider that the common language by which these two divergent groups could meet is the language of everyday life and of our respective faiths. Our common commitment to faith provided a place to begin developing the relationships that can teach us about each other's ideas, and to communicate the religious atmosphere in which those ideas are lived out, more than any book learning can provide. That said, from the Mennonite point of view it might seem that a focus on religious thought, as a locus for genuine encounter and mutual learning, shuts out the great majority of churchgoers who might want to become involved in interfaith relationships. This is why recognition of the larger context of the exchange program, as well as refugee and earthquake relief work, as the backdrop for the academic conferences is particularly important. It is necessary to appreciate that "dialogue" is much more than the conversation about a specific conference subject matter; it is fostering an opportunity to authentically encounter each other.

As Bryant describes in "A View from Outside," one unique contribution to dialogue is the sustained nature of the relationship between the two communities and the connections made over time that help us to know who each other is as we speak about our faith and faith community. One Mennonite scholar, new to the Shi'ite dialogue partners, remarked early on in the conference, "I'm in a room full of mystics." Spending time among Shi'ite worshipers, one finds they operate from within an Islamic atmosphere, shaped through the study of Qur'an, Sunna of the Prophet and the Imams, prayer, and a kind of theoretical mysticism (irfan). As people of faith, that makes theology, particularly spirituality, an important place to have our mutual conversation.

The presentations in this volume demonstrate how little we can presume to know about each other, even if we have a shared language of faith. Two notable moments illustrate this. After Irma Fast Dueck's presentation on Mennonite worship, Mahmoud Namazi Esfahani asked, "If God is Father, Son, and Holy Spirit, how do you know which one to pray to when you worship?" Also, after Muhammad Legenhausen's presentation, a Mennonite inquired, "If it's hard to discern the Holy

Spirit, then I wonder how the Holy Spirit is discerned in the choosing of a leader?" Legenhausen replied, "Good question. This has been discussed for centuries and centuries . . . about how to recognize an Imam. So, . . . a few things. First is character. Nobody can go up and say 'I'm the one.' It has to be something that the previous Imam said about them – that they would be Imam. Character . . . being known 'by their fruits,' and thirdly by knowledge." His response prompted more questions. Thomas Finger asked whether the three qualifications for choosing an Imam refer solely to the twelve Imams, or whether these qualifications come under consideration for the "source of emulation." "Is it similar or something different?" he asked. To Mennonite surprise, Legenhausen replied, "Completely different. The source of emulation means the smartest guy around who knows about God's love."

Jon Hoover suggested that the *Gelassenheit* (yieldedness) in Arnold Snyder's presentation might be similar to the Islamic notion of *tawakkul* (a process of surrender to Allah). According to Yusuf Daneshvar Nilu, [a Muslim participant], *tawakkul, taslim,* and *tafwiz* are similar aspects of submission to God, so it could be that taslim is a conceptually closer equivalent to *Gelassenheit*. The Shi'ites asked questions to determine the philosophical framework for the notion of *Gelassenheit*, to which it was replied that "they [the Anabaptists] were not dogmatically careful." It was a repeatedly observed difference, and significant, that this seemingly shared language of theology was incomplete, because while we have some shared vocabulary we do not always understand words in the same way. Other points of clarification concerned understanding the mystical metaphysics of Shi'ite beliefs: How is God understood to be in relation to the human worshiper? At what point is a person "absorbed" into God, or the Love of God? Is monism acceptable in Shi'ite thought? What relevance does the material world play with respect to spirituality? Can we reach the deeper reality of God, absorption in the Love of God, without attention to how we live in the corporeal/material world?

In the observer/participant circles, the Mennonite-Shi'ite interactions were limited because a significant number of local Shi'ite participants dropped out of the conference, citing their concern of being seen attending via the internet and Persian TV broadcasting.

Through this conversation the Mennonites learned more about the realities of life in the Iranian diaspora community. Discussions in the observer break-out groups ranged from clarifying basic Christian and Muslim beliefs to discussing the meaning of the Trinity, with Shi'ite surprise at the wide divergence among Mennonite participants with respect to what the Trinity means. Another striking difference was noted between the role of the Spirit and the source of authority in the respective communities. "For Shi'ites the authority is found in the Imam; for Mennonites the Spirit is in . . . the community's discernment," was one comment. The observer groups discussed how dialogue could focus more on the social realities of our religions – "those who abuse the religion and give religion a bad name."

There was commiseration about how Islam and Christianity are demonized today. Mennonites noted the honour which Muslims give to Jesus, and wondered "why Christians have not taken into account the revelations of Mohammad?" The Mennonites were asked to explain how they develop a sense of what they must do, their religious duties to be faithful, in comparison with Muslim obligations to learn the prophetic traditions, give alms, pray five daily prayers, and go on the pilgrimage to Mecca. How is repentance for sin realized by Mennonites? For example, if a Shi'ite missed fasting some of the required days, he would be obliged to feed the poor for the number of days he did not fast. There was also noteworthy conversation around worship differences. It was stated that a Persian (Shi'ite) person holds that "the Qur'an and poetry both are holy," to which it was observed that Mennonites "express holy passion through hymns." A heartfelt inquiry asked whether Christians and westerners know mourning: "Do they mourn those who suffered or were significant saints and prophets?"

There was an important transition in MCC personnel that occurred as soon as the conference was finished. Ed Martin, inarguably the instigator and facilitator of this unique relationship, was stepping down as Director of the MCC South East Asia desk. Margaret Nally, a participant in MCC learning tours to Iran and chair of the MCC Ontario board, led us in a memorable and symbolic litany that afforded time for personal expressions of appreciation to him.

These are cameo moments in the give-and-take that was part

of the lively, rich exchange that occurred at the conference itself. Communication beyond the content of the essays and discussions was also taking place in the way faith was embodied in the individual person. One observes how faith shapes the interlocutor as a person, and how their virtues and shortcomings are negotiated. These are critically important but frequently ignored aspects of dialogue: seeing how specific beliefs are embodied by those who hold them, things that essays in books rarely reveal. A poignant example comes to mind when Snyder remarked in his presentation, "I would just say that living in love, nonviolently, was a spiritual condition, it grew out of our spirituality – not just ethics. We do this [not only] because Jesus said so . . . but in fact it grew out of the basis of spiritual yieldedness in our tradition, which is at the heart of who we are as a spiritual people – as a religious people." He went on to reflect on this in the context of the protest at the beginning of the conference: "I want to say that we were uncomfortable as Mennonites, to be protected by all these people [police officers] when we ourselves profess nonviolence. That hurt. That hurt us very deeply to be in that situation . . . ."

The Shi'ites observed that Mennonites were articulating their reasons for being in this contested dialogue as part of their commitment to follow Jesus' teaching, "love your enemies."[8] But this vocabulary is hurtful, as it does not fairly represent the relationships of the dialogue and the student exchange. The decision to foster a dialogue of life by inviting a local Shi'ite presence to the conference resulted in major challenges. One of the local Shi'ites invited to participate in the observer circle took it upon himself to inform the broader Iranian diaspora community about Dialogue III, knowing there would be people who would take offense at an initiative involving IKERI. Since the purpose of the conference was to learn more about one another's religions, not to discuss the Iranian government, the implications of the decision to foster a dialogue of life, given the current political climate in and between Iran and her diaspora community, were grave. Serious protest emerged within the diaspora community, which resulted in the "Two Faiths, Two Peoples in Dialogue" public panel being shut down, as the conference itself nearly was.

MCC and Conrad Grebel University College were working behind the scenes intensely for several months prior to the conference, because some people tried to keep the event from taking place by attempting to block the dialogue partners' entry visas to Canada, by sending petitions to the various agencies involved, and by public protest. The protest started right at the beginning of the conference and was politically motivated with aggressive, inaccurate accusations publicly directed to the Shi'ites on the panel. The events of that first night created hurt between the Mennonite and Shi'ite dialogue partners, and required group debriefings and ongoing conversations well beyond the end of the conference. As one Shi'ite put it, if MCC wants to hear other sides to the political stories about Iran, that is its business, "but that does not give it a right to make me confront such people and be slandered in public . . . to impose a confrontation with . . . [those who were] invited for a completely different purpose." In a letter to the Shi'ite participants the Mennonites stated, "We are sorry that you were named as 'criminals' and 'torturers' by the protesters and that these comments were then picked up and repeated by our Mennonite media. We know you to be people of integrity and deep faith. We do not know you in the way you were depicted by the protesters. As Mennonites, who frequently distance ourselves from our own governments' public policies, we know very well that one cannot and should not equate citizens with accusations against their governments. And yet, we allowed this to happen to you at our event."

After the conference ended, a number of social events took place, including travel to Niagara Falls, a local butterfly museum, and Captain John's fish restaurant. Our guests visited their former thesis advisors at McGill and Carlton Universities, met with a Christian Peacemakers Team director, lectured at local Shi'ite community centres, and shared informal visits with Mennonite and Shi'ite families. There was an amusing moment at Niagara Falls while we were waiting for "The Maid of the Mist," when some tourists were overheard talking about the Muslim guests (dressed in white button-up shirts and black trousers, and bearded). One asked her friend who they were. The other replied, "I don't know who they are . . . maybe they're Amish?"

An evaluation form given to conference participants raised a number of important questions. Would the political climate allow for public sessions to take place now, or even in the future? Why were Mennonite and Shi'ite women's voices not more equally included among the presentations? It was noteworthy that scholars and other participants unanimously affirmed the idea of having another dialogue between the two groups in the future. Indeed, more than one Mennonite scholar reported the conference to be one of the best they had attended. One participant reported that when the Shi'ite scholars were asked "why they value these dialogues so highly," they replied that "Ayatollah Mesbah says the dialogues are important for two reasons: our understandings of God are being transformed, and if we had been engaged in such dialogues over the years we would not be in the impasse we are in now." The following statement seems an apt summary of what was discovered and affirmed in "the dialogue of life" at Dialogue III:

> Any way we look at it, dialogue is an adventure in which the participants are not sure how things will turn out. They are content merely to have confidence in each other, to begin talking and to take action together. They need a certain range of freedom which will permit each party to experiment, taking into full account, of course, the other party and its community. New relationships are thus formed, and whatever their depth of significance at the beginning, they are bound to evolve, grow and bear fruit. Dialogue, involving as it does the free interplay of human initiatives, carries with it a dynamism that even its most severe critics are obliged to recognize.

> Whether they like it or not each party in dialogue is revealed to the other. Everyone should be aware of this as a risk to be taken.... It is even good to experience times of suspicion and of frustration which will oblige the interlocutors further to clarify to themselves the reasons for their encounter and the motives of their cooperation.... This requires a severe pursuit of truth and a true love for people, along with a faith that has been tested and a generous measure of spiritual wisdom.[9]

## Endnotes

1   J. M. Hensman, *The Dialogue of Life.* The question: "How do we live our lives together?" The answer: "By passing over and coming back." Retrieved January 18, 2010, from <http://eapi.admu.edu.ph/eapr99/mhensman.htm>.

2   American Friends Service Committee, April 2007 e-newsletter.

3   For more background, see Roy Hange, "A Dialogue of Civilizations: The Encounter of Iranian Shi'ites and North American Mennonites," in *Borders and Bridges: Mennonite Witness in a Religiously Diverse World*, eds. A. E. Weaver and P. Dula (Telford, PA: Cascadia Publishing House, 2007), 105-116, 174; and Susan K. Harrison, "Interfaith Friendship: A Bridge to Peace," in *Windows to World's Religions: Selected Proceedings of the Global Congress on the World's Religions after September 11*, ed. Arvind Sharma (New Delhi: D. K. Printworld (P) Ltd, 2009), 35-51.

4   With special thanks to the Mennonite Savings and Credit Union for a grant towards making the hospitality project possible. The introduction to the project stated that: "Our objectives in providing hosting before and after the academic conference are several: 1) to demonstrate our Mennonite commitment to hospitality and good will through the actions of caring for our Shiite friends in this way; 2) to provide opportunities for other Mennonites in Ontario to meet our Shiite friends and share in our blessing from friendship with them; 3) to provide an opportunity to further educate our Shiite guests about our Mennonite Christian values by providing opportunity for our Shiite guests to encounter our community at its best, in its everyday life together; 4) to provide ample opportunity for one-on-one interactions.

5   The hospitality itinerary included these highlights: New Hamburg MCC relief sale: sharing in a significant Mennonite community event; St Jacobs, *The Mennonite Story* museum: sharing a part of our religious history; travel along the Niagara escarpment, and going to Niagara falls together: sharing the beauty of Ontario; visiting Kanata Iroquois village and the Mohawk Chapel: sharing the First Nations story in Ontario. There were also plans to have the Shiites visit Mennonite congregations during Sunday morning worship and to be hosted by local Mennonite families for the noon meal.

6   As much as possible, each academic conference has sought to keep the same scholars involved, so that a sustained conversation and deeper level of learning can be fostered over time. For this reason the presentations were assigned in advance to scholars involved in previous dialogues.

7   The three public events were originally: Sunday, May 27 at Conrad Grebel University College, "Mennonites and Shi'ites on Spirituality: A Dialogue," featuring Muhammad Legenhausen and Arnold Snyder – postponed to Monday morning; Monday, May 28, "Two Peoples, Two Faiths in Dialogue" – disrupted and cancelled due to protests (see Dave Rogalsky, "Building Bridges of Understanding" in *Canadian Mennonite* (June 25, 2007, 33-34); and Thursday,

May 31, "Mennonites and Shi'ites: Continuing the Conversation" at Victoria University, Toronto – cancelled due to the inability of Mennonite participants to attend because of another conference inadvertently cross-scheduled.

8   Matt. 5: 43-48; 7:12; Rom. 12:14-21.

9   M. Borrmans, *Guidelines for Dialogue between Christians and Muslims*, trans. R. M. Speight (New York: Paulist Press, 1990), 33, 34.

# A View from Outside: Shi'a Muslim - Mennonite Christian Dialogue III

## M. Darrol Bryant

I had learned of the planned Shi'a Muslim - Mennonite Christian Dialogue III conference late in 2006. I immediately wrote a note to my colleague and friend, A. James Reimer at Conrad Grebel University College, requesting permission to be part of this event. He let me know that he would see what he could do, explaining that the Conference was purposely limited to people from these two specific religious communities. I was neither a Shi'a nor a Mennonite, though I did say to Reimer that having been a colleague of Mennonites for thirty-five years – I was at the neighbouring Renison University College in the University of Waterloo, and all of us teach Religious Studies as part of the University's Department of Religious Studies – and living in the largely Mennonite town of Elmira, I must have had some aspects of being a Mennonite rub off on me. I also indicated that while I could respect this limitation, I nevertheless really wanted to be present at the event, since interfaith dialogue was such an important aspect of my life. Over the years I had been involved in more than thirty cross-cultural and interfaith events with Buddhist, Hindu, Sikh, First Nation, and Jewish, as well as Muslim, communities.[1] I was finally allowed to participate as a member of the Listening Committee. We were a group of four who were asked to listen to the presentations and discussions, and then to report to the Conference on what we were hearing. We acted as a feedback device.

The Conference began on a rather grim note. A group of Iranians now living in Canada arrived in Waterloo on the first day to protest the event. Fearing the possibility of violence, the Waterloo Regional Police were out in full force, including members of the local SWAT team wearing flak jackets and carrying weapons. This was immensely troubling for the Mennonite community with its traditions of nonviolence. Nevertheless, when the Conference began that evening in the Great Hall of the College, the protesters were also allowed in. They carried signs – all of which said there should be no exchange with the guests from Qom, since they were oppressors – and milled around the edges of the Hall as James Pankratz, the Academic Dean of the College, welcomed everyone to the event. He was cognizant of the protesters and indicated that there would be a time for them to speak but they would need to observe the decorum of the event. It was, I thought, a fine opening moment and a fair response to the presence of the protesters. The confrontational atmosphere was reminiscent of moments I had experienced on university campuses in the 1960s when studying at Harvard Divinity School, and later at the end of the '60s at Waterloo Lutheran University and the University of Waterloo and in the early '70s at the University of Toronto.

When Pankratz invited one of the guests to speak, the protesters shouted him down and would not let him continue. After repeated attempts to bring some order to the event, Pankratz announced that the meeting was over and the Conference would resume the following day with only the invited guests present. We cleared the Great Hall and some of us went outside in the hope that we might speak to some of the protesters.[2] Outside, the 20-30 protesters with their signs remained shouting their displeasure with the meeting and insisted that there should not be any exchange with the "terrible" people (they were not so polite) from Qom. It is true that the Khomeini Institute in Qom is a centre of conservative support for the Iranian Revolution. But it is not clear to me why that makes members of that Institute and community unworthy of exchange and dialogue.

It was not the first time that I had experienced attempts to politicize meetings and attempts at dialogue. In 1969-70 I had worked for the Lutheran World Federation in Geneva, Switzerland, in relation to the planned 5th Assembly of the Lutheran World Federation that was to be held in Porto Allegre, Brazil. There were those who felt the event should not take place in Brazil, as it would indirectly lend credibility to the military junta then ruling the country. While I was initially sympathetic to this objection, I finally came to the view that the meeting of the international Lutheran community should take precedence over any alleged political credibility that might accrue to Brazil's governing powers. It seemed to me then, as it does now, that every meeting for purposes of dialogue and exchange, either within a given religious tradition or across traditions, can always be faulted by one or another group for its presumed political implications.

Indeed, one of the biggest challenges to dialogue arises from those who seek to politicize such events. In the 2007 case, there was a concerted effort to demonize the participants from Qom in ways that ran counter to the experience of Mennonites who had worked with this community for more than a decade. To decide de jure that such folks are unworthy is a dangerous business, especially when one attempts to impose this decision on a community that has always sought, as Mennonites have, to heed Jesus' injunction to love their neighbour and even to love their enemies. The participants from Qom were not their enemies, but friends they had discovered over their long association.

This became obvious the following morning, when the Conference met for its first full day and welcomed the rest of the contingent from Iran that had been delayed and arrived late in the night. As I watched them greeting one another, it was obvious that these were friends meeting friends and delighted to be in each other's company. This was, in my view, the first distinctive feature of the 2007 Conference. It was rooted in the fact that relationships between these Shi'a Muslims and Mennonite Christians had developed over time. More typically, interfaith events involve people from different religious communities meeting for the first time, a situation that greatly affects both the nature and depth of the ensuing conversation. In this case it was obvious that everyone had a great deal of trust in each other, a trust that allowed them to explore contentious differences as well as shared convergences. I commented on this aspect of the Conference when I gave some remarks from the Listening Committee on the last day of the event.

A second striking feature of this event was the degree of focus present. This was facilitated partly by the fact that participation was limited to two specific religious communities. This meant that the Conference eliminated intra-Christian discussion – "That may be *your* Christianity, but *my* Christianity says ..." – as well as intra-Muslim discussion. Such intra-group conversations can enrich a meeting, but they can also take away from its focus. Another aspect of this tight focus was the single theme – spirituality – that was addressed in myriad ways by speakers from both communities. A range of issues was explored under this heading – from the mythic to the mystical and the political, from the ritual to the ethical to the prayerful and communal – as the papers here attest. Yet they all circled back to a single theme. So every time we had an occasion for exchange about the papers, they revolved around one or another aspect of spirituality, both Shi'a and Mennonite.

In some ways "spirituality" was a more difficult topic for the Shi'a than for the Mennonites, as it is not as familiar a category for Shi'a thinkers, though it has become such a vital strand of the contemporary discussion in the West and among Christians. But the Conference theme had been worked out in advance, which also points to the long term involvement of these two communities with one another. It also meant that there was a lot of learning taking place during the Conference, as we listened to both Mennonites and Shi'a unfold their understandings. I know that I learned a lot, and other participants did as well as the Listening Committee members who sat in on the discussions that followed the presentations, noted in their feedback to the broader group.

The theme also allowed for the crossing of a number of boundaries that are often significant in cross-cultural and cross-religious dialogue. When academics meet, there is often a tendency to bracket religious and devotional questions; when religious leaders meet, there is a tendency to bracket contentious theological issues; and when lay people meet, there is a tendency to focus on practical issues and bracket the more difficult theoretical matters. Here the conversation ranged back and forth across these boundaries, giving richness and depth to the conversation that unfolded over the days of our gathering. People felt free to ask about each other's religious practice, to raise troubling theoretical and theological issues, and to explore practice while relating it to one another's theological and philosophical stance. I don't think this would have been possible without the shared history that lay behind this event.

When I began my own involvement in the dialogue of men and women from the many religious communities of humankind more than thirty-five years ago, many assumed that dialogue was impossible. And there are still those who denigrate this vitally important contemporary development. Yet today virtually every religious community in Canada has a statement on the importance of dialogue. Dialogue has become acceptable, but real meeting and real exchange remains difficult. Why is that? One reason is that there continue to be those who pay lip service to dialogue, yet then say, "but not with those people." I have always felt that dialogue is the new name for love of neighbour; it is a willingness to meet the Other, let each community define itself, and engage in a multi-faceted conversation. This I have noted elsewhere is a first rule of dialogue. If we decide in advance that this or that group can or cannot be part of the dialogue of dialogues, then we have broken faith with the fundamental premise of dialogue itself. If we respect these minimal requirements, then we can build the bridges of understanding and relationships of trust that facilitate healing in our broken world.

The Mennonite community is to be commended for its willingness to go where few others have dared to tread, namely into dialogue with the Shi'a community. And that applies reciprocally for the Shi'a community that was willing to engage Mennonite Christians in dialogue. It is always risky to meet, since preconceptions might be overturned, stereotypes shattered, and fears altered; everyone will be changed by the encounter.[3] It seems to me that they have discovered something vitally important to our global community: that peace in the human family begins with a hand outstretched in welcome to one another and with a word that acknowledges the dignity of all.

## Endnotes

1   See M. Darrol Bryant, *Religion in a New Key* (Kitchener, ON: Pandora Press, 2nd ed., 2001); M. Darrol Bryant and S.A. Ali, eds., *Muslim-Christian Dialogue: Promise and Problems* (St. Paul, MN: Paragon Press, 1998); and "Interfaith Encounter and Dialogue in a Trinitarian Perspective" in Peter Phan, ed., *Christianity and the Wider Ecumenism* (New York: Paragon Press, 1990), 3-20. I also recently edited with Susan Hodges Bryant, and contributed to,

*Mahayana Buddhism: History and Culture* (New Delhi: Tibet House, 2008).

2   See the contribution in this volume by Susan Kennel Harrison for a glimpse of the hurt and dismay felt that evening by other participants – Mennonite and Shi'a – in the conference.

3   Eugen Rosenstock-Huessy once proposed respondeo etsi mutabor (I respond, though I will be changed) as the motto for our planetary era. It would replace the cogito ergo sum (I think, therefore I am) of Descartes in the modern era. See especially *The Christian Future, Or the Modern Mind Outrun* (New York: Harper and Row, 1966) and *Speech and Reality* (Norwich, VT: Argo Books, 1970).

# An Ode: to the Shi'ah-Mennonite Dialogue III

## Susan Kennel Harrison

Group of five, six or seven
seeking how to get to heaven!

Closely watched by security,
learned men of purity.

Presenting, explaining, mingling at lunch,
books, break-outs, questions a bunch.

Sharing ideas and giving tribute,
tawheed and trinity raising dispute.

Van rides, laughter, telling stories,
gardens, butterflies, riding lorries.

Singing, reciting, going to pray,
boat ride, waterfalls, lots of spray!

Rough beginning, endearing ending,
friendships, colleagues, together seeking,
truth and integrity, God transcending,

Pilgrims on the journey of life,
seeking together to move beyond strife.

Journey safely home our friends,
Dialogue III now ends ....

*The Lord bless you and keep you; the Lord make his face to shine upon you, and be gracious to you; The Lord lift up his countenance upon you, and give you peace.*
Numbers 6:24-26.

Ed. Note: Susan Kennel Harrison has been involved with the student exchange program and academic conferences since 1999. She was the guide for the post-Conference events in 2007. This was written at the airport for the Iranian Conference participants.

# Contributors

**Dr. Mahmoud Namazi Esfahani** is a Professor of Islamic Philosophy and Theology at The Imam Khomeini Education & Research Institute. He completed a BA in Islamic Jurisprudence at the Ilmiyah Seminary of Qom in 1986 and a BA in Islamic Economy at the Baqir al-Uloum Foundation (1990). In addition he completed an MA (1994) and his PhD (2003) in Islamic Studies at McGill University. Namazi's primary area of scholarly interest is Islamic Philosophy with a focus on Mysticism, and Theology. He has published a monograph, translated two articles from English sources into Persian and published numerous articles in scholarly journals, both English and Persian. His research interests involve Islamic Philosophy, Philosophy of Religion, Theology, Ethics and Qur'anic Studies.

**Dr. Mohammad Fanaei Eshkevari**, is an Associate Professor of Philosophy and Mysticism, at the Howzeh seminary in Qom, Iran. Fanaei completed a BA in Islamic studies at the Theology School in Qom (1990), an MA (1994) and PhD (2000) from McGill University. His areas of scholarly interest include Comparative Philosophy, Islamic Theology and Mysticism. He has published eight books in the above subjects and numerous articles in scholarly journals.

**Dr. Irma Fast Dueck** is an Assistant Professor of Practical Theology, Canadian Mennonite University. BA from the University of Waterloo, MDiv from the University of Winnipeg, and a ThD from Victoria University at the University of Toronto. Prior to coming to CMU, she was a graduate/teaching assistant at Emmanuel College; an instructor at Canadian Mennonite Bible College; Assistant Pastor at Bethel Mennonite Church; and University Chaplain for the Conference of Mennonites in Manitoba. Along with her teaching duties, she is also the Director of CMU's Institute for Theology and the Church.

**Dr. Thomas Finger** is presently an independent scholar living in Evanston, IL, USA, devoting his time to writing, to ecumenical and inter-faith work, and to teaching world religions part-time. His PhD is in the Philosophy of Religion and Systematic Theology from Claremont Graduate University (1975). He has taught and published in Theology, Church History and Christian Spirituality. He has represented the Mennonite Church USA on the Faith & Order Commission of the National Council of Churches since 1983, working jointly with the Interfaith Commission for 8 years of that time. He is the author of *A Contemporary Anabaptist Theology* (2004), *Self Earth and Society* (1997), *Christian Theology: an eschatological approach* (2 vols., 1985, 1989), and several articles on inter-faith relations.

**Dr. Aboulhassan Haghani** is a Professor of Qur'anic Science in the Imam Khomeini Education and Research Institute in Qom, Iran. He is also the Director of International Affairs in the Imam Khomeini Education and Research Institute in Qom. He completed his BA in Islamic Theology and Law at the Seminary of Qom, MA in Developmental Psychology and MA in Islamic Studies at McGill University. He co-wrote a two-volume book on *Developmental Psychology* and translated a volume on the *Philosophy of Psychology*, and numerous articles.

**Susan Kennel Harrison** is a PhD Candidate in Theology at Victoria University at the University of Toronto, Ontario. She completed her BA at Goshen College (1987), holds an MDiv from the Associated Mennonite Biblical Seminary (1992), as well as a ThM from Victoria University (2004). Susan has also studied Islam and Arabic in North America and the Middle East. Her primary areas of research are Mennonite Peace Theology, Theologies of Interreligious Pluralism, Interfaith relations, Scriptural Reasoning, and Ecumenism. She has served as a Pastor, Chaplain, and coordinated MCC's student exchange between Iran (IKERI) and Ontario (TST) for 9 years. In addition to writing and teaching about interreligious dialogue, she co-leads a scriptural reasoning group at the University of Toronto, serves on the advisory boards for the *Society of Scriptural Reasoning, Bridgefolk* [a Mennonite-Catholic encounter] and the *Abraham's Tent* initiative at Eastern Mennonite University.

**Dr. Jon Hoover** is an ordained minister in the Mennonite Church USA and a Lecturer in Islamic Studies at the University of Nottingham (UK). He holds an MA (1991) from Associated Mennonite Biblical Seminary and a PhD (2002) from the University of Birmingham (UK). His publications include *Ibn Taymiyya's Theodicy of Perpetual Optimism* (2007) and a number of articles on Islamic Philosophical Theology and Christian-Muslim relations. His research interests are Islamic Theology and Christian-Muslim relations.

**Dr. Harry J. Huebner** is Professor of Philosophy and Theology at Canadian Mennonite University in Winnipeg, Canada. He is a graduate of the University of St. Michael's College in Toronto with a PhD (1982) in theology. He is co-author of *Church as Parable: Whatever Happened to Ethics?*(1993) and author of *Echoes of the Word: Theological Ethics as Rhetorical Practice* (2005). He has edited several books and contributed several articles in books and journals on the subject of Christian ethics. His research interests are in Philosophical Theology and Ethics.

**Dr. Muhammad Legenhausen** lectures on Western Philosophy and Christianity at the Imam Khomeini Education and Research Institute. His BA is from the State University of New York at Albany in 1974. His MA (1978) and PhD (1983) in Philosophy were completed at Rice University. He is the author of *Islam and Religious Pluralism* (1999) and numerous articles some of which have been collected as *Contemporary Topics of Islamic Thought* (2000). He has translated (from Farsi) Ayatollah Misbah Yazdi's *Philosophical Instructions* (1999) and (from Arabic) has translated the narrations collected in *Jesus Through the Qur'an and Shi'ite Narrations* (2005). His research interests are in the Philosophy of Religion, Ethics and Islamic Philosophy.

**Dr. Ali Mesbah** is an Assistant Professor of Philosophy at the Imam Khomeini Education and Research Institute, Qom, Iran. Mesbah completed a BA in Islamic Theology and Law at the Seminary of Qom, and a certificate in Social Sciences at Dar Rah-i Haq Institute (1986), an MA in Developmental Psychology at Baqir al-'Ulum Cultural Foundation (1990), an MA in Comparative Philosophy

(1994), and PhD in Religious Studies (2003) at McGill University. His primary area of scholarly interest is Philosophy of Religion. He has published – with the cooperation of others – a two-volume book on Developmental Psychology, and numerous articles in scholarly journals. Research interests include the relation of Religion to Social Sciences, Hermeneutics, and Religious language.

**Dr. A. James Reimer** teaches Religion and Theology at Conrad Grebel University College, University of Waterloo, Ontario, and at the Toronto School of Theology. He was the founding Director of the Toronto Mennonite Theological Centre. He received his BA (honours) in History and Philosophy from the University of Manitoba in 1971, an MA in history from the University of Toronto in 1974; and a PhD in Theology from University of St. Michael's College in 1983. He has written many scholarly articles and numerous books, including *The Emanuel Hirsch and Paul Tillich Debate* (1989), translated and published in German (1995); *Mennonites and Classical Theology* (2001); and *The Dogmatic Imagination* (2003); *Paul Tillich: Theologian of Nature, Culture and Politics* (2004). He is the co-editor of *The Influence of the Frankfurt School on Contemporary Theology* (1992) and *Das Gebet als Grundakt des Glaubens* (2004). His areas of specialty are theology in the Nazi period, Modern and Contemporary Christian thought, and Systematic theology.

**Dr. Aboulfazl Sajedi**, Professor of Philosophy of Religion, Imam Khomeini Education and Research Institute. Completed a BA in Islamic studies (1986), an MA in Psychology (1990) both at Imam Khomeini Education and Research Institute, an MA in Philosophy (1995) at McGill University, and a PhD in Philosophy of Religion (2000) at Concordia University. He has published books on group work including *Developmental Psychology with reference to Islamic Sources*, and studies of *The Language of Religion and Qur'an*, and *The Qur'an and the Educational System of Youth*. He has translated several books into Persian including, Dan Stiver, *The Philosophy of Religious Language, Sign, Symbol and Story* and  Robert M. Grant and David Tracy, *A Short History of the Interpretation of the Bible*. He has published more than 25 articles in scholarly Journals. His primary areas of scholarly interest are the Philosophy of Religion, Philosophy, Islamic Theology and Psychology.

**Dr. David W. Shenk** is an internationalist with particular interest in the role of religions in modern societies; that interest has taken him to over 100 countries. He has lived in East Africa for nearly 30 years as well as four years in Lithuania in the former Soviet Union. He has served as an administrator and consultant with Eastern Mennonite Missions in Pennsylvania, USA, and taught courses in world religions and Islam in at least a dozen academic institutions in North America and internationally. Shenk is an author of over a dozen books including *A Muslim and A Christian in Dialogue.* His PhD is from New York University in Religious Studies Education with course work in Anthropology. His many research interests include Interfaith Dialogue.

**Dr. Mohammad Ali Shomali** is a lecturer and the Head of Dept. of Religions at the Imam Khomeini Education & Research Institute, Qom. He has been a visiting research fellow of the University of London and taught in the Faculty of Oriental Studies at the Cambridge University. His publications include: *Self-Knowledge* (1996 & 2006, translated into Malay, Spanish and Kiswahili), *Ethical Relativism: An Analysis of the Foundations of Morality* (2001, translated into Malay), *Discovering Shi'a Islam* (2003, Fifth edition 2006, also translated into 12 languages), *Shi'a Islam: Origins, Faith & Practices* (2003, translated into Spanish & Swedish) and *Principles of Jurisprudence: An Introduction to Methodology of Fiqh* (2006). He has also compiled *A Selection of Ethical Texts* (2006), a textbook for students of a Masters program on ethics at Payam-e Nur University, Iran. He is a co-editor of *Catholics & Shi'a in Dialogue: Studies in Theology & Spirituality* (2004) and *Catholic-Shi'a Engagement: Reason & Faith in Theory and Practice* (2006). Shomali is also the editor in chief of the *Message of Thaqalayn: A Quarterly Journal of Islamic Studies.*

**Dr. C. Arnold Snyder** is a Professor of History, Conrad Grebel University College. Snyder completed a BA in Religious Studies at the University of Waterloo (1974), an MA (1975) and PhD (1981) from McMaster University. His primary area of scholarly interest is Church History, particularly in 16th-century Europe. He has published three monographs, translated a volume of Anabaptist sources into Spanish and published numerous articles in scholarly journals. Research interests include Anabaptist History and Thought, Spirituality and Peace, and themes related to Church History.

**Dr. M. Darrol Bryant** is a Distinguished Professor Emeritus and Director of the Centre for Dialogue and Spirituality in World Religions, Renison University College, University of Waterloo. He received his BA in Philosophy and Political Science from Concordia College, an STB in theology from Harvard Divinity School, and his MA and PhD from the Institute of Christian Thought, St. Michael's University College. He has authored and edited more than twenty volumes in the field of religious studies including *Religion in a New Key, Muslim-Christian Dialogue: Promise and Problems, Woven on the Loom of Time: Many Faiths and One Divine Purpose, A World Broken by Unshared Bread,* and *Mahayana Buddhism: History & Culture.* His areas of research have been in the dialogue of religions and Christian thought.

## Joint MCC-CGUC Conference Planning Committee:

Dr. Lydia Neufeld Harder, chairperson, adjunct faculty in Theology, CGUC

Susan Kennel Harrison, conference coordinator

Arli Klassen, Director Mennonite Central Committee Ontario (MCCO)

Dr. James Pankratz, Academic Dean, CGUC

Dr. A. James Reimer, conference presenter


## Academic sub-committee:

Dr. Lydia Neufeld Harder, chairperson, adjunct faculty in Theology, CGUC

Susan Kennel Harrison, conference coordinator

Dr. Nathan Funk, Assistant Professor of Peace and Conflict Studies, CGUC

Dr. A. James Reimer, conference presenter

Dr. Yousef Daneshvar Nilu, former MCC/IKERI exchange student, Scholar from Qom


## Listening Committee:

Dr. M. Darrol Bryant, chairperson

Dr. Nathan Funk, Assistant Professor of Peace and Conflict Studies, CGUC

Susan Kennel Harrison, conference coordinator

Dr. Yousef Daneshvar Nilu, former MCC/IKERI exchange student, Scholar from Qom

# Building an understanding; Once the protesters departed, Muslim and Mennonite scholars meeting in Waterloo exchanged kind words

## Mirko Petricevic Record Staff

© 2007 *Waterloo Region Record, Ontario Canada*

On the morning this week after angry protesters shouted down a meeting of Mennonite scholars and Muslim clerics at Conrad Grebel University College in Waterloo, the mood in the room could not have been more different.

As the Muslim clerics entered the college lecture hall on Tuesday, their Mennonite hosts sprang from their seats, shook their guests' hands and hugged them like dear, old friends.

It was their third meeting, part of a nine-year peace-building program between the Mennonite Central Committee and the Imam Khomeini Education and Research Institute, which is based in Qom, Iran.

Critics object to the relationship because the institute has strong ties to the Iranian government, which in turn has a poor human rights record.

Although protesters prevented the academics from speaking on Monday, during the following two-and-a-half days they shared meals, presented papers and taught each other about the foundations of their faiths.

It's not possible to summarize the breadth and depth of their dialogue here.

But the following are snippets from the presentations they made, mostly gleaned during brief interviews:

## An Overview

The division between Sunni and Shiite Muslims is often explained as simply a disagreement over political leadership, said Hajj Muhammad Legenhausen, who lectures on Western philosophy and Christianity in Qom.

However, there's a more fundamental difference based in their approaches to spirituality, Legenhausen said.

Shiites generally teach there are five spirits that work on human beings. Ordinary humans are aware of four — faith, strength, appetite and motion.

Only a few people, prophets and imams, have the guidance of an angel.

"The prophet is purified by seeing what others don't," Legenhausen said. "You can't understand properly what the Qur'an has to say unless (it's delivered) through the spirit that you find in the guidance of the imams."

Arnold Snyder, professor of history at Conrad Grebel, gave an overview of how early Mennonites, in the 16th century, practised their faith.

Rather than putting their trust in a few designated priests for spiritual guidance, they turned to Scripture.

Memorizing Scripture was an important practice. Their proficiency in learning verses by heart is documented in court records of heresy trials of early Mennonites.

Sometimes, frustrated jailers removed Bibles from an accused person's prison cell to keep him or her from memorizing more.

But that didn't completely remove the Gospel from the Mennonites.

"They still had the Bible between their ears," Snyder said.


## On Trinity and on Knowing God

Islam emphasizes the singularity of God, said James Reimer, teacher of religion and theology at Conrad Grebel.

Christians also reject polytheism in favour of monotheism, he said.

However, Christians use the language of the Trinity — Father, Son and Holy Spirit – when describing God.

Reimer argued that contemporary Mennonites must retrieve a "very strong emphasis" on the Trinity to underpin their social ethics.

"The three have everything in common – Father, Son and Holy Spirit – they are one and equal with each other," Reimer said. "That becomes our analogy of how human beings should have everything in common and be one with each other."

In his presentation, Ali Mesbah described the world as being only a tiny part of reality.

"The tip of the iceberg, so to speak. The main part is hidden from our senses," said Mesbah, a professor of philosophy at the institute in Qom.

"The essential part of the world is the spiritual, hidden, unseen, world."

Mesbah likened understanding reality to reading a passage of writing.

There is the surface meaning – what the words literally convey.

But there's also a sub-text which relates a deeper meaning, Mesbah said.

"Religion is one of the main sources (for) providing humans with deeper meaning."

## On Spiritual Poverty

When the Prophet Muhammad asked followers the meaning of bankruptcy, some replied it was a state of economic failure, said Mohammad Ali Shomali, head of the religions department at the institute in Qom.

But the Prophet answered that in the afterlife, people will be shown their personal balance sheets.

"Certain people find it's empty of good deeds," Shomali said. "This is the most painful poverty."

Spiritual poverty – super-humility in the face of God – is a goal, he said. We achieve that poverty when we totally understand that all our blessings come from God. All we have is just a loan from God that must be repaid.

"And if you are not careful, you may become bankrupt," Shomali said.

Thomas Finger, an independent American scholar, said spiritual poverty is not the same as economic poverty, but Mennonites can't really talk about one without dealing with the other.

Having spiritual poverty means you have come to a state when you're willing to give up wealth or anything that clutters your life, Finger said.

But if a person responds to God, his or her economic situation often improves. So the challenge is to retain an attitude of reliance on God as you accumulate wealth, he added.

"That's a struggle always to put those in perspective."

## On Mysticism

Sufism is sometimes understood as being the equivalent of Muslim mysticism.

But that's only partly true, said Mohammad Fanaei, an associate professor of philosophy and mysticism at the Houze seminary in Qom.

Fanaei said mysticism is the deeper understanding and practice of religion and that there's no genuine mysticism outside of religion.

Religion has esoteric (inward spiritual) teachings and exoteric (outward, ritual, sharia and theology) teachings. "These two are complementary to each other. We cannot replace mysticism with religion or vice versa," Fanaei said.

The word "sufism" describes different orders, groups or schools of mysticism, but mysticism is also practised outside organized groups, he said.

David Shenk, author and former administrator of the U.S.-based Eastern Mennonite Missions, presented a paper alongside Mohammad Fanaei.

Muslim mystics teach the notion of ascending spiritualities in which a person exercises spiritual disciplines which help elevate him or her into ever higher realms of spirituality, Shenk said.

Eventually the believer becomes absorbed into divinity.

But in Christianity, Shenk explained, the union is "God taking initiative, in Jesus, coming to meet us. He comes down to meet us.

"So it's not that we ascend, but we receive the gift of grace which he pours out to us in Christ."

## On Ritual and Morals

Having a high level of morals leads to harmonious social relations, says Aboulfazl Sajedi, a professor of the philosophy of religion.

Prayers, conducted five times a day, help cultivate positive relationships because they begin with the words: In the name of God, the most compassionate, the most merciful.

"A good Muslim is someone who is going to be close to God," Sajedi said. "Meaning that (he) should acquire God's attributes as much as he can."

Frequent prayers are constant reminders to strive to acquire God's attributes. A person's innate nature is moral, he added, but the material world separates a person from his or her nature.

Mennonites use rituals as much as other religious groups, said Irma Fast Dueck, a professor of practical theology at Canadian Mennonite University in Winnipeg.

When her congregation takes communion, nobody leaves the pews. Instead, plates of bread are distributed. But nobody holds the plate and takes a piece of bread themselves. Instead, everyone serves their neighbour, Dueck said.

"That's Mennonite theology at its best. The communal emphasis. Serving each other."

And nobody eats the bread until everyone in the congregation has been served a piece. Then, worshippers eat as a community, as one body of Christ, she said.

## On Politics and Spirituality

Shiite spirituality provides self-corrections to the relationship between humans and the material world, said Mahmoud Namazi Esfahani, professor of Islamic philosophy and theology.

Before the Islamic revolution in Iran in 1979, society was too capitalistic, Esfahani said.

"Islam says possessing wealth . . . is no problem. But if you belong to it in a way that it is (worldly) entities that direct you, it's not acceptable."

The revolution, led by Ayatollah Ruhollah Khomeini, was a self-correction, Esfahani said.

Khomeini wasn't driven by the desires of the material world, Esfahani said.

"It is natural for the faithful to follow a pious faqih (senior jurist) who has nothing in mind except to erect the will of God."

Mennonites traditionally had an uneasy relationship to government, said Harry Hueb-ner, professor of philosophy and theology at Canadian Mennonite University in Winnipeg, Man.

Though the tension has mostly subsided, it still continues today.

Some, like Old Order colonies, isolate themselves. But more contemporary Mennonites look to a 1995 confession of faith which promotes engagement with government.

"Profound love of God . . . has implications in all aspects of life," Huebner said. "Every facet of life."

That belief is based partly on the story of the Good Samaritan.

"Loving God and neighbour is really the spirituality and politics brought together."


## On Prayer

"We believe that everyone needs to connect with Allah, to talk with Allah," said Aboulhassan Haghani, director of International Affairs for the institute in Qom.

"But how can we talk with Allah?"

Haghani said Shiite Muslims look to the prophets and historic imams.

"These prophets know better (than) us," Haghani said. "So we should follow them."

Thursday nights, Shiites read a supplication by Imam Ali, the first Shiite leader after the Prophet Muhammad.

"Oh Thou who art the most holy! Oh Thou who existed before the foremost! Oh Thou who shall exist after the last!" reads the prayer, which takes 25 minutes to read.

Jon Hoover, assistant professor of Islamic Studies at the Near East School of Theology in Beirut, presented an examination of The Lord's Prayer in which Christians call for God's Kingdom to come and for His will to be done.

That indicates God hasn't yet completed His work on Earth, Hoover said.

And the part calling on God to "lead us not into temptation" is a call for God to finish the job, Hoover added.

"We have a strong foretaste of the Kingdom in the life, death and resurrection of Jesus," Hoover said. "So I prefer to speak of the Kingdom already here in Christ, and to some degree in the church, but not yet complete."

*On Spirituality*

Participants and observers at Dialogue 2007, Conrad Grebel University College, Waterloo Ontario, Canada.

Picnic at the Park, Mississauga, Ontario, Canada

Mr. Haghani pouring Water into the cup of Ed Martin, part of a tribute and farewell ceremony for Ed. (see Susan Harrison essay)

Dr. Ali Mesbah speaks while Dr. Aboulhassan Haghani Khaveh observes.

# Shi'ah Muslim - Mennonite Christian Dialogue III

## January 9, 2007

Greetings!

This letter is an invitation to you to attend the Shi'ah Muslim-Mennonite Christian Dialogue III to be held in Waterloo, Ontario on May 27-May 30, 2007. This conference is co-sponsored by the two institutions, Mennonite Central Committee (MCC) and Conrad Grebel University College (CGUC), and is part of a growing relationship between Mennonites and Shi'ah Muslim scholars from Qom, Iran. MCC first initiated a formal student exchange with the Imam Khomeini Institute for Education and Research (IKERI) of Qom in 1998. Since then relationships have been built through learning tours, academic conferences and personal interactions. If you are unfamiliar with this dialogue you may want to check out the *Conrad Grebel Review*, Vol. 24, No. 1 (winter 2006) for a sample of papers from the last conference held in 2004 in Iran.

This year's conference will take place at Conrad Grebel University College and includes papers by the seven scholars from Iran and an equal number of Mennonite scholars. The overall conference theme is "Spirituality" and planned around questions that members of the 2004 conference collected and exchanged to form the direction of the main presentations and discussions for 2007. The format of the conference will include ample time for interaction and discussion on these major papers. Topics range from "The Role of Ritual in the Cultivation and Strengthening of Morals" to "The Relationship between Spirituality and Politics". A primary focus will be on what each faith community understands as spirituality in the first place.

Relationship building that leads to better understanding of our respective faith communities is also part of the purpose of the conference. Therefore, we expect all participants to be present for the meals and for the evening sessions (which will usually be of a somewhat different nature: a panel discussion, listening committee report etc.) The strength of these events has been the fostering of relationships among people of different faiths as well as the creation of ongoing informal theological dialogue. Consequently, there will also be additional activities on the two days before the conference and the two days afterward. These include attending a Mennonite Relief Sale together; a Mennonite worship service; an Old Order Mennonite home; a Shiite mosque; Niagara Falls; and visiting the Toronto School of Theology. Persons of both faith communities will benefit from these informal occasions to connect and further shape our mutual understandings, and develop ongoing conversation partners.

This conference represents an opportunity for us all to learn more about the Shia faith (as well as our own) and to develop ongoing relationships with Muslim scholars. We are inviting a limited number of persons to be part of this conference to listen, to learn and to participate in the discussion. We hope you will welcome this opportunity.

Please consider this invitation seriously. A registration form and a brief overview of the program is included. We hope all participants will seek to attend the whole conference including all or some of the pre or post conference events. Space is limited so an early response will assure you a place at this dialogue.

Sincerely, Lydia Neufeld Harder, Chair of the Planning Committee On behalf of Conrad Grebel University College and Mennonite Central Committee.